Studies in Cultural History

When Fathers Ruled

When Fathers Ruled

Family Life in Reformation Europe

Steven Ozment

Harvard University Press

Cambridge, Massachusetts
and London, England
1983

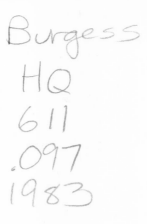
Library of Congress Cataloging in Publication Data

Ozment, Steven E.
    When fathers ruled.

    (Studies in cultural history)
    Includes bibliographical references and index.
    1.   Marriage—Europe—History.
    2.   Family—Europe—History.
    3.   Husbands—Europe—History.
    4.   Fathers—Europe—History.
    5.   Children—Europe—History.
    6.   Reformation—Europe—History.
    I.   Title.   II.   Series.
    HQ611.097   1983   306.8'094   83-6098
    ISBN 0-674-95120-4

For Andrea

Preface

THIS STUDY represents a new scholarly departure for me, as I have not published works on family history before. Scholars who have already blazed trails in this field have been generous in sharing published and unpublished materials, among them John Boswell, Barbara Ritter Dailey, Ronnie Po-Chia Hsia, Robert Kolb, Klaus Lindner, H. C. Erik Midelfort, Thomas F. Miller, Kathryn Norberg, Thomas Robisheaux, Thomas Max Safley, and Merry Wiesner Wood. I have been especially stimulated by the magisterial studies of Lawrence Stone on England, Natalie Zemon Davis and Jean-Louis Flandrin on France, and Gerald Strauss on Germany, although from my particular vantage point in German and Swiss sources I have not always agreed with the generalizations they have drawn about the early modern family. I owe special thanks to Dr. Maureen Lynch for her evaluation of the chapter on childbearing from the point of view of modern gynecological and obstetrical practice; to Robert M. Kingdon for a critique of the manuscript as a whole; to Aida Donald for encouraging the project in the first place and guiding it through the editorial process; and to Peg Anderson, whose consummate skill with the English language has enhanced the book in many ways.

I have attempted in this book to avoid both a history that holds unconscious demographic and economic forces in such awe that we learn little more about the human family than what it has in common with herding animals, and a history so preoccupied with man's self-transcendence and self-control that the family is treated as if its true home were that of the angels. All scholars have deep convictions in this matter — my own bias is that humankind is more the master of its fate than mastered by it — and I do not expect to make converts on so personal an issue. I do, however, mean to argue that historians best understand the early modern family at the crossroads of values and structures, where freedom meets necessity, ideals confront nature, and minds self-consciously choose.

Sections of chapters 3 and 4 have appeared in article form as "The Family in Reformation Germany: The Bearing and Rearing of Children" in the *Journal of Family History* (Summer 1983), copyright 1983 by the National Council on Family Relations. I am grateful to the editors for permission to reproduce this material.

Newbury, Massachusetts
February 1983

Contents

Illustrations

All of the illustrations except *A Woman in Labor* and *The Nursery* are reprinted with permission from Max Geisberg, *The German Single-Leaf Woodcut: 1500-1550*, vols. I, III, and IV, revised and edited by Walter L. Strauss (New York: Hacker, 1974). *A Woman in Labor* is from *Alte Meister der Medizin und Naturkunde in Facsimile-Ausgaben und Neudrucken nach Werken des 15.-18. Jahrhunderts* (Munich, 1910). *The Nursery* is from Th. Hampe, ed., *Gedichte vom Hausrat aus dem XV. und XVI. Jahrhundert* (Strasbourg, 1899).

When Fathers Ruled

· 1 ·

In Defense of Marriage

ACCORDING TO contemporary observers, marriage and the family were in a crisis in late medieval and Reformation Europe. Humanists, reform-minded Catholics, and especially Protestants decried the amount of domestic litigation, particularly that of contested first marriages, and a casual demeaning of marriage and family life they perceived all around. It was surely not accidental that these "defenders of the estate of marriage," if such they may be called, appeared at a time when perhaps 40 percent of all women were single (an estimated 20 percent spinsters, 10–20 percent widows),[1] and infant and child mortality high (perhaps one-third to one-half of all children died by age five).[2] Nor was it accidental that women found new advocates in an age when their physical vulnerability had made them the main target of politically self-aggrandizing secular and ecclesiastical witch-hunters (perhaps 80 percent of the estimated 100,000 people executed for witchcraft and harmful magic between 1400 and 1700 were women, the vast majority older spinsters and widows).[3] Both humanist and Protestant commentators closely associated the prejudice against marriage and family with exaggerated clerical ideals of virginity and celibacy and the religious culture these ideals nourished.[4] Many accused the medieval church of forcing virginity upon unwilling and incapable youth, while at the same time stereotyping marriage as a distinctly inferior and burdensome institution.[5] For Martin Luther and his followers the cloister became the symbol of the age's antifeminism; by suppressing monasteries and nunneries and placing women securely in the home as wives and mothers, the reformers believed they had liberated them from sexual repression, cultural deprivation, and male (clerical) domination.

Reformers also discerned threats to marriage and family in the laws of the medieval church, which formed a major part of the moral governance of late medieval cities and towns. On the one hand, church law was seen to encourage immature and impulsive unions by recognizing as valid so-called "clandestine" marriages that had occurred without parental permission and apart from public witness. On the other, the medieval church was accused of placing legal obstacles to mature and reasoned marriages by arbitrarily defining numerous "impediments" to marriage between people related by various blood, legal, spiritual, and familial ties. It became a major goal of new Protestant and secular marriage ordinances in the sixteenth century to end such secret unions and define impediments more realistically.

These various measures gave marriage and family life a new importance in Reformation Europe, which may be described as the heyday of the patriarchal nuclear family. Today many ridicule this model of marriage and family, with its seemingly total subjection of the wife to home and husband, of the home to the production of children, and of the children to the will of their parents, an alleged domestic parallel to the growing political absolutism of the age of Reformation. Several recent studies, from Philippe Ariès's *Centuries of Childhood* (1960) to Lawrence Stone's *The Family, Sex and Marriage In England 1500–1800* (1977), argue that little genuine affection existed in the early modern family, either between husband and wife or between parents and children, that for wives and children the traditional family was a kind of bondage that stifled self-realization.

This book is an attempt to reconstruct contemporary attitudes toward marriage and parenthood in Reformation Europe, primarily in Germany and Switzerland, and to illumine something of the rationale behind the early modern family as here represented. My sources are heavily weighted toward self-conscious assessments by contemporary observers and participants, who report contemporary beliefs and practices and also reflect them in their own lives. They include medical tracts by experienced physicians designed to guide midwives and expectant mothers in both prenatal and postnatal care; "housefather" books, massive guides to estate management, containing much advice on marital relations, childbearing, and child rearing; vernacular pamphlets,[6] a growth industry at that time, in which moralists of every religious and political persuasion commented and advised on all aspects of family life; family chronicles and housebooks,[7] probably the richest sources for family history, directly conveying both their authors' familial activities and their innermost attitudes toward them; single-leaf woodcuts,[8] a largely unexplored source that briefly and strikingly summarizes generations of criticism and advice for spouses, parents, and children; popular sermons, mines of social commentary by those who observed human behavior most critically; vernacular catechisms and etiquette books, especially those designed for home use,[9] which set forth the values parents and tutors gave lip service to and attempted to instill in children and youth; city ordinances, especially those of newly Protestant Europe, which rewrote the marriage laws and reshaped the institutions that governed domestic life in cities and territories; and finally, the records of marriage and morals courts, which reveal still further the difficult transition from ideals and values to actual behavior and habits.

I have drawn on examples from each of these sources and cannot claim to have exhausted any one genre; indeed, in some cases I have only skimmed the surface of vast pools of information, which future studies will surely penetrate more deeply as the field of family history matures. On some subjects, particularly canon law and the operation of marriage courts, I am much indebted to the labors of other scholars. I believe these various sources permit us to approach family life in Reformation Europe on the level at which people actually lived, at least as far as organized burgher society is concerned. Through these sources we can listen sympathetically as people comment on themselves and their times both by word and by deed, speaking their minds and venting their emotions on the subjects of marriage and parenthood.[10]

Celibacy and Marriage

Three years before his own marriage, Martin Luther wrote a treatise, *Vom ehelichen Leben* (On the estate of marriage, 1522), his first lengthy discussion of the subject, in which he complained that "marriage has universally fallen into awful disrepute," that peddlers everywhere are selling "pagan books which treat of nothing but the depravity of womankind and the unhappiness of the estate of marriage"—a reference to classical misogynist and antimarriage sentiments and to the bawdy antifeminist stories that were popular among Luther's contemporaries.[11] The connection between the celibate ideal and misogyny was revealed in Sebastian Franck's collection of popular German proverbs (1541), which preserved a proverb used by St. Jerome to defend the single life: "If you find things going too well, take a wife"—a proverb Franck paired with another: "If you take a wife, you get a devil on your back."[12] Parents, said Luther, were buffeted by such sentiments and by the religious propaganda in praise of celibacy; in response they turned their children away from marriage and encouraged them to enter the cloister.

Luther was not alone in making such complaints. An observer in Augsburg reported in 1534 that marriage there had become a "weak, despised, and rejected estate," which the young, especially men, fled in fear; everywhere women were said to make fools of men (the biblical stories of the downfall of Adam, Samson, and David at the hand of a woman were current), and both sexes looked on the birth and rearing of children with "superstitious dread."[13] Caspar Gütell, Protestant pastor in Eisleben (Saxony), commented on his contemporaries in a sermon published in the same year: "Having seen how much effort, anxiety, pain, need, care, and work are involved in marriage, they would not recommend it to a dog, and to save their children from it, they give them over to the Devil by forcing them into the cloister. Thereby they gain for them an easy life on earth, but they dispatch their souls to hell."[14]

Although contemporary Catholic parents did not consider the cloister a danger to the souls of their children, they did tend to view it as a place for the weak, or in some way failed, child who needed special protection. Although Hermann von Weinsberg was later very proud of his illegitimate daughter Anna when she became mother superior in the family convent in Cologne, he originally viewed her entrance into the cloister as fitting for one with her social handicap.[15] He also was not surprised when a frail niece who had left the cloister to live with her mother found life in the world so stressful that she sought to enter another cloister.[16] And he recommended the religious life to a sickly nephew who, he was convinced, would not be able to lead a "more vigorous" life in the world.[17] In his old age Martin Luther explained his own entrance into the cloister at Erfurt in 1505 as an act of weakness occasioned by his then "pusillanimous temperament," which his parent's very strict discipline had unintentionally brought about[18]

Protestant pamphleteers accused the secular and clerical critics of marriage of desiring personal and sexual freedom in the single life and of conjuring false fears and excuses to escape the responsibility and self-discipline imposed by monogamous marriage. "Because they prefer whoring and Sodomy, not a few want to avoid holy matrimony," argued the Eisleben pastor Gütell.

> For this reason they say: "It would be nice to get married but how will I live? I have nothing; if I take a wife things will really get tight. And marriage brings with it many new troubles and cares and requires much effort and work. The wife complains or gets sick; the children wail and scream, this one demanding something to drink, another something

to eat . . ." Here [in having to assume these new respon-
sibilities] is truly the greatest obstacle to marriage.[19]

Concern for the estate of marriage was not confined to the ranks
of Protestants and humanists. An anonymous tract, written in 1545
by self-critical Catholic clergy to urge the newly convened Council
of Trent to allow the clergy to marry, accused the Catholic clergy
themselves of undermining marriage and family life by their lax and
hypocritical sexual lives and confessional practice. The authors
pointed out that the clergy openly had sexual amours and that many
lived publicly in concubinage, a widespread practice in the fifteenth
and sixteenth centuries. According to the authors, the sight of
celibate priests whoring and committing other sexual sins, yet
receiving only small fines and continuing to perform their clerical
offices, only encouraged weak and immoral laity to take their own
seductions and adultery lightly, especially when they, too, for the
penance of a few groschen, could obtain absolution from a priest for
such acts.[20]

Protestant pamphleteers were quick to condemn clerical sexual
hypocrisy and a penitential system by which the church profited
from the irrepressible desires of human nature (bishops regularly
fined priests for whoring and forced those living in concubinage to
pay annual penitential fees and "cradle taxes" when children
arrived).[21] According to Eberlin von Günzburg, a Franciscan convert to the Reformation and after Luther the most prolific Protestant
pamphleteer, many priests felt torn apart by this contradiction. He
recorded a fictitious assembly of "seven pious but disconsolate priests
whom no one can comfort," who were said to have met secretly to
discuss the most burdensome aspect of their vocation. The first to
speak declared it to be without question celibacy, and he recounted
in graphic detail his own unsuccessful struggle to maintain it — his
sensuous dreams, nocturnal emissions, masturbation, and lechery.
He told of an affair with a married woman that became doubly
grievous to his conscience because he continued to befriend her
cuckolded husband. Guilt-ridden, he ended this relationship and
took a concubine, an arrangement that continued to burden his conscience not only because of its illegality but also because he forced
her to practice birth control. After her death he took another concubine through whom he claims to have fathered seventeen
children. Although church authority officially disapproved of such
arrangements, he pointed out that it also tolerated them so long as
priests paid the prescribed penitential fee (*hurenzinss*). The laity
had awkwardly adjusted to such clerical whoring, "like stableboys

become accustomed to dung." The priest was convinced that by his own example he had taught his parishioners that whoring is no sin, and he lamented the hardships imposed on his children by the stigma of illegitimacy. His was a true dilemma:

> Thus am I entangled: on the one hand, I cannot live without a wife; on the other, I am not permitted a wife. Hence, I am forced to live a publicly disgraceful life, to the shame of my soul and honor and to the damnation of many who have taken offense at me [that is, by refusing to receive the sacraments from his hands]. How shall I preach about chasteness and against promiscuity, adultery, and knavish behavior, when my own whore goes to church and about the streets and my own bastards sit before my eyes?[22]

Protestant apologists for marriage concerned themselves also with the burdens these contradictions led priests to impose upon the laity, especially upon married women and adolescent girls. Heinrich of Kettenbach, another Franciscan convert to the Reformation and a Lutheran pamphleteer, accused confessors of impregnating sexually aggressive women who could not be satisfied by their husbands, alleging that a single confessor might service as many as twenty such women — wives, daughters, and maids, "like a steer a herd of cows." Kettenbach further accused confessors of impregnating young girls who had been forced by parents or circumstance into nunneries, proof of which, he claimed, was visible in moated cloisters where the drains ran free (infanticide was here alleged). He accused confessors further of "debasing respectable women and girls who are simple and pious" by their interrogations during confession, causing them "often to leave confession without hope of salvation, godless, dishonored, soulless, having become whores in their own minds, because there, in confession, their hearts have been secretly and subtly stolen, betrayed, and sold."[23] Kettenbach also alleged that confessors were not above passing the names of adulterers on to the Fiscal, the powerful administrative office of the bishop, whose agents privately extorted from them a gulden or two on threat of exposure.[24]

Protestants were faced with what they considered to be a crisis in domestic relations, one that could be traced to the institutions of medieval religion. To correct the situation, they exalted the patriarchal nuclear family as the liberation of men, women, and children from religious, sexual, and vocational bondage. Humanists and

Protestants were not the first to defend the estate of marriage; medieval theologians and preachers had earlier done so when confronted by extreme ascetical sects like the Cathars, who questioned the propriety even of procreation.[25] The Protestant reformers were, however, the first to set the family unequivocally above the celibate ideal and to praise the husband and the housewife over the monk and the nun in principle. Repeatedly one reads that God respects marriage as much as virginity, that an unhappy marriage is preferable to unhappy chastity, that celibacy, while more desirable than marriage for those few who can freely and happily maintain it, is a supernatural gift God rarely bestows.[26] Commenting on his own experience under vows, Eberlin von Günzburg described the celibate life as a daily nagging of conscience and unrest of mind, a state in which all joy became a suffering, all consolation saddening, all sweetness bitter, a condition that dulled and deadened the senses, hardened the heart, restrained natural honesty, made one uncivil, inhumane, and frequently susceptible to feelings of remorse, at times so twisting one's judgment that one came to hate salvation and the good in one's life and to long for misfortune.[27] Erasmus deemed vows of celibacy "blind superstition" arising from inadequate knowledge of human nature. Well before the Protestants made it their issue, Erasmus had ridiculed the church's condemning of clerical marriage, while it tolerated and profited from clerical concubinage, and he praised family life over the cloister. Erasmus was also concerned that celibacy inhibited the growth of population in the west at a time of Turkish expansion; not only was celibacy a contradictory ideal in light of God's command to procreate, it also threatened to become self-destructive if large segments of society embraced it.[28]

No tribute to the estate of marriage was more eloquent than that of the fifteenth-century Bamberg humanist and canon Albrecht von Eyb:

> What could be happier and sweeter than the name of father, mother, and children [that is, a family], where the children hang on their parents' arms and exchange many sweet kisses with them, and where husband and wife are so drawn to one another by love and choice, and experience such friendship between themselves that what one wants, the other also chooses, and what one says, the other maintains in silence as if he had said it himself; where all good and evil is held in common, the good all the happier, the adversity all the lighter, because shared by two.[29]

Not only did the creation of woman and the blessing of marriage make it possible for humankind to know, love, obey, and enjoy God into eternity, but marriage also controlled the sins of concupiscence and fornication by giving each person a handy, regular, and legitimate sexual partner.[30] Men and women have been so created for marriage that they resist it at their peril (*muss dran*), declared the Thuringian Lutheran Justus Menius; it is both the rule of nature and the command of God; to ask whether one should marry is like asking whether one should breathe, eat, drink, or attend to other natural needs and functions: "Every man should and must have his wife and every woman her husband."[31] One who truly understands marriage, still another reformer maintained, does not fret over how much must go into it, as do its critics, but rather marvels at how much comes out of it.[32] Boomed Luther, still unmarried: "When a father washes diapers or performs some other mean task for his child, and someone ridicules him as an effeminate fool . . . God with all his angels and creatures is smiling."[33]

According to its defenders, marriage stabilized both individuals and society as a whole. By creating families, von Eyb pointed out, marriage filled a land with homes and communities, instruments of civil peace, and by turning strangers into relatives and friends, it reduced enmity, war, and hostility.[34] Marriage not only created sound bodies, good conscience, property, honor, and families, Luther insisted, it also helped pacify entire cities and lands by bringing order and purpose to sexual commerce.[35] As marriage laid the foundation of household government (*Oeconomia*, *Haushaltung*), family life in turn imparted to a new generation the values by which society at large was governed.

The profound social significance that Protestants attached to marriage was illustrated by the marriage services of newly reformed Wittenberg (1524) and Nuremberg (1526), both of which elaborated the second chapter of Genesis. The new service in Wittenberg stressed that marriage was "a far different thing than what the world presently jokes about and insults"; on the one hand, it is the end of a man's loneliness, as he and his bride become "one thing, like a cake"; on the other, it is a penitential institution in which the wife freely accepts the pain of childbirth and subjection to her husband, and the husband the pain of daily labor and worry over his family's well-being.[36] Before the prospective bride and bridegroom formalized their vows in Nuremberg, they were read the story of the first marriage, the subsequent fall of Adam and Eve, and mankind's consequent guilt and need for penance and redemption.[37] The couple's assumption of the responsibility, self-discipline, and suffering of marriage — the husband's "toil" and the wife's "labor" — was presented as part of the process by which mankind recovers from its fallen condition. Although this was not the most cheery of nuptial messages, both services exalted marriage as the foundation and nucleus of society and the divine instrument for its stability and reform. Little wonder that Lutherans described parents as "priests" and "bishops."

The home, then, was no introspective, private sphere, unmindful of society, but the cradle of citizenship, extending its values and example into the world around it. The habits and character developed within families became the virtues that shaped entire lands.

Where today children were raised to be god-fearing, obedient, and virtuous, the reformers expected tomorrow to find a citizenry capable of self-sacrifice and altruism, as well.[38] In the great housefather books of the seventeenth century, written as comprehensive guides to the management of home and manor, direction of a household was presented as the highest human art. A father not only provided for the present and future needs of his immediate family but also extended his household throughout the fatherland, as its members assisted church and school, friends and neighbors, the poor and the needy.[39]

The Liberation of Women from Cloisters

Throughout the Middle Ages and well into the Renaissance, women were depicted as the physical and mental inferiors of men, and marriage was considered an institution best shunned by knowledgeable males. A broad spectrum of scholastic, theological, medical, ethical, and legal texts assumed the inferiority of women and on this basis defined and proclaimed for them a circumscribed place in life.[40] This point of view embraced deep misogynist and antimarriage sentiments that had existed since antiquity, but that had gained a special resonance in the high and later Middle Ages through the church's promotion of the celibate life. Although accepted theories about the nature and place of women did not always originate with the Christian clerical classes, it was largely through them that such theories gained religious sanction and popular currency.

To the medieval cleric, unmarried virgins and continent widows were always spiritually superior to wives and mothers, and marriage was a debased state in comparison with the life of the cloister.[41] Jean Gerson, probably western Europe's most influential theologian in the early fifteenth century, elaborated such a conviction when he

urged his six sisters to live together and avoid marriage. He instructed them to consider the many advantages, both in this life and
in the life to come, of virginity and celibacy in contrast to the endless
"solicitudes and cares of marriage" they had witnessed in their
parents' lives. Gerson had no doubt that if the choice were fairly
weighed, his sisters would choose to remain single and chaste, like
him and their three other brothers. "For there is no service in the
world more pleasing to God, no way of life more loved by him, than
total virginity of body and mind." He turned aside protestations of
unfulfilled sexual desire with the assurance that "for every [sexual]
pleasure there are four pains." Since four of his sisters were in their
late teens or twenties, he assured them that they had already passed
through "the most difficult period of temptation by evil flesh" as he
directed their minds to the temporal and eternal rewards of continued continence.[42]

This belief was deep and persisting. In the fourth rule of the
Spiritual Exercises (1548), Ignatius of Loyola commanded loyal
Catholics "to praise highly the religious life, virginity, and continence; and also matrimony, but not as highly."[43] In medieval
religion, continent monks and nuns spiritually excelled husbands
and wives, fathers and mothers, just as the clergy spiritually excelled
the laity and the religious vocation excelled all secular callings.

Bias against sex and marriage pervaded canon law. Canonists as
a group have been described as "restrained in their enthusiasm for
marriage as an institution," accepting it as a cure for fornication and
an aid to social stability, but not recognizing it as an intrinsically
desirable state.[44] Behind such feelings lay the sexual prejudices of the
church fathers, especially St. Augustine and St. Jerome, who viewed
the taking of pleasure in any creaturely thing as idolatry, the mark
of humankind's fallen nature. Whereas an upright person took
pleasure only in God and used the things of the world to God's glory,
fallen men and women were enslaved to their lusts and passions, no
longer masters of their wills, and eager to worship the world in place
of its creator. In what area of human experience did one delight in a
creature more totally and intensely than in carnal pleasure? Where
was fallen man more self-indulgent and forgetful of God than at the
point of sexual ecstasy? Christian clerics viewed sexual emotion as
the supreme commentary on humankind's fallenness, empirical
proof of the loss of that reasoned self-control and obedience to God
that had originally characterized Adam and Eve.[45] According to the
canonist Huguccio (d. 1210), an extreme Augustinian on this issue,
sexual intercourse could never occur without sin, even among married people, since pleasure always accompanied it. A famous tract in

praise of marriage by the sixteenth-century Catholic humanist and reformer Juan Luis Vives (d. 1540) reflected the persistence of such belief—and revealed its irony and self-contradiction when the author recoiled from sexual intercourse as a "beastly activity" that turned the mind away from spiritual contemplation.[46] Even Luther, arguably the sixteenth century's most outspoken defender of marriage and sexual intercourse within it, one who criticized the church fathers for being deceived by "unclean celibacy" into denigrating marriage, seems to have believed that sexual intercourse between spouses, while not "unchaste" and to be enjoyed with a good conscience, still remained to some degree sinful.[47] The majority of canonists were more consoling than Huguccio and the stricter Augustinian tradition. They "excused" sex in marriage and acknowledged its goodness, provided that spouses engaged in sex consciously for the sake of procreation or to pay the marital debt—motives that placed sex safely under God's commandments to be fruitful and multiply and avoid illicit fornication.[48]

Canonists also played a role in promoting the popular perception of women as temptresses. Whereas in Roman law it was presumed that men were the sexual aggressors and women their victims, canon lawyers, again under the influence of the church fathers, stressed the sexually predatory nature of women. They found support for their views in contemporary medical opinion, which depicted women as sexually insatiable by nature; some medical authorities believed, for example, that without regular moisturizing with male semen, the uterus would dry up—hence woman's constant need for sex. These same legal theorists were also impressed by the biological fact that girls reached puberty at an earlier age than boys (women, like weeds, explained the canonist Hostiensis, mature earlier than desirable plants.)[49] Because of woman's assumed overpowering sexual desire and her weak, pliant mind and will, medieval theologians, following a logic peculiarly their own, generally subjected her to the strictest standards of sexual morality, standards their own theories denied she could maintain. In nunneries the restrictions on contact with the world were far greater than in monasteries,[50] although woman's greater physical vulnerability must also have been a factor. According to some, a woman's mastery of the cloistered life was a higher achievement than a man's success in the monastery because her nature placed greater obstacles to the fulfillment of religious vows.

The impact on the laity of such teaching can be seen in the prying into the sexual activity of married penitents during confession. Confessors who followed the rules laid down by canonists inter-

rogated married couples about their sexual habits and prescribed
penances for a large variety of sexual sins. "How One Sins in the
Marital Duty," a section of a vernacular catechism published in
1494, cited the following "sexual sins of marriage" in commentary
on the third deadly sin (impurity) to prepare the laity for confession.
Laity were said to sin sexually in marriage by unnatural acts and
positions, contraception, and masturbation;[51] by desiring sex with
another while performing it with one's own spouse; by desiring sex
with another while not performing it with one's spouse; by refusing
the marital duty without an "honest" reason, thereby possibly causing one's spouse to "fall" (that is, to enter an illicit relationship in
order to satisfy his or her thwarted sexual desires); by having sex in
forbidden seasons (the menstrual period and final weeks of pregnancy were specified, but abstinence was also generally expected
during lactation and the penitential seasons of the church calendar);
by continuing to have sex with a known adulterous spouse (a prohibition Luther found particularly outrageous); and by having sex
out of sheer lust for one's spouse (*von wollusts wegen*) rather than, as
God had commanded, in order to flee the sin of concupiscence and
to populate the earth.[52] It was also commonplace in late medieval
tracts and sermons to depict marriage as itself a "religious order,"
one oriented to the world and having its own moral rules and
spiritual discipline.[53] Such modeling of marriage on the ascetic
ideals of the religious was doubtless flattering from the point of view
of the clergy, but many laity considered it an inappropriate standard and found the Reformation's criticism of it most appealing.

Because canon lawyers generally assumed the existence of an
emotional bond of affection between spouses and because they subjected men to the same sexual obligations and prohibitions as
women, they have been depicted as advocates of sexual equality who
"made it possible to view sexual intercourse as an act that embodied
some of the finest and highest human values."[54] A more measured
judgment, I believe, would be that the canonists, by so exalting
celibacy and the cloister as the supreme forms of individual and
communal self-realization, indirectly demeaned marriage and
family as an imperfect, second-class estate.

In challenging the celibate ideal, Protestant critics were particularly concerned to expose the repressive nature of the nunnery,
to free nuns from their cloisters, and allow them to rejoin society.
They believed that women suffered more under vows than men,
were more readily bullied by their superiors, and had far greater
difficulty in breaking their vows and taking flight. Their concen-
trated attack on nunneries in the 1520s also reflected the Protestant

reformers' own recent appreciation of the joys of marriage and their rejection of the convent as a proper solution to the social problem of unmarried women.

Here we should pause to remember that for the vast majority of women in late medieval times, especially those in the lower and middle strata of society, a vocation was the least of their worries. Women filled many different occupations, although concern for propriety and unfair competition occasionally led city governments to restrict the type of work women could do (for example, in Würzburg wives, maids, and children were prohibited from selling the *wurst* made by their husbands, masters, and fathers). Unmarried single women labored as nurses, midwives, maids, barmaids, prostitutes, small shopkeepers, bearers of water, stone, and coal, weavers, flax workers, street sweepers, and guild assistants.[55] Women belonged to guilds (in Lübeck they became craft masters), and those with a skilled trade before marriage continued it after marriage. When Gotschalk von Weinsberg, a carpenter, married in Cologne in June 1585, his wife not only brought a 200 thaler dowry, but she continued after the marriage to run a successful shop selling fish, butter, and cheese, apparently at the same location as Gotschalk's carpentry shop.[56] Women regularly marketed their husbands' produce (some were engaged in international trade) and could be described as true business partners with their husbands. Usually a widow continued to operate her deceased husband's business, although certain guilds required younger widows to remarry as a condition of continued membership. From butchers to goldsmiths, women were found in virtually every craft and large numbers of single and married women worked in their homes as piece workers for the textile, food, and drink industries. All women were expected in addition to maintain their households; employment in a skilled trade was no excuse for neglecting essential housework.[57]

Gainful, meaningful work was more of a problem for unmarried women in the upper social strata. For these women the main alternative to marriage was the cloister, sometimes because of genuine religious enthusiasm, but just as often because the family was unable or unwilling to provide the dowry necessary for a suitable marriage, especially for younger daughters. In northern Europe large numbers of such women, from well-to-do mercantile and aristocratic families, found their way into nunneries and beguinages, or lay sisterhoods. Between 1250 and 1320, for example, the city of Cologne established more than a hundred beguinages, each housing ten to twelve women, in an effort to catch the overflow of women, including those from the lower and middle strata, who could not find places in convents of the established orders. In fifteenth-century Strasbourg eight nunneries existed, and only one Dominican monastery.[58]

Families placed their sons and daughters in cloisters between the ages five and seven, and for some children the cloister became a cruel life of hard labor, boring routine, beatings, and fear of sexual sin and assault.[59] That children placed involuntarily in cloisters could grow up to resent their parents for it is suggested by a carnival song of nuns sung in mock derision of the cloister in late medieval Tuscany:

> It was not our intention
> To wear this black . . .
> We had little knowledge
> When we put on these robes.
> But now that we're grown up
> We know our error . . .
> I curse my father
> Who wanted me held here.[60]

Although the lay "appetite for the divine" had not slackened on the eve of the Reformation, and the doctrinal authority of the church continued to be respected,[61] the number of women entering cloisters appears to have been in decline. This was in part a response to growing lay criticism and anticlericalism, which focused especially on the religious orders' inability to maintain their high ideals of poverty and chastity, a failure attested by the steady evolution of monasteries into major landholders and business enterprises and by rampant clerical whoring and concubinage. Noblewomen seem also to have taken advantage of new educational opportunities and social freedoms to find self-expression in other activities, including nontraditional religious movements.[62] With the growing success of the Reformation, the number of women entering cloisters declined precipitously and irreversibly in many parts of northern Europe. Whereas approximately 3,500 nuns had filled English convents in 1350, only 1,900 were counted in 1534 when Parliament began to implement the reforms that would by the end of the decade dissolve all monasteries and nunneries. In Lutheran lands the young were denied entrance into the cloister altogether in the 1520s. The few continuing cloisters died a natural death with those women who had been permitted to remain — predominantly older women without family and friends to take them in, who could not have survived on their own in the world, and deeply devout religious women who were prepared to resist expulsion at any cost.[63]

Modern scholars of the family, and particularly of women's history, frequently view the closing of the cloisters in Protestant lands as a major loss for women. They argue that the nunnery had provided ambitious women who were desirous of power and independence with a more attractive vocation than marriage, a place where they could escape constant subjection to men and rise to positions of authority as abbesses or prioresses.[64] One scholar describes nunneries as "a boon for women of the Middle Ages" that gave unmarried upper-class women an education, social commerce with their peers, and myriad responsibilities, while also serving as boarding houses for the wives and widows of the nobility.[65] Another writes somewhat more cautiously: "Despite androcentric and patriarchal assumptions, the institution of monasticism was for the Christian woman a real and concrete option, a little world occasionally run by and for women, where a woman had an alternative to the authority of father and husband."[66] Still another declares that the elimination of a separate identity and organization for women in the religious life was a loss that made women "a little more vulnerable to subjection in all spheres."[67]

Our sixteenth-century defenders of marriage would have dismissed such portrayals of the cloister as romantic at best and papist propaganda at worst. The tradition they opposed also depicted the cloister as a higher calling, especially for women, who otherwise would have remained, at best, mere wives. In the experience and observation of these writers, many of whom had been monks and nuns, abbesses and prioresses were far less independent and powerful in their cloisters than any honorable wife and mother in her home. With rare exception, nuns had to submit to the discipline of supervisory monks, who either lodged nearby or made regular visits to the convents and beguinages under their jurisdiction. An example of what this might involve was the convent of Maria of Bethlehem in Cologne, a beguinage supervised by observant Franciscans, who used it as a refuge when passing through town. When the monks arrived, usually unexpectedly (the chronicler described their visits as "raids" [*uberfall*], the sisters had to prepare their meals, making personal sacrifices if the larder was poorly stocked, and do their laundry ("shirts, pants, and bedclothes"), receiving nothing in return. The sisters split into factions opposed to and accepting these visits. Several, including the abbess, complained to the civil and ecclesiastical authorities about such rude treatment, but the monks had cultivated special relationships with certain other nuns (described by the chronicler as their "spiritually converted sisters"), who favored their visits (a "strange

business" [*seltsam handel*] according to the chronicler, whose family
had founded the convent and whose sister was there enclosed). The
monks finally alienated so many of the sisters that one night in 1538
when they came knocking they found themselves locked out. The en-
suing commotion led to an official investigation, the upshot of which
was to prohibit the Franciscans from taking refuge in the convent,
which thereafter came under the supervision of a special visiting
committee. A secular priest was assigned to minister to the sisters'
spiritual needs.[68]

As modern scholars sympathetic to the nunnery as an important
vocational option for women have acknowledged, cloistered women
were far more strictly regulated than cloistered men. In the so-called
double monasteries that existed until the fifteenth century, the nuns
did all the housekeeping and maintained the kitchen, cellar, and
economy of the two houses; rarely was a convent not under the
supervision of male clergy and regular male discipline.[69] Religiously
inspired women were attracted to heterodox convents, like those of
the Catharist Beguines, and to heterodox religious movements, like
Lollardy, Hussitism, and the seventeenth-century English sects, in
part because of the greater informality and spiritual egalitarianism
there in contrast to traditional religious life, which permitted them
to assume important cultic and administrative responsibilities.[70] Not
only did the nunnery offer no safe escape from male rule, it imposed
sexual self-denial and created guilt among the unsuccessful, burdens
no honorable wife was forced to bear, as the defenders of marriage
were quick to point out. The ex-Franciscan Eberlin von Günzburg
charged that nuns living under the authority of "foolish, ignorant,
and inexperienced monks" knew more unhappiness than women did
in marriage. In the early 1520s he advised aristocratic fathers to permit their daughters to marry day laborers rather than venture upon
the greater mismatch of the cloister, and he urged magistrates to
transform nunneries into preparatory schools for marriage and
homemaking.[71]

In the 1520s fathers and friends of women in cloisters, occasionally urged on by Protestant reformers, planned and executed
"escapes." These heroics, sometimes accomplished with swords
drawn, were celebrated in the pamphlet literature, which sought
both to expose the religious life and to inspire others to similar deeds.
One such rescuer was Leonhard Koppe, a Torgau burgher, whose
exploits were celebrated by Luther. Koppe regularly delivered herring to the cloister at Nimbschen near Grimma, where his daughter
was a nun. This cloister also held Katherine von Bora, Luther's
future wife, who had lived there since she was fifteen (she was

twenty-four at the time of her departure in 1523). Twelve Nimbschen nuns, including Koppe's daughter and Katherine, came under the influence of the Reformation and with Koppe's help fled the cloister (Koppe apparently smuggled them out in empty herring barrels). Three of the freed nuns returned to their families in electoral Saxony, but the other nine were natives of ducal Saxony, which had remained militantly Catholic under Duke George. Koppe took them to Wittenberg and placed them in Luther's charge. Luther arranged their marriages to eligible bachelors and in the process ended up with Katherine (who appears to have had her eye on him from the start), after twice failing to wed her to others.[72]

In a pamphlet entitled *Why Nuns May Leave Cloisters with God's Blessing* (1523), Luther praised Koppe's deed as an example for all parents with children in cloisters, comparing it to Moses's deliverance of the children of Israel from Egyptian bondage and Christ's "theft" of mankind from the Prince of the World. Luther urged parents to heed their daughters' petitions and consider their plight, insisting that it was the cloistered women themselves, not outsiders, who initiated such escapes. Placed in convents while still "young, foolish, and inexperienced girls," they grew up to find themselves without help in the most difficult struggle of their lives, one Luther was convinced they could not win, namely, the suppression of their sexual nature, something even women armed with God's true Word and special grace seldom conquered.[73] Only "unmerciful" parents and friends and "blind and mad" bishops and abbots, he concluded, would permit girls to suffer and waste away in cloisters, for "a woman is not created to be a virgin, but to conceive and bear children."[74]

In Nuremberg in 1524 the Lutheran reformer Andreas Osiander celebrated a heroic rescue of cloistered nuns by Johann of Schwartzenberg, a nobleman whose daughter was the prioress of a convent near Bamberg, where she had lived for some twenty years. Schwartzenberg learned that his daughter and her sisters were being bullied by their monkish supervisors, who monitored their daily devotions and regularly censured their reading in an attempt to keep out Protestant propaganda and vernacular Scriptures. When his daughter protested these intrusions into their lives, they paid her no heed, even though she was the prioress. Schwartzenberg assembled what amounted to a small commando unit of like-minded fathers and sympathizers, who invaded the monastery and forcibly rescued the disconsolate sisters.[75] Osiander, whose eight-page preface dwarfed Schwartzenberg's two-page account of the episode, raged against "tyrannical mendicants" and the nuns who passively become their concubines "in the bedrooms of their consciences."[76]

Opponents of the religious life campaigned actively through the press on behalf of women in cloisters. A sophisticated example is a pseudonymous pamphlet circulated in 1524, addressed to "all abbesses and prioresses of nunneries and beguinages," which provided detailed instruction on "how to make cloisters Christian." This guide to the dissolution of the traditional cloister anticipated procedures that were sanctioned by law when secular authorities later dissolved cloisters in Lutheran countries. The authors called for ending all masses, vigils, holidays, and canonical hours; having a preacher to interpret God's Word daily to the sisters; and stocking the library with the books of Luther, Philip Melanchthon, and Johann Bugenhagen. At matins, vernacular readings from the Psalms and the two Testaments were to replace traditional Latin prayers, and Luther's new German Mass was to replace the traditional Mass, while the Eucharist was to be administered in both kinds. A list of appropriate hymns and liturgical readings was appended. Regarding discipline for misconduct, the authors called for an end to public and corporal punishment; no more straw crowns to ridicule, no more bans (that is, periods of ostracization), no more periods of imprisonment.[77] Fasting and special dress were no longer to be required. Above all, no celibate vows were to be made, nor any woman forced to remain in a cloister against her will: "Let the poor virgins be unbound so that none is any longer obligated by such devilish belief [celibacy]. Let them stay in the cloister only so long as they freely choose, and when one wishes no longer to remain, let her follow the example of her friends, take a husband, and serve her neighbors in the world."[78]

Those who left the cloister were advised to "fortify" their consciences in advance; because excommunication and persecution awaited them, it was imperative that they understand clearly what they were doing and why. Here the authors recognized the personal and social pressures a woman faced when she broke with such a long-standing habit. In appendices to the pamphlet they instructed dissident and renegade nuns being punished by excommunication and other ecclesiastical threats to complain to their secular magistrates, who had an obligation to protect them.[79] The psychologically perceptive authors also warned that those who were leaving the cloister to marry should expect an attack of conscience. To prepare for such a radical transition, the writers suggested that the women first study all the passages of Scripture that recommend and praise the estate of marriage.[80] Recognizing that for the time being some cloisters would have to continue to care for old nuns who, either by desire or by circumstance, could not leave and live in the world, the authors still looked forward to the day when all cloisters would be transformed into Christian schools that reared children in Protestant doctrine, discipline, and self-respect (*Zucht, leer und eere*).[81]

No propaganda proved more effective in exposing the cloister than the testimony of former nuns, whom the reformers encouraged to write and publish accounts of their lives under vows. One such account, published in Wittenberg by Luther in 1524, told the story of Florentina of Ober Weimar, the daughter of a nobleman who had been placed in the cloister at age six. Florentina recounted in great detail the maturation of a noncomprehending and nonconforming sister. Confirmed at eleven while still too young to understand fully what the religious life would require of her (*in unwissender jugent eingesegenet*), at fourteen she discovered that neither her talents nor her nature enabled her to maintain vows of chastity, poverty, and obedience.[82] After confessing this discovery to the mother superior, she was firmly instructed to put such thoughts from her mind and accept her eternal marriage to Christ.[83] At the end of her novitiate she was given an opportunity to leave the cloister, but she claims that she felt compelled by her peers and superiors to say what they wanted to hear[84] and thus became a nun against her true feelings and to the continuing distress of her conscience.

With the coming of the Reformation, Florentina appealed to Luther for advice and assistance, and therewith her trials began in earnest. Whey they learned of her letter, her superiors placed her in solitary confinement and required her to confess in writing over a period of several weeks all "secret or public, solitary or group transgressions" against the Rule and the ordinances of the cloister over the past three years. They also forced her to confess the same orally before all the sisters in the chapter. Then she was "banned" to her cell for a period of three days, during which time she had to lie prostrate at the singing of the hours. Thereafter she came under the so-called "lesser ban" (*klaynen bann*), which permitted her to attend choir but required her to prostrate herself as the sisters entered and exited over her. As a three-day penance, she sat at mealtime on the floor before the prioress with a straw garland on her head. Then she had to choose five people who henceforth served as her "parole officers" (*die mein burgen sollten werden*), to whom she vowed never again to do anything that would alienate her from the religious life. Perceiving that her heart was not in such a promise, the mother superior assigned a special "deputy" to watch over her day and night, wherever she went and whatever she did. The other sisters were instructed to treat her as an untrustworthy prisoner.[85] Florentina further reported that for seven weeks, on Wednesdays and Fridays, as many as ten persons at a time would "specially discipline" her, apparently a form of group interrogation and verbal chastisement.

A second series of punishments befell Florentina at a later date, after the discovery of a note from her to an Evangelical nephew, Caspar von Watzdorf, who was apparently working for her release. According to Florentina, she was now punished in ways so insulting, shameful, and debasing that pious people should neither read nor hear about them.[86] She claims to have been flogged by the mother superior and four others until they grew weary and then placed again in the cloister prison, where she remained for eight days, with her legs in chains for one day and night. When permitted to return to choir and the refectory, she was made to stand with the children. Locked in her cell by day, she was denied both visitors and conversation. Florentina expected such treatment to be her lot forevermore. But thanks to great fortune, which she now considered to be providential, the sisters charged to watch her neglected one day to lock her cell door and she escaped to tell her story, which, according to her benefactor Luther, revealed the truth about nuns and nunneries.

Another exposé of the cloister by one who had reluctantly been there came from the hand of Ursula, duchess of Monsterberg. In Wittenberg in 1528, Luther published her letter to Saxon officials in defense of her flight with two other nuns from their cloister in Freiberg. Apologizing in a brief postscript for making public still another exposé of the cloister when a claimed "surplus" already circulated, Luther explained that this one was "too important" to keep private. Saxon officials had criticized Ursula's departure from the religious life as "light-hearted impertinence"; given her prominence and their traditional piety, they had been genuinely upset and embarrassed by it. Stung by the charge, Ursula addressed her letter to dukes George and Heinrich and any other Saxon official in whose disfavor she now stood. At both the beginning and the end she insisted that every word was her own, written without coaching or counsel from anyone else, so that all might know that "I have not acted either frivolously or precipitously, but with good cause and after careful deliberation."[87] The professed independence of her act notwithstanding, Ursula had thoroughly absorbed Luther's new theology. She wrote that Christians are married to Christ by faith and that those who place their trust in celibate vows and the works of the cloister betray that faith; this recognition, she claimed, is what has disturbed women in cloisters and prompted them to flee. "Our salvation is not such a venal thing that we can sell it or market it for human favor, for we know there is no abiding place on earth."[88] She recalled having watched with horror as sisters in the cloister died uncertain of God's mercy and in fear of his judgment, having failed to find consolation in their vows and religious works.[89] According to Ursula, the works of the cloister proceeded from unhappy hearts and created bad consciences. She acknowledged her own fear and guilt over the importance she once attached to Mary and the saints, an error she ascribed largely to the failings of her sex, as she now rejoiced that God had given a new understanding of Christ to "women [like myself] who have been by nature weak, pliable, and fickle."[90]

Unlike most male pamphleteers against the cloister, neither Florentina nor Ursula dwelt on unfulfilled sexual desire and the emotional benefits of a companionable marriage. (I suspect this was an oversight based more on modesty than on lack of concern.) Others did directly contrast marriage and family with the celibate ideal. An example was an exchange of letters between a married woman and an older acquaintance in a nunnery whom the married woman had attempted to "enlighten" by sending her Protestant books and sermons, a common tactic in the ideological warfare of the 1520s. The sister responded by burning the books and sermons ("much bad was mixed in with the good," she claimed), and she denounced the attempt to convert her by declaring it better for a nun to be chained in her cloister against her will than to be permitted to abandon her habit and marry.[91] The wife's reply circulated as an anonymous pamphlet, which summarized the episode and carried on its title page a portrayal of a nun burning books. Condemning the nun's indocility, the wife retorted that God had nowhere commanded men and women to withdraw to cloisters, but rather "to marry, work hard, love our children, and serve our neighbors"; in the realization of Christian perfection the home far surpassed the cloister. "How many thousands of people can one find who are married and have beautiful, lovable children and lead a manifestly better Christian life than those who are in cloisters! These people, who suffer in poverty with their children and earn their living by the sweat of their brow, keep God's commandment according to his word."[92]

In a similar vein Bernhard Rem, who described himself as the "organist" of the Fuggers, having long worried that his cloistered daughter Feronica and her friends were "worshiping God without understanding" and failing to lead a proper Christian life, urged them to flee the cloister of St. Katherine in Augsburg. According to Rem, the original purpose of the cloister was to provide a school of Christian doctrine and discipline, where youth might be taught obedience and Holy Scripture and raised in the fear of God — not to create a so-called "state of perfection" that bound youth to vows and rules they could not keep, while inculcating in them a sense of superiority over all other Christians. "If the life of the cloister were really as important as you presume," he wrote to the sisters, "then we would all have to become monks and nuns."[93] Rem proclaimed that the original purpose of the cloister was now better served by the home and that marriage was the sisters' best defense against the Devil, sexual desire, and the sin of pride. Because there is so much idleness in the cloister, in contrast with the activities of the home, "the Devil has many more opportunities there to plant evil thoughts."[94] Rem also believed that the cloister, unlike the home, did not prepare the sisters to "think freely and enjoy a properly reflective life." "When a nun prays or sings the Psalter in Latin, it is like the speech and song of a parrot; this is not the cloister of the days of St. Jerome, when nuns were properly taught the Word of God and could confidently resist temptation."[95] When a sister is "walled in" from the world, her carnal desires are not "walled out"; she experiences the demands of the flesh as powerfully as any layperson, only without the aid of marriage.

Finally, Rem wrote, the cloister, like the synagogue, teaches the sisters self-righteousness; some sisters remind him of a cat with a breadsop, so utterly self-content have they become. In contrast, he pointed to the pious housewife who spends her day washing diapers, grinding millet, feeding her household, and rearing her children with love and devotion, yet does not think that any of these activities make her pious or save her, looking solely to Christ for her salvation. "This woman does her work for the good of her neighbor, confesses her sins, trusts in God's mercy, and honors God in all things."[96]

Not every sister was as distressed by the religious regimen nor as eager to escape the nunnery as Florentina of Ober Weimar and Ursula of Monsterberg. Rem's daughter, to his great dismay, proved to be one of those who did not wish to leave. The sisters of St. Katherine's, and especially his daughter, took offense at the way he characterized their vocation and presumed to dictate temporal and eternal happiness to them. Assuring him that they had not placed their hope in their own works but in God, whom they freely served in the cloister, the sisters accused Rem of trying to confuse and demoralize them (*woltest uns gern verirren und klainmutig machen*) and suggested that he examine his own self-righteousness. Boasting that they had many good books in the cloister, they refused henceforward to accept any more books from him.[97]

The church did not simply leave nuns to their own devices in the face of the Protestant campaign. Catholic pamphleteers came to the defense of the cloister, albeit belatedly and perhaps with too heavy a hand. A striking example was a pamphlet attack on Katherine von Bora, the prototype of the renegade nun, by Joachim von der Heyden, secretary to Duke George of Saxony. Von der Heyden denounced Katherine as one who had forsaken her cloister, donned layman's clothing "like a dancing girl," fled to the University of Wittenberg, and there, before the eyes of all, become "a little rat servant," living openly in disgrace with Luther before finally marrying him.[98] She was accused of having led many other sisters astray by her example, women who now found themselves far more impoverished (*ermer dan arm*) than they had ever been in the cloister and scorned by others as the most despicable of people (*die vorechtlichsten lewth*). Whereas before they had lived in "respectable, handsome, and happy cloisters," with their bodily needs well attended, many now grubbed for their lowly fare "by sin and shame," some even in public houses, having been "lured out of the cloister like fish by a false bait," promised new bodily and spiritual freedom by the Lutherans, only to find their bodies and spirits "entombed in a terrible dungeon."[99]

Von der Heyden urged renegade nuns to return to their cloisters and do penance. To this end he appended excerpts in translation from St. Ambrose's *Instruction for a Fallen Nun*, a censorious work that compared a nun's flight from her cloister with the transformation of a dove into a serpent. Von der Heyden encouraged a sense of guilt. He had no sympathy with such excuses as "I could not contain my sexual desires" or "I was forced by others." Regardless of the circumstances, the forsaking of celibate vows was the worst imaginable form of adultery, a crime so great that von der Heyden declared his inability to conceive a sufficient punishment or a worthy death. "Your father now curses his bodily organ from which you issued and your mother the womb in which you were carried"; the parents' only consolation was the knowledge that they did not force upon their daughter the vows she now spurned, and hence they bore no responsibility for her disgracing the religious life.[100] He prescribed a penitential confession for the woman who finds it within herself to

return to her cloister: "The sin and the evil are mine, mine, mine
they are; a like transgression has not been found among humankind;
what I have done is terrifying, horrifying godlessness." [101]

Other Catholic apologists, instead of appealing to the consciences of lapsed nuns, sought to stir up political support for their
views. In 1528 a Cologne citizen, Johann Lansburg, protested to the
emperor against the "Lutheranization" of German cloisters, and his
letter became a popular vernacular pamphlet. Lansburg lamented
the process, all too familiar by 1528, by which monasteries and nunneries were stripped of their traditional images and artifacts, and
monks and nuns were subjected to Lutheran sermons before being
sent into the world on modest pensions (except those who were too
old or too stubborn to be pensioned off). Lansburg recalled the
divine mandate and long history of monasticism. As proof that the
celibate life was not only feasible, but even highly desirable, he cited
the fact that so many men and women had chosen to live in cloisters;
centuries of history contradicted the Lutheran claim that chastity
was an ideal beyond human nature. And how insulting was such a
claim to courtiers, merchants, and workers, as well as lords and
princes, who often had to be away from their wives on business for
long periods of time and, assuming that the Lutherans were correct
about the force of sexual desire, must conclude that their wives were
unfaithful to them in their absence. Turning the tables on the
Lutherans, Lansburg suggested that their arguments against
chastity were designed to excuse their own predilection for
"whoring."[102]

Protestants, totally unmoved by such arguments, dismissed as a
fiction the alleged social plight of unmarried noble and burgher
women, many of whose families had for generations found in nunneries or beguinages a vocational alternative to marriage for their
daughters.[103] As far as the reformers were concerned, opportunities
for marriage abounded; the rapid marriages of so many former
monks and nuns in the 1520s seemed proof enough. New ordinances
now prohibited boys and girls from entering cloisters and permitted
all present monks and nuns who could be persuaded to do so to
depart their cloisters and, if they wished, to marry.[104] Fathers were
instructed by the new clergy to find proper mates for *all* their
daughters. Those young women who still desired to lead a virgin's
life and seemed genuinely capable of doing so were advised to live at
home quietly without vows, supported by their parents.[105]

Both experience and belief had set Protestants unalterably
against the celibate life.[106] To them it contradicted both the Bible
and human nature, and created more personal and social problems

than it solved; as an alternative vocation to homemaking, the cloister was deemed inhumane and antisocial.

Disciplining Marriage

In the sixteenth century, Protestants discerned threats to the stability of marriage and family not only in the celibate ideal and the cultural values it nourished, but also in the marital legislation of the medieval church. Their specific targets were the church's recognition of the validity of so-called secret marriages — marriages that occurred in private without public witness and parental consent — and the church's refusal to sanction marriages it deemed incestuous by virtue of certain blood, legal, spiritual, or family relationships between the contracting partners.

Secret marriages had a secure but complicated place in canon law. Since the high Middle Ages boys and girls of legally marriageable age (fourteen for boys, twelve for girls) had been permitted to perform the sacrament of marriage effectually themselves. Marriages were made by God; priests only proclaimed his will for a couple after the fact. If a couple in private, following their hearts' desire, freely and directly promised to love one another and live together until death, then in the eyes of the church a valid marriage had occurred, especially if the couple had also consummated their vows by sexual intercourse. Although the union was not yet fully licit (that required solemnization in church), the two were said to have been joined together by God in a union no person, whether guardian or magistrate, could put asunder.

Since such marriages occurred privately, without witnesses and apart from any public institution, they could be only as real as those involved agreed they were; therein lay the grave problems of secret marriages. The courts were filled with cases of contested betrothal: girls seduced on alleged promises of marriage, parents challenging the secret unions of their children, bigamous "Casanovas" accused of secretly promising marriage to two or more women, and, possibly most embarrassing of all, men and women sincerely attempting to make public their private vows, only to be challenged by someone claiming to have been secretly promised marriage by one of the partners. Here was a fertile seedbed of domestic strife and litigation, keeping priests and local ecclesiastical courts very busy and, according to their critics, prosperous.[107] In the episcopal courts of late medieval Troyes and Châlons-sur-Marne, there were fifteen separate categories of marital litigation, fully half of which stemmed from informal betrothal.[108] Strasbourg in late medieval times witnessed repeated protests against its ecclesiastical courts, particularly their expansive system of domestic fines and punishments, which seemed at some point to touch every marriage in town.[109] Before the Protestant reformers made secret marriages an issue, Erasmus had condemned them as a major social evil and urged church officials to require both publicity and parental consent for a valid marriage.[110] Within the medieval church itself, such unions had a mixed reputation, but opponents were stymied by the canonical rule "consensus facit nuptias."[111]

The laws that recognized secret marriages had evolved from the teaching of two major twelfth-century legal theorists, Gratian and Peter Lombard.[112] Gratian, somewhat ambivalent toward such marriages,[113] held that a couple's private exchange of vows did not make a valid marriage until they were sexually consummated (*copula carnalis*), after which point the marriage also became sacramentally sealed. Prior to sexual commerce a marriage existing on vows alone could be dissolved and the parties set free to marry others, if they so chose. Germanic law also viewed cohabitation and sexual commerce as establishing a couple's social equality, along with mutual property rights and legal protections. In distinction from Gratian, Peter Lombard was impressed, as most canonists would be, by the example of Mary and Joseph, whose marriage had been consummated by verbal consent alone without sexual commerce. Lombard argued that a marriage was both valid and sacramentally sealed at the moment a couple who were of age and without impediments freely promised one another in good faith to be man and wife, what came to be known as "*present* vows of marriage" (*sponsalia per verba de praesenti*).[114] Lombard distinguished such vows from a couple's penultimate promise to exchange final marriage vows in the *future* (*sponsalia per verba de futuro*), or what we would today call an engagement.

In the later Middle Ages, church law deemed a present exchange of vows in private ("I, Hans, take you, Gretel, today as my wife"; "I, Gretel, take you, Hans, today as my husband") to constitute a valid marriage (Lombard); to be sacramentally sealed, it had to be sexually consummated (Gratian). This meant that an unconsummated marriage based on present vows had the character of permanency in the eyes of the church but was not yet spiritually permanent in the persons of the married couple themselves. Such a marriage could be dissolved if one of the spouses chose to enter a cloister, that is, to take a higher vow, or if the pope granted a dispensation from the church law that deemed a person validly married. Sexual commerce after an exchange of vows, whether present or future, always carried with it the presumption of full marital consent, so that a sexually consummated promise of marriage, assuming all the requisite legal requirements (proper age, absence of impediments) had been met, established an indissoluble bond of matrimony both in the eyes of the church and in the souls of the spouses. Penultimate promises to marry in the future ("I, Hans, promise to take you, Gretel, next June to be my wife"; "I, Gretel, promise to take you, Hans, next June to be my husband") could be dissolved either by mutual consent, or if either party did one of the following: made *present* vows with a third party; moved away to another land; slept with a third party; turned apostate or heretical; or fell victim to leprosy.[115]

The church's recognition of private marriages reflected a certain personalizing of marriage vows in the later Middle Ages that was also attested in secular law, albeit hardly so radically as by the church. Germanic law began to recognize betrothal (*desponsatio*) as a contract between a bride and her suitor, rather than as an arrangement entered by a suitor and her guardian independently of the bride's knowledge and wishes.[116] The so-called *Muntehe* or *Brautkauf* of traditional German law, according to which the person holding legal authority (*Munt*) over a woman (her parent or guardian) arranged as he saw fit to transfer (*Brautkauf*, "bride purchase") this authority to a prospective husband, remained intact in the sense that parents could disinherit a child who married against their wishes.[117] But no one advocated that men and women be forced to marry against their wills; indeed, there is every indication that far more men and women married with little outside consultation than married by parental fiat.[118] By declaring marriage to be preeminently a sacrament and a spiritual matter between God and the spouses themselves, the church released marriage in principle from arbitrary parental control, although it did not thereby intend to encourage marriages in defiance of parents and a public church service.

Despite a new recognition of the bride's wishes in secular law and the church's sanction of secret marriages, parental influence over the choice of mates remained very strong in late medieval and early modern Europe. This was not simply, or even primarily, an expression of the "paternalism" of the age, as modern scholars have tended to argue. For both children and parents in a society that prized community, a marriage that united families and friends was preferable to one that divided them, so there was an abiding concern on *both* sides to contract marriages pleasing to the spouses as well as to their parents.

Also in the later Middle Ages the church began to play a more prominent role in the marriage ceremony itself. Whereas the priest's blessing upon a marriage had traditionally been a secondary act that publicized and made licit an earlier exchange of vows, usually at home with the couple's family, the priest now began regularly to transfer a bride to her husband before the church doors (therein approximating the traditional authority of parent or guardian) and to pronounce the church's blessing upon the couple at the church altar.[119] Such formal ceremonies continued to make a marriage fully licit in the eyes of the community at large by publicizing it, but now also brought about a close association in the popular mind between getting married and "going to church."

The Protestant reformers condemned the recognition of secret marriages as an encouragement to marry on the basis of sexual desire alone. Youth who exchanged vows because of sexual attraction (*auff ausserlich schöne des leibs*) defeated one of the main purposes of marriage, argued the Eisenach reformer Jacob Strauss, which was to tame the old Adam in human nature, not strengthen it. "When the honeymoon is over and one has to contend with the body of a sick spouse, then we discover how lasting is the fidelity of a marriage based on lust."[120] According to the Swabian reformer Johannes Brenz, a "valid" marriage could only be one contracted in a "sensible, legal, and godly manner" (*billich rechtlich und Göttlich*).

> When two young people secretly and without the knowledge and will of their parents, in the disobedience and ignorance of youth, as if intoxicated, wantonly and deceitfully, sometimes aided and abetted by a matchmaker, lying flattery, or other unreasonable means, join themselves together in marriage, who would not agree that such a union has been brought about by Satan and not by the Lord God?[121]

What Satan had joined together, Brenz had no doubts society could put asunder with impunity; it was the *circumstances* of marriage vows, not the vows per se, that gave marriage its validity.

Brenz agreed with the proponents of secret marriages that God had not made children to be bondservants of their parents, but he insisted that God intended children to use their freedom "to do what is right and to be obedient." Only wicked and unchristian parents should be defied; pious children could always reach an accommodation with "good Christian parents." As for the argument that what happened between the sexes in matters of the heart was the "mysterious providence of God," Brenz despaired that from such a point of view it would be impossible to distinguish the secretly married from common fornicators.[122]

Deploring a "more superficial and unheeding" approach to marriage among his contemporaries, the Strasbourg reformer Martin Bucer laid the blame squarely on the church's recognition of secret marriages:

> that supremely godless dogma that the compact of matrimony made verbally by the contracting parties, as they say, binds at once, if only those who contract are of the age of puberty, and that such a pact is not invalidated if it is made without the knowledge or consent of the parents, out of blind love and the desire of the flesh, and for the most part out of the deviousness of seducers and the wantonness of the seduced.[123]

For Bucer, what was at stake here was not a child's freedom to follow his heart's desire, but a child's sense of responsibility to family and society. A secret marriage showed "immeasurable levity" in a matter of utmost seriousness, as if a valid contract affecting not only the body, temporal goods, and property, but also one's very soul, could be made without advice and counsel and off the public record.[124] A half century later, after the battle against secret unions had long since been won, the Puritan Richard Baxter still advised young people set upon marriage that "such a change of your condition should be seriously fore-thought on and all the troubles foreseen and pondered . . . [don't undertake it] in a pang of lust."[125]

Where the Reformation succeeded, secular government intruded itself into the sphere of spiritual marital jurisdiction and effectually challenged the validity of secret marriages. (Later in the century it did the same in Catholic lands.) New secular marriage ordinances and lay-dominated marriage courts either supplanted or severely restricted canon law and the episcopal courts, which had traditionally held jurisdiction over domestic marital conflict. The new legislation and courts reflected the successful transition from ecclesiastical to secular jurisdiction over religion and morals that had begun in the fourteenth century and became a general feature of sixteenth-century life in many Catholic as well as Protestant lands. In most cases the new laws required witnesses and parental consent

for a valid marriage, making it more difficult to get married than it
had been in the later Middle Ages. The goal, however, was to place
marriage on a more secure foundation, both legally and personally,
and reduce the legal grounds for contesting its validity. Despite the
hostility to secret marriages, however, the new marriage courts continued to recognize sexually consummated private vows as a valid
marriage, and magistrates and pastors urged family support in such
situations; youth in Protestant lands who were prepared to go to
such lengths could still enter valid secret marriages in initial
defiance of family and society. On the other hand, by stressing the
necessity of public ceremony and parental consent for a proper
Christian marriage, the new Protestant preachers progressively succeeded in making publicity and communal approval a matter of
conscience as well as of law for newlyweds who were prepared to
heed their message.[126] The moral influence of the church was now
unequivocally against secret unions.

   The changes in marriage law and practice brought about by the
Reformation were not always clear-cut and uniform. In some
Lutheran cities and lands the traditional episcopal marriage courts
continued, only they were now staffed by self-proclaimed "skillful
honest officials" rather than the old church authorities. In a majority
of Lutheran cities and territories the traditional courts were
dissolved and marital affairs placed entirely in the hands of new
secular judges. These judges usually came from established governing councils or agencies and received counsel from clerical advisers
who were often highly influential, but distinct from and subordinate
to the judges.[127] After the collapse of episcopal authority in the
1520s, secular governments initially relied heavily on the new Protestant clergy for counsel and direction in marital affairs. In
Lutheran Strasbourg and Nuremberg, for example, Protestant
clerics decided marital disputes in the mid-1520s much as the old
church courts had done. Very soon thereafter, however, all matters
relating to marriage and divorce came under the jurisdiction of
secular tribunals, which, despite clerical protests that continued for
the rest of the century, refused to allow the clergy an authoritative
place among the judges.[128] Lutheran clergy regularly advised the
court and molded popular and official opinion on domestic issues
through sermons and pamphlets. But no longer did the clergy
directly originate marriage laws and independently adjudicate
domestic conflicts as the old episcopal courts had done. The Protestant governments of Strasbourg and Nuremberg were no keener on
giving Protestant clergy jurisdiction over the moral life than they
had been on letting Catholic bishops continue to exercise it.

The secular governments were assisted in this policy by Luther himself. Having rejected the sacramental status of marriage as unbiblical, and having praised secular princes as "emergency bishops" who were responsible for religious reform,[129] Luther called upon magistrates to establish purely civil courts to adjudicate conflicts. A majority of Lutheran theologians, however, favored a less radical departure from the old ways, and throughout the sixteenth century they doggedly fought to regain a measure of independent clerical jurisdiction over marriage.[130] Although they were unsuccessful in this attempt, their efforts did reestablish the "ancient canons" alongside Scripture and secular law as a source of Protestant marriage legislation in the second half of the century.[131] The actual institutional solution reached by the major Protestant groups — marriage boards with laymen in the majority and clergy restricted to an important, but secondary, advisory role — was a compromise between conservative and liberal elements on both sides. No compromise was made on the key point of jurisdiction over marriage, however, which henceforth remained in the hands of secular government.

Like the canonists before them, the Protestant reformers considered free mutual consent in a present exchange of vows to be the constitutive act of marriage. The church service celebrated and confirmed the marriage, and by its public proclamation and recording of the marriage also secured it in law. Among Protestants marriage ceased to be a sacrament that indelibly imprinted each spouse and fell under the jurisdiction of the church. The sacramental status of marriage, they argued, had done marriage no good. As Heinrich von Kettenbach put it:

> You [papists] say, "Marriage is a sacrament," but then you go on to reckon the spiritual fruit of virginity to be a hundredfold, that of widowhood sixtyfold, and that of marriage thirtyfold [Kettenbach here extrapolates from Matt. 13:8]. How does it help married people when you make marriage a sacrament, but then treat it as the least spiritually fruitful state a person can be in? . . . I believe that God has so established marriage that a pious married person, even one who has been married three times, is more esteemed by God than a monk or a nun who has been chaste for thirty years. Therefore, I reckon the spiritual fruit of marriage to be a hundredfold, that of monks and nuns [the equivalent of] three ripe pears.[132]

Protestants, however, continued to view a proper marriage as a
"spiritual" bond that transcended all natural relationships. For
Luther, marriage was a *divine* ordinance set in *worldly* law, a part
of the charge God had independently given to secular governments.
Because it was a divine charge, the church had a duty to assist
government in maintaining its quality according to biblical standards, and in Lutheran cities and towns the clergy and magistrates
cooperated to a considerable extent.[133] Bucer, on the other hand,
held marriage to be a more strictly political or civil matter. Unlike
Luther, he did not see in it an intrinsic spiritual character directly
established by divine ordinance; marriage was rather a secular event
under the auspices of secular authority, and it gained a spiritual
quality only through the church's added blessing. According to
Bucer, the church raised marriage above a purely natural relationship by "Christianizing" it, that is, by influencing the moral
behavior of spouses as best it could. In Strasbourg this often meant
clerical criticism of and confrontation with a city government that
was perceived to be all too lax in enforcing Christian standards.[134]
The Strasbourg marriage ordinance of 1534 reflected Bucer's point
of view by describing the celebration of a marriage in church as
"Christian and agreeable to God," that is, obligatory for a proper
Christian marriage but not essential to a valid and licit marriage according to Strasbourg civil law. Over time, however, Strasbourg
magistrates as well as clergy found the common goal of domestic
harmony best served by formal church weddings, which put marriage incontestably on the public record.[135]

Despite often subtle differences in their theologies, mainline
Protestants generally agreed that marriage properly fell within the
purview of secular government, yet at the same time they expected
secular governments to discipline and maintain marriage by biblical
norms. To this end the reformers demanded a significant role in for-
mulating and maintaining domestic policy, albeit at a distance,
often grudgingly acknowledged by them, from the reins of true temporal power.

One of the best-documented examples of a Protestant marriage
court in action and of the treatment of secret marriages at Protestant
hands is Zwinglian Zurich. The Zurich court came into existence in
1525, replacing the bishop's court in Constance, which had traditionally handled transgressions and claims in marital disputes. With
the creation of the court, Zurich became its own moral arbiter of
such matters, its own bishop, as it were. The court was composed of
six members: two each from the Small Council and the Large Council, the city's governing bodies, and two pastors (*Leutpriester*). The

court met twice weekly on Mondays and Thursdays, unlike the bishop's court, which had met daily, but with many recesses for the numerous religious holidays. Between 1525 and 1531, its formative years, the court held 537 sessions and heard 1,116 complainants, the majority of whom were women (at a ratio of more than six to four). Most complaints (well over 800 cases) came from people under thirty years of age, a not surprising statistic since the court dealt primarily with contested marriages and divorce petitions.[136] The court could rule, but it had no power to enforce its rulings. The power of enforcement belonged solely to the councils, which also heard appeals of the court's decisions but rarely overturned them (only four of twenty-nine such appeals were successful between 1525 and 1531).[137]

Aggrieved parties normally took the initiative to appear before the court and acted as their own spokespersons. A client could be represented by a lawyer, but a lawyer was not required for the successful prosecution of a claim. Parents and guardians regularly appeared as character witnesses, as did friends and relatives.[138] The court as a rule heard accuser and accused separately; when testimony proved to be manifestly contradictory, the parties were brought face to face and cross-examined. The court also summoned its own witnesses and experts, especially in cases involving contested virginity and in divorce petitions alleging physical impairment of sexual function or impotence. In theory the court permitted any relevant information that was deemed helpful to complainant and defendant, with certain exceptions. Servants, for example, were not permitted to testify against their masters, of whom, it was assumed, they would be jealous; the court also took into account friendship, kinship, and moral reputation when assessing the testimony of witnesses.[139] But in principle the court committed itself to a full and fair hearing—this in conscious reaction to the old episcopal court's popular reputation for arbitrariness.

During the late 1520s the court took steps to end both clerical and lay concubinage. Clergy living with concubines were given two weeks to marry or separate on pain of losing their benefice. Single lay people living together had one month to publicize their marriage vows in church or face the substantial fine of one mark silver each. Prostitutes received fines, and chronic offenders were exiled (usually after the third offense), but in Zurich, unlike Lutheran Wittenberg, a "Frauenhaus" continued to operate, apparently because of ambivalent feelings within the Zurich councils over its social utility. The court, however, exercised tight surveillance and fined married men who were seen entering and leaving.[140]

Secret marriages continued to be a disruptive force in Zurich's domestic life during the early years of the Reformation, partly because of the difficulty of controlling premarital sex and partly because of the expectations engendered by traditional practice. Between 1525 and 1531, 135 women appeared before the court allegedly as virgins deflowered (*entmagtet*) upon promises of marriage.[141] According to the Zurich marriage ordinance (1525), a man who was shown to have willfully "deflowered, shamed, or impregnated a [single] daughter, maid, or virgin" upon false promises of marriage was required to provide a bridegroom's dowry and marry her, borrowing the dowry from the "Jewish butcher" if his parents or guardians refused to provide it.[142] Behind this stern law lay concern for innocent girls of previously impeccable reputation who were possibly rendered hopeless spinsters because of the public scandal.[143] But the long tradition of secret marriages, which equated sexually consummated private vows with a valid marriage, also played a role in such directives. Any accused Zurich male who contested such a charge invariably denied that the woman in question was a virgin and that he had ever intended to marry her. "I went to her as to a whore," said one. "When I penetrated her, it was like putting my foot in an oversized boot — she was not tight [that is, she was no virgin]", protested another.[144] Character witnesses testified on the women's behalf in forty-three cases and proved decisive in fourteen. In sixty-two cases the court ruled that virgins had indeed been deflowered, but *not* upon false promises of marriage. The offending males were punished by fines scaled to the degree of culpability. In those cases where it was determined that the woman had enticed the man or that she had known he was already married (if he was), then she shared the punishment.[145] If sexual relations had followed verbal promise of marriage and the woman had been a virgin of good reputation, the couple was apparently persuaded to marry. Also in Nuremberg, if a serious marriage vow was found to have preceded sexual intercourse, the court forced marriage upon an unwilling man; guards accompanied those who refused to go voluntarily to the altar, and an official answered "Ja" for them.[146] While such "shotgun" weddings were extremely rare and contradicted the Protestant ideal of companionable marriage, they were in line with counsel given earlier by Luther himself. Noting that "in our day strong aversion exists to marrying a despoiled woman," Luther urged couples who had "secretly become one flesh" to remain united even against the wishes of their parents, since the injustice of scandalizing an innocent woman for life was too great for a Christian conscience to bear.[147]

One of the moral purposes of the church's recognition of the validity of secret marriages may have been to provide seduced women, especially those who were pregnant, a way to salvage their reputations by gaining a valid marriage.[148] But as Protestants were quick to point out, such an approach to the problem of premarital sex and pregnancy contributed to the plight of such women at least as much as it alleviated it. The church's recognition of private vows served both seducer and seduced, as the seducer found it easier to succeed with a "victim" who had reason to believe she might gain a proper marriage by surrendering.[149]

In cases where neither side desired to force marriage upon the other, the problems of premarital pregnancy appear to have been worked out as privately as they had been created, without recourse to the courts. This was probably easier to do in old Catholic cities than in the highly charged moral atmosphere of newly reformed Zurich and Nuremberg. In Cologne, for example, the family of Hermann von Weinsberg raised his illegitimate aunt, Agnes Kort, and his grandmother raised an illegitimate daughter, named Geirt, of his father's.[150] When Agnes Kort grew up ("twenty-five and not very resolute") and succumbed to the charms of one Johann van Zulch, a student in the Cronenbursa where she lived and worked as a maid, the families involved reached a private solution; the pregnant Agnes and her seducer were betrothed on paper by her uncle, who acted as her legal guardian, and the marriage proper was made conditional upon Johann's completion of his education in Paris and Orleans and his continued willingness to marry her at that time, when he would presumably be able to support her. Although a child was born and took the father's name, Johann and Agnes, despite their professed intention to marry, never reunited, and each eventually married another.[151] When Hermann impregnated his parent's maid (Greitgin Olup) after a long affair, the family began making arrangements in the second month of pregnancy. They terminated Greitgin's services and restrained Hermann from further involvement with her. The child, a daughter who grew up to be the apple of her father's eye,[152] was taken at birth by Hermann's family and baptized, receiving the name Anna from a maid of one of Hermann's sisters, who attended the baptism with other family members. Hermann's family arranged for a nurse, and Hermann assumed support payments to both the child and the mother.[153] It even became a matter the family could joke about. A few months after Anna's birth, Hermann's father commented that within a nine-month period he had had three grandchildren in three different combinations: an illegitimate child by a legitimate child (Anna by

Hermann); a legitimate child by a legitimate child (the child of his properly married daughter Merg); and a legitimate child by an illegitimate child (the child of his properly married illegitimate daughter, Geirt).[154]

To fight the scandal of premarital sex and pregnancy, Zurich denied outright the validity of private vows of marriage. The new ordinance of 1525 required for a valid marriage at least "two pious, honorable, and incontestable witnesses." These might be town officials or the couple's parents or legal guardian, without whose "favor, knowledge, and will" a marriage was also deemed invalid, although Zurich permitted children to marry against their parents' will after they had reached their majority (nineteen).[155] To avoid what the authors describe as "the slanders, deceit, and litigation of secret marriages," a valid and licit marriage had still further to be publicly witnessed and recorded in church within two weeks of an exchange of vows. A virgin allegedly seduced upon false promise of marriage henceforth had only six and a half weeks to bring a formal complaint against her seducer, not the year or longer permitted in pre-Reformation practice.[156]

As the years passed, the requirement of credible witnesses evolved to the point that a couple's appearance in church became tantamount to marriage itself in the popular mind. Vows made earlier, even though duly witnessed by officials or parents, were perceived as secondary in importance to the public celebration and recording of the marriage in church, although the letter of the law still treated a couple's preliminary vows outside of church as the legal basis of a valid marriage. The growing importance of the church ceremony (*kilchgang*, "going to church") is further indicated by the court's encouraging betrothed couples to postpone cohabitation and coition until *after* the public church service — in the court's opinion, the surest way to end the strife of a contested secret marriage.[157] After 1534 encouragement gave way to insistence; those who "mingled themselves sexually" before a public celebration of their marriage vows were fined ten pfennig, and those too poor to pay must spend a night in jail.[158] The Augsburg and Nuremberg marriage ordinances of 1537 also carried provisions for punishing couples who prematurely consummated marriage vows.[159] In midcentury Geneva such "anticipatory sex" between betrothed couples brought excommunication from church.[160] As the years passed, in Protestant cities and towns premarital sex and pregnancy came to be considered seduction, fornication, or adultery (assuming one party was married), each transgression carrying an appropriate punishment;[161] but premarital sex in consummation of purely private vows ceased to be a proper basis for a serious marriage suit in court.

These lessons were not lost on the Catholic church, long deeply divided on the issue. In 1563 the Council of Trent capitulated to internal and external critics of the church's arguably mischievous marriage laws by requiring that marriage vows be made in the presence of a priest and that banns be proclaimed three times in advance of the church celebration, something long demanded by regional courts. And, as in the Protestant churches, Catholic priests henceforth maintained up-to-date registers of all marriages.[162]

By the seventeenth century the only licit marriages recognized in Zurich were those publicly vowed and recorded in church.[163] The city much earlier achieved some of the intended disciplinary effect of prohibiting private vows, especially as concerned protecting women from unprincipled lovers. In the late 1520s the court could report many examples of women who refused to have sex with their fiancés until they had been "taken to church," or at least until a firm date for "going to church" had been set, "so that [these women] are not deceived like so many other women have been in the past."[164] In Zwinglian Basel, whose laws were strongly influenced by Zurich, the postponement of cohabitation and coition until after the church service was more successfully achieved among the upper classes than among the lower, a circumstance reflected in other areas of church discipline. Here too the magistrates pressured all couples to "go to church" by denying legal protection to unpublicized marriage vows.[165]

Despite the assurances of Protestant apologists, children wanting to marry did occasionally find themselves in hopeless conflict, even with "good Christian parents," over the choice of a mate, and were faced with the unhappy prospect of either denying their heart's desire or defying their parents. Between 1525 and 1531 the Zurich court heard ninety parental challenges to the secret marriages of underaged children (under nineteen).[166] Such conflicts between parents and children also occurred in Lutheran villages.[167] This problem was exacerbated in many places because the legal age at which children could marry without parental consent was raised, an apparent reflection both of demographic changes and of parental and governmental efforts to discourage immature (non-self-supporting) marriages.

It has long been argued that beginning in the late fourteenth century, western Europeans generally married at progressively later ages, creating by the sixteenth century what has been described as a distinctive, widespread "late marriage pattern" reflected in both law and practice. In the sixteenth and seventeenth centuries, for example, first marriages among British peers occurred at average ages of 24.3 (men) and 19.5 (women); among Genevan ruling families at 27.2 and 21.4; and among the Württemberg elite at 25.3 and 21.4.[168] Protestant reformers, however, proved to be remarkably flexible in dealing with the legal age of marriage, largely because they were guided by often inflexible standards of sexual and domestic morality and undaunted by demographic fact and social custom. In the 1520s the Lutheran Johannes Brenz suggested a legal marriage age of twenty-five for both men and women, whereas Luther, fearing for the mental and moral health of men unmarried after age twenty and of women not married between fifteen and eighteen, urged marriage at a much earlier age.[169] In 1534 Nuremberg set the legal limits for marriage without parental consent at twenty-five (men) and twenty-two (women).[170] In Strasbourg these limits were nineteen and fifteen in 1500, rose to twenty-four and twenty in the 1520s and 1530s, and peaked at twenty-five for both sexes in 1565.[171] On the other hand, Basel lowered the legal age from twenty-four (men) and twenty (women), set in 1529, to twenty and eighteen between 1532 and 1533.[172] If parents were willing to support an immature marriage that seemed advisable under the circumstances (for example, to regulate sexual promiscuity or to legitimate a child), children could still marry as early as the canonical ages (fourteen and twelve) with the blessing and even encouragement of Lutheran theologians.

When underaged children married against their parents' wishes, the parents could not unilaterally dissolve the marriage. Disapproving parents faced an often complicated legal process, and courts were reluctant to dissolve such marriages even though the letter of the law was on the parents' side. Most such marriages were already sexually consummated, and Protestant theologians and jurists, like their late medieval counterparts, held such unions to be true, if not yet proper and licit, marriages. Both pastors and magistrates preferred belated parental acceptance and support, the solution that best served domestic harmony, assuming that differences in the age and/or social status of the spouses were not so great as to embarrass a majority of the members and friends of one or the other family and thereby engender enmity between them. When, however, parents remained unalterably opposed and the circumstances clearly justified their protest, marriages of minor children were declared void and the couples separated. In Zurich successful parental challenges seem to have been related to the adamancy of paternal disapproval and to the youthfulness of the children involved. In such cases the couple separated until they reached their majority (age nineteen). Zurich, however, permitted orphaned children without parents or official guardians to betroth themselves before witnesses as early as age sixteen (men) and fourteen (women), clear recognition of at least the propriety of marriage for children under nineteen.[173] When the Nuremberg court ruled against the parents and permitted a contested marriage to stand, the parents were not obliged to furnish a dowry and could limit the child's inheritance to a "minimum"; they could disinherit a child altogether if it could be shown that he or she had married a "dishonorable" person.[174] In Strasbourg a secret marriage could not be annulled if that would entail "injury" either to the well-being of the children or to the reputation of the parents — a test that appears to have taken into account the degree of emotional attachment between the newlyweds, sexual consummation of the union, and the possibility of pregnancy.[175] Generally in all German lands parents did not have the right to contest a sexually consummated private marriage in which both parties professed a desire to maintain the union.[176]

Ideally, parents were not supposed to bully their children into unwanted marriages nor children to inflict undesirable in-laws upon their parents. Both theory and law attempted to respect the needs and wishes of *both* sides. The official concern to reconcile love and gain, that is, to respect a child's freedom and wishes, while at the same time appreciating a parent's legitimate self-interest in his child's marriage, found expression in a statute in the Augsburg ordinance of 1537. "Children are not to be forced against their will into a marriage they find unpleasant and undesirable; parents should take the greatest care to respect and advance what is to the profit and well-being of their children's persons and possessions."[177]

Learning of parents who had compelled their children into unwanted marriages, with sad consequences for all, Luther devoted a special treatise to the subject: *That Parents Should Neither Compel Nor Hinder the Marriage of Their Children and Children Should Not Become Engaged without the Consent of Their Parents* (1524). On the one hand, Luther condemned the abuse of parental authority over children as "outrageous injustice" and urged civil officials to prevent and punish it. On the other, he instructed Christian children to obey the laws that subjected them to their parents, even when such obedience meant suffering. However, conceding that most children were "weak Christians" and rarely capable of approaching this matter as the Christian martyrs might, Luther went on to counsel alternatives to passive resignation. First, children should appeal to secular authority for justice if their parents thwarted their heart's desire. Here Luther stood on traditional ground, since throughout the Middle Ages boys and girls of canonical age (fourteen and twelve) had the right, however infrequently exercised, to dissent formally from unwanted arranged marriages.[178] In Protestant cities such appeals were ordinarily pursued by adult friends and relatives, sometimes even by one parent against the other.[179] If a formal appeal to secular authority did not bring a positive result, then Luther advised unhappy children to do as Christians in the past had done when tyrannized: pack up, flee to another land, and there marry at will.[180] Luther believed that parents had a basic duty to provide good marriages for *all* their children; each father was "duty bound to get his child a good mate who will be just right for him, or who seems to be just right for him."[181] If parents ignored this responsibility, then children could in good conscience take matters into their own hands. Luther charged that it was precisely the parental shirking of this duty that had filled Europe with so many cloisters and created so many unhappy monks and nuns during the Middle Ages.[182]

Luther also recognized that parents had some options when children persisted in marrying whenever and whomever they pleased without parental consent. Parents might "hinder" a marriage to "this or that particular person" when they were convinced that it threatened a child's welfare, although no parent could legally and morally withhold marriage altogether from a child who was ready for it.[183] Short of directly forbidding a marriage, parents might treat such a conflict as a learning experience for their child. Here Luther advised that parents counsel their child against the marriage, frankly stating why they objected to the proposed spouse; should the child remain unmoved by their arguments and still desire the marriage, then the parents, without approving the union, might permit it nonetheless so that the child might discover by hard experience the wisdom of parental counsel. "For who can possibly ward off all evil when good [parental] advice and sound judgment are ignored?"[184] Luther described this approach as acting in good conscience and placing a willful and disobedient child in God's hands. He appears to have preferred it to outright prohibition of a marriage, no doubt because he understood the difficulty of separating young lovers determined to be together and the hopelessness of forcing two people to live together when the will to do so was utterly lacking. If, as Luther believed, men and women were supposed to "find in marriage the things they naturally desire, namely, sex and offspring, a life together and mutual trust" (*generatio et proles, item cohabitatio et mutua fides*),[185] then to force two people together *or* apart against their consent and desire threatened both the intrinsic purpose of marriage and the social order beyond it. In matters of marriage, as in matters of faith, the Reformation opposed bullying the heart and conscience.

A case in point, illustrating the new Protestant values, may be cited in conclusion. In 1529 at age thirty, Thomas Platter, later a well-known printer in Basel and Zurich and rector of Basel's Latin school, married Anna Dietschi, the maid of his Zurich tutor, Oswald Myconius. Platter had converted to Protestantism in the mid-1520s under the influence of Zwingli's preaching (he writes of being "yanked up by my hair"), greatly disappointing his pious Catholic relatives, who had envisioned a traditional clerical career for him. After the marriage his uncle confronted him at church in the village of Visp (Wallis), where he and Anna then lived and worked, he as a ropemaker and scholar, she at spinning wool. (Thomas was in conflict with the clergy of the village church, who remained traditional and critical of his "Luthery.") "Have you brought a wife with you to Visp?" his uncle asked when they met, and when Thomas acknowledged that he had, his uncle exclaimed: "O, the power of the Devil! Would that you had rather brought a whore" (which Thomas might well have done had he become a priest). Defending his marriage and exhibiting his new Protestant faith, Thomas promptly replied: "Sir, you will not find in the Bible that it is better to have a whore than a wife."[180] According to Thomas, a long time passed before he and his uncle, a self-proclaimed "*bibliacus*, who understood little of the Bible," spoke again.

According to one line of argument by modern scholars, the medieval church's recognition of secret marriages had liberated children from arbitrary parental authority and had affirmed freedom of choice in matters of the heart, especially for women.[187] It "permitted persons, if they were sufficiently desperate, to escape from the complex of family, financial, and feudal concerns which surrounded marriage and to enter a valid marriage without the consent of their families"; thereby it "enhanced the status of the individual, and particularly of the woman, at the expense of both civil and ecclesiastical society."[188]

This is a charitable interpretation of what may more accurately be described as the church's fear of unregulated sexual intimacy and its lax, yet also highly enterprising, accommodation to it in the hope of bringing premarital sexual behavior under church influence if not outright control. Concubinage and sexual promiscuity were widespread in the later Middle Ages; still in the sixteenth century an estimated one-third to one-half of urban populations were unmar-

ried adults (one-third in the countryside).[189] The vast majority of
couples who approached priests to bless and publicize secret marriages were not sexually inexperienced, as the sizable litigation over
contested secret marriages makes clear. Also the church's recognition of such marriages had been avowedly reluctant. In 1215 the
Fourth Lateran Council discouraged informal unions by demanding
that couples publicly declare their marital intentions well in advance, that is, make *sponsalia de futuro* and pursue orderly public
marriages in church, and by forbidding priests to "officiate" at secret
marriages.[190] But such marriages were not thereby legally prohibited, nor were they declared invalid until the Council of Trent in
1563 ruled against them, acting on what had arguably long been the
church's own best judgment in the matter.

Modern scholars have also interpreted Protestant hostility to
secret marriage as an expression of the "paternalism" of the age. The
invalidation of secret marriages and the raising of the legal age at
which children could marry independently allowed parents to impose stronger controls over their offspring, and for a longer period of
time.[191] In this argument, in which (perhaps uncharitably) parents
are alleged to look upon their children as little more than extensions
of their own will, the regulation of secret marriages becomes a
development in lockstep with the growth of political absolutism in
early modern Europe; on the assumption that a docile child would
grow up to be a docile subject, the strengthening of parental control
over children was also a strengthening of the ruler's control over his
subjects. Scholars cite the example of France, where in 1556 a royal
edict decreed that parents could disinherit children who had married without their permission and at the same time established the
legal age for marriage without parental consent at the unprecedented levels of thirty for men and twenty-five for women.[192]
It has also been argued that the popular appeal of the Lutheran
Reformation in rural villages lay in its alleged harking back to a
German legal tradition that had given parents "total authority" over
the marriages of their children.[193]

There is no question that for both secular and ecclesiastical
authorities, social control was part of the inspiration for legislation
against secret marriages. In an extreme example, like newly
reformed Zurich, one can even get the impression that the Protestant
marriage courts came into existence to encourage people to spy on
their neighbors. In Zurich, if a woman had a male visitor while her
husband was away on business, or if a woman was seen entering a
private place with a man and closing the door behind them, or if a
passerby heard a suspicious disturbance in a house, or if a knock at

the door was greeted by a quick running about inside, such things were reported to the court, and those involved were interrogated. To discourage premarital sex and illegitimacy, the Zurich court decreed that unwed mothers be ostracized, and it harassed those who befriended these women.[194]

Moral surveillance was considered essential to domestic and social order in both Catholic and Protestant towns. While Protestant Zurich, and later Protestant Geneva, deserve their reputations for being especially efficient at it, such surveillance was a general feature of early modern urban life. One may mock it as Puritanical and theocratic, but one must also appreciate a city's expectation that its citizens be honorably married and faithful to one another, or if unmarried, be circumspect about their sexual habits and domestic relations. We would not today readily ostracize unwed mothers, but then neither would we be inclined to grant respectability to behavior that we, by our modern standards, considered to be a moral outrage or an unfair burden on public charity. By requiring parental consent, public witnesses, and a church ceremony for a valid marriage, Protestant courts theoretically enhanced the role of parental and church authority in matters of the heart. But contemporaries also welcomed the new laws as a clarification of the conditions of marriage, a securing of its foundations, and a reduction of individual anxiety and domestic strife over it.

In practice the new laws neither eliminated the old problems nor gave parents total control over their offspring. Since Protestants too recognized a *copula carnalis* as validating marriage vows, they too accepted many secret marriages that had occurred without parental consent. Sufficiently bold children could have their way almost as easily under Protestant regimes as under Catholic, despite the new marital legislation. Nowhere were parents legally permitted to coerce their children into unwanted marriages; even in France after the edict of 1556, courts often found in favor of children who exercised their right to appeal a union opposed by their parents.[195] The new laws probably did increase the persuasive power of parents and give solace to those who were genuinely fearful of their children's assumption of responsibilities for which they were neither emotionally nor financially prepared. Among the questions left unanswered by modern defenders of secret marriage as "children's liberation" are the exact ages and material circumstances of children whose marriages were delayed or rescinded at their parents' insistence.

In the end the Protestants, too, were left with human nature and also found it to be intractable. Still in midcentury (1546) Pastor Veit

Dietrich in reformed Nuremberg could complain that children, especially the children of the wealthy, were marrying without their parents' foreknowledge and against their wishes.[196] But the laws that regulated marriage did change; past practice ceased to be legal practice. Therein lay at least the possibility of reshaping human behavior.

If the traditional church sanction of secret marriage encouraged domestic strife and litigation by making marriage too casual, the church's long list of declared "impediments" to marriage made it unnecessarily difficult to get married. The church traditionally forbade marriage within a broad spectrum of relationships. In the twelfth and thirteenth centuries, when church authority reached a certain pinnacle, the number of impediments requiring dispensation had become so extensive that, according to one scholar, both lords and peasants found they were forbidden to marry "all the marriageable girls they could possibly know and a great many more besides."[197] Protestants accused the church of multiplying kinship barriers "as far as the mind could reckon relationships,"[198] and they ridiculed such dispensations as an outrageous charade, the church greedily granting with one hand what it had piously denied with the other.[199]

At the beginning of the sixteenth century impediments to marriage by reason of consanguinity and affinity still extended to the fourth degree of a relationship, that is, to third cousins. Just how complicated and disruptive of the social and political order such laws could be was illustrated on a grand scale by the protracted divorce suit of Henry VIII against Catherine of Aragon.[200] In addition to denying marriage to those related by blood or marriage, the church also deemed improper marriages between couples of different religions, unless the non-Christian converted. Premarital impotence was a legal impediment to marriage, although impotence developing after marriage (*impotentia superveniens* in contrast to *inpotentia antecedens*) was not a ground for annulment. Previous secret vows to another person prevented a proper Christian marriage, as did vows of chastity and holy orders. Nor could one properly marry one's betrothed if one had had sexual relations with another after the engagement (the illicit carnal union was said to create an *impedimentum ligaminis*, the "impediment of a tie or bond" with another). Godparentage or sponsorship at baptism established a "spiritual affinity" between godparent and godchild that prevented both their marriage to one another and the godchild's marriage to any child or sibling of the godparent. The legal relationship of adoption created a similar impediment. A person found guilty of the sexual crime of fornication or adultery, or of plotting murder to set free a married lover, was forbidden to marry the object of affection or any of that person's relatives. Coercion invalidated a marriage, even when used to save a seduced virgin from scandal and ruin. Marriage vows made in error also lacked validity; for example, mistaking another person for one's intended spouse, perhaps while inebriated, or as the result of deception, or exchanging vows with a professed freeman who later proved to be a bonded serf. Even defective eyesight and hearing impeded a proper Christian marriage, according to the church; without dispensation a blind and dumb person could not validly marry.[201]

Marriages in which impediments remained concealed and unresolved were vulnerable to dissolution if one spouse should become alienated and contest the marriage on such grounds (could some have found it consoling to have in reserve such an "out" from a marriage?), or if a third party had reason to challenge it. Rather than have their marriage haunted by an undispensed impediment, many, especially those whose position in society was closely tied to their public reputation, found it prudent to bargain with the church.

In treatises written in the early 1520s, Luther condemned the church's impediments as "only snares for taking money and nets for catching souls," and he characterized the "Romanists" who dispensed them as "merchants selling vulvas and genitals."[202] He examined the eighteen traditional grounds for either preventing or annulling a marriage, as set forth in the most popular confessional manual of the period, the *Summa Angelica*, published in thirty-one editions between 1476 and 1520. Luther accepted impotence as "the only sound reason for dissolving a marriage," but he also believed that marriages made in error should not be forced to stand, and he favored coercing a man to marry a girl who would otherwise be ruined by the scandal associated with seduction and premarital pregnancy. As for the impediments of consanguinity and affinity, he confined himself strictly to the prohibitions stated in Leviticus 18:6–18, which permitted many previously forbidden marriages: "First cousins may contract a godly and Christian marriage, and I may marry my stepmother's sister, my father's stepsister, or my mother's stepsister . . . I may also marry the sister of my deceased wife or fiancée, etc."[203] Elsewhere Luther wrote:

According to Leviticus 18, there are only twelve persons a man is prohibited from marrying: his mother, stepmother,

full sister, half-sister by either parent, granddaughter,
father's or mother's sister, daughter-in-law, brother's wife,
wife's sister, stepdaughter, and his uncle's wife. Here only
the first degree of affinity and the second degree of consanguinity are forbidden . . . Therefore, if a marriage has
been contracted outside of these degrees, which are the only
ones which have been prohibited by God's appointment, it
should by no means be annulled on account of the laws of
men.[204]

Luther ridiculed the "invented" spiritual and legal affinity that
underlay the impediments to marriage established by godparentage
and adoption: "Take as your spouse whomsoever you please,
whether it be godparent, godchild, or the daughter or sister of a
sponsor . . . and disregard those artificial, money-seeking impediments."[205] As for the impediment of religious disparity: "Just as
I may eat, drink, sleep, walk, ride with, buy from, speak to, and eat
with a heathen, Jew, Turk, or heretic, so I may also marry him."[206]
No impediment seemed to enrage Luther more than that of sexual crime, perhaps a reflection both of a certain guilt about his own
sexual feelings and of his personal resentment of sexual repression.
Had not King David married Bathsheba after committing adultery
with her and plotting her husband's murder?[207] Criminal behavior
did not suspend either a person's sexual need or the possibility of
divine forgiveness. Pointing to the unhappiness created by this particular impediment, Luther cited two cases that to him exemplified
the perversity of the church's marriage laws. In the case of a man
found guilty of fornication, the church forbade him to marry not
only his accomplice, but also her sisters, aunts, nieces, and cousins.
And if a man was convicted of incest for having had sexual relations
with his wife's sister, his mother-in-law, or another woman related
to him in a direct blood line, the church forfeited his right to have
sex with his wife, even though he was expected to continue to live
with her as a husband. This, Luther concluded, was penance
beyond human nature, punishment no marriage could survive, an
act analogous to throwing wood on a fire and commanding it not to
burn.[208]
To Luther, a lack of realism and of charity underlay many of the
church's marital impediments. They were a web of mercenary
mischief, opposed to basic human need, lacking a foundation in
Scripture, and constantly complicating domestic life. By restricting
kinship barriers to those stated in Leviticus and by rejecting

altogether so-called spiritual and legal impediments, Luther and his followers hoped to advance both social and church reform.

Protestants initially succeeded in reducing the overall number of impediments; many that were based on affinity fell away permanently, especially those deduced from spiritual affinity. But changes in marital practice did not come easily to an age subject to habit and beholden to tradition, and later Protestant magistrates and theologians proved to be more sensitive to the social and political consequences of such changes than Luther had been in the early 1520s. Nuremberg's leading reformer, Andreas Osiander, found that rescinding many traditional impediments to marriage had given rise to unforeseen and quite undesirable results, in his view largely because of the weakness of human nature. Commenting in a private memorandum prepared in 1537 for the city's magistrates, Osiander reported that people now not only married within relationships that had long been unjustly forbidden by the pope, but that many "false saints" attempted to go even further and marry also within those relationships clearly forbidden by God in Scripture, letting fall *all* kinship barriers to sex and marriage. According to Osiander, incestuous whoring and adultery threatened even the most immediate family members, as debauchery, previously aided by the availability of papal dispensation and absolution, now, to his great dismay, found an ally in the very success of the Reformation.[209]

Osiander's fears were shared by Nuremberg's even more conservative magistrates, who worried also about the political consequences for the city of alienating the Catholic emperor on so touchy a matter. They essentially supported the traditional marriage laws regulating kinship barriers. When the city secretary, Lazarus Spengler, defended the city's refusal to allow a man to marry his deceased wife's sister, which was permitted by Lutheran teaching, he reported derogatory remarks about Nuremberg's reformed marriage laws, among them, that the city "permitted . . . its citizens to marry each other like dogs, without any discretion . . . judgment, and differentiation among the degrees of relationship."[210] That was indeed serious criticism for a city sensitive to its imperial obligations.

Osiander's reaction was perhaps typical of embattled reformers: he multiplied the prohibitions anew, charting no fewer than fifty relationships in which he found marriage and sexual commerce forbidden by divine and secular law. Unlike Luther, he interpreted the prohibitions in Leviticus 18 and 20 thematically, "according to their logic," which led to the inclusion of all possible blood relatives (*blut-*

freundin) "who might be shamed" by marriage or sexual relations with each other. He established four basic rules for extrapolating forbidden relationships, which he offered to the authorities as guidelines:

> 1. If a woman is forbidden me because of blood kinship, her brother or husband is forbidden my sister; as I cannot marry my father's sister, my sister cannot marry her father's brother, etc.
>
> 2. Male and female gender make no difference in blood relationships; my mother's sister is as close to me as my father's sister, etc.
>
> 3. What is forbidden to an ascending line is also forbidden a descending line; as I cannot marry my mother, so I cannot marry my daughter, etc.
>
> 4. If a man cannot take my wife after I die, I cannot take his after he dies; I cannot marry my stepmother, nor can my father marry his daughter-in-law, etc.[211]

Using these rules, Osiander deduced nineteen forbidden relationships from Leviticus 18 and 20 (only twelve of which were literally stated there); fifteen such relationships from the laws of Moses; and sixteen from the network of relationships around one's grandparents.[212]

Practice elsewhere also resisted the freer course made possible by theology and law in the 1520s and 1530s. Among Strasbourg's lawyers and theologians, canon law progressively regained an influential place beside Scripture and secular law as a source of marriage legislation. In 1560 the city forbade marriages within ascending and descending lines and collaterally to the third degree, and the government (the *Ammeister* or *Grosser Rat*) now issued dispensations from impediments much as the old church authorities had done, although not on so grand a scale.[213] In a city or territory that reversed the Reformation altogether, the reversion to traditional marriage law and practice was often massive. After the Reformation ended in Constance in 1548, for example, the revived diocesan court adjudicated 1,439 cases of traditional impediments between 1551 and 1620, including many cases of affinity long rejected by Protestants. Despite both long-standing Protestant and new Tridentine legislation (in 1563) against secret marriages, the court heard 3,981 cases, almost half of all the city's marital litigation, over a nearly seventy-year period.[214]

Despite the conservatism to which it often succumbed, the Reformation still dramatically changed traditional attitudes toward the insititutions of celibacy and marriage during the course of the sixteenth century. In Protestant territories monasteries and nunneries were dissolved and their physical structures and endowments given over in most instances to public charitable and educational uses. Marriage laws became simpler, clearer, and more enforceable, and were applied less arbitrarily. A new freedom and privacy came into the lives of the honorably married who had no sins to hide, while for the sexually unprincipled and wayward, correction was now nearer at hand from the new, vigilant marriage courts. If governmental monitoring of moral and domestic life increased through the agency of conscientious marriage courts, so too did the security of marriage, its new publicity and communal oversight now its best defense. Reversing the practice of centuries, the Reformation made it more difficult for the immature and unestablished to enter a valid marriage; at the same time those with a just and proper cause could, for the first time, divorce and remarry with the church's blessing.[215]

Most significantly, home and family were no longer objects of widespread ridicule, a situation that lasted until modern times. The first generation of Protestant reformers died believing they had released women into the world by establishing them firmly at the center of the home and family life, no longer to suffer the withdrawn, culturally circumscribed, sexually repressed, male-regulated life of a cloister. And they believed children would never again be consigned at an early age to involuntary celibacy but would henceforth remain in the home, objects of constant parental love and wrath, until they were all properly married.

·2·

Husbands and Wives

The Duties of Spouses

THE MORALISTS of Reformation Europe depicted marriage as a shared responsibility between husband and wife, whose expectations of one another were clearly defined. The basic duties of the husband were to provide for the welfare of his wife and children, to protect his household from any who would harm it, and to rule over his family and servants with a firm but just hand.[1] The man of the house was expected to be steady, a model of self-control, and able to moderate his own appetites and drives; otherwise he could not successfully command those around him to moderate theirs. The classical doctrine of the "mean" pervaded the instructional literature for spouses and parents, as it did also the educational manuals for teachers.[2] The most popular housefather book of the seventeenth century portrayed the exemplary husband as one who was "god-fearing, wise, understanding, and experienced, who has God ever before his eyes, prays and works diligently, does harm neither to his neighbors nor to the members of his household, and is able to maintain the love, friendship, and good will of all around him."[3] Above all, the husband was supposed to *rule*. He alone was master of his house, the one on whom all domestic discipline and order finally depended. Those around him could offer counsel and advice, which he would be wise to take ("Many eyes see better than only one," Johannes Coler pointed out, quoting Cato; "if your wife has good counsel, follow it"); but none could directly challenge his decisions save with the greatest tact and caution. "For as a body can have but one head, so a household, if it is to prosper, can have but one lord and master" (*muss allein Herr im Hause sein*).[4]

In popular literature the bad husband invariably appeared as a man without self-discipline who was unable to rule over his own house, and the bad wife as one who forgot her place and improperly aspired to manly rule. An anonymous vernacular pamphlet from the early 1520s depicted in rhymed couplets the alleged common complaints of wives about their husbands and husbands about their wives, behavior that was said to undermine marriages and households. A wife lamented that her husband ignored her poverty and the disrepair of their house, while regularly squandering their money at the pub. Arriving home at midnight, he would raise hell, pass out, awaken early with complaints and demands, then slouch off again to the tavern. When she complained about his behavior, he would strike her and suggest she leave. A husband, in turn, bewailed a wife who was always cross and stubborn, quick to contradict, and ready to curse at length if he dared to scold. If he reached for a strap, she would grab a brick; if he made a fist, she would take a club. When she did not have her way, he had to go without meals and sleep alone. "She fights over everything, just as if she wants to be the man." She accused him of infidelity when that was the farthest thing from his mind, and she spurned him when his earnings dropped, or he was unemployed. Generally the bad wife demanded more than a husband could provide and was loath to work.[5]

Contrary to the impression often given by modern historians,[6] paternal authority in Reformation Europe did not necessarily mean that a man was free to dominate his household as he pleased. Enormous moral and legal pressure was brought to bear on housefathers who flagrantly abused their mandate. Among neither Protestants nor Catholics was the ordered and disciplined home a tyrannized home. In a popular mirror for the nobility of Hesse, the Lutheran Antonius Corvinus urged noblemen to treat all subordinates in such a way that they would win their love as well as instill fear: "For one fears but does not love tyrannous rule, whereas good government is both loved and feared."[7] Marriage counselors dwelt on this point when they instructed husbands in the treatment of their wives, a subject of such frequent commentary that the reader suspects a determined campaign against an abuse. All condemned the husband who "plays the lion" in his household. Only in the most grave matters (*es die hohe Not erfordere*) should a housefather ever deal severely with his wife, children, or servants to exact obedience.[8] The Saxon Lutheran Justus Menius instructed husbands to rule their wives cleverly, using their heads (*sol synne im kopffe haben/und klug sein*), and not follow the "mad, vicious mob" who attempt to rule at home by a "perverse craft" that relies more on force than on intelligence (*mehre werens/denn lerens*). "The Holy Spirit has not inspired that insanity which believes a husband should prove his manhood by repeated grumbling, insults, curses, and blows to a poor, defenseless, weak woman; the Spirit rather wants husbands to

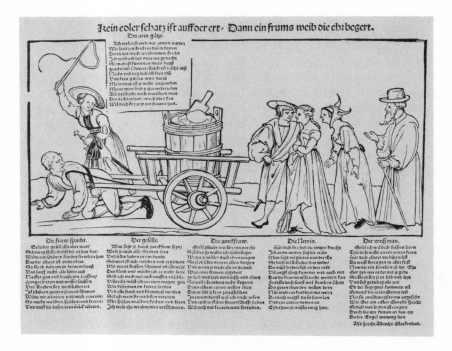

A Husband Who Does Not Rule

There Is No Greater Treasure on Earth Than a Devoted Wife Who Prizes Her Honor

The poor god [husband]

Oh woe, oh woe is me, poor fool.
How I must work to draw this cart!
And why? Because I took myself a wife.
Would that the thought had never
    crossed my mind!
A shrewish scold has come into my
    house.
She has taken my sword, my pants, and
    my purse.
Night and day I have no peace —
And never a kind word from her.
My loyalty does not please her.
She finds my every word hostile.
But such is the fate of many a man:
He may not possess, know, or be able to
    do anything,
But still, in time, he will have a wife.

The wife speaks

Ey, dear fellow, is what you say true?
(Be still or I will part your hair!)
If you want to have a beautiful and
    devout wife,
Who obeys you at all times,
Then stay at home in your own house
And stop carousing about.
How can one expect beautiful young
    women
To maintain their wifely dignity,
When they are forced to go about
    naked,
Begging from door to door, hungry,
Subsisting on water?
If you will not work and support me,
Then you must wash, spin, and draw
    the cart
And be beaten upon your back.

The single fellow [to his girlfriend]

What do you think of this scene, my
    fine lady?
Would you also like to be a shrewish
    scold
And in your hand hold sword, pants,
    purse, and rule?
And bite and strike and cut your man
    with words?
I could not and would not suffer such.
Should we brawl and fight with each
    other,
Perhaps I would end up pulling a cart
Like this poor man
Who has lost all joy and pleasure,
My free life wasted away
With spinning, washing, cooking, and
    carting.
I would rather forswear marriage
    altogether.

The girl

Boy, believe me on my word of honor,
I have no desire for such power.
If we have an honest disagreement,
You will remain the man in all things.
I ask only that you grant me
Those things that belong to a wife,
That you love and honor me and we
    suffer want together.
More I shall not demand
And in all things I will do your will,
Of that you should not doubt.
I will devote my life to serving you
And love you in constant friendship.
And you will not be scolded by a single
    word.

The foolish woman

Be careful of your life, young man.
I, a poor foolish woman, speak the
    truth.
One hears many good things about
    marriage,
But it is more properly called Pain.
Lifelong you must suffer
Much anxiety, uncertainty, worry, and
    want;
From this no one who marries is spared.
But now if you see a pretty girl,
She will do your will
For a bottle of wine.
And when you are done with her,
You are free to go
And take another.
But a wife is forever.

The wise man

Young man, I will give you better
    advice.
Do not listen to this foolish old woman.
Beware the wiles of whores,
Who are always there to deceive you.
Go and take a wife;
God will guide your lives.
Stay with her in love and suffering
And always be patient.
If you have much worry and care,
Look on it as God's will.
Provide for your wife by the sweat of
    your brow
As God has commanded in the first
    book of Genesis.
Patience and suffering are the doors
Through which we come to the place
Where the angels dwell.

love, care for, and honor their wives as their own flesh, just as Christ
does his church."⁹ "There are many filthy beasts," Menius wrote in
still another tract on the subject, "who can themselves neither crow
nor lay eggs, yet they demand nothing less from their poor wives, insisting that they run the household with absolute perfection. They
think they can set everything on a right course if they just complain,
curse, insult, bully, and strike their poor wives and smash whatever
they get their hands on . . . Scripture has condemned such loutish
behavior."¹⁰ Sebastian Artomedes, a seventeenth-century Lutheran
pastor noted for his sermons on the Christian household, described
the husband no man should ever be:

> There is many a pug who is convinced he would not be a
> real man, if once in many weeks he spoke a kind word to his
> wife. He stalks about the house and sits at table like one who
> is mute, speaking to his wife only when he decides to rattle
> her ears and sink her heart by reprimanding whatever she
> has said or done, even when her actions are well-intentioned
> and blameless. Such monsters should have become monks
> and hermits rather than husbands, for they are more at
> home in the forest with wild animals than in a house at the
> side of a rational wife.¹¹

A wife, then, was no maid or common servant of her husband.
As he was the "father of the house," she was the "mother of the
house" (hausmutter), a position of high authority and equal
respect.¹² None wrote more eloquently of this than the English
Puritans. According to Robert Cleaver, "The husband is not to command his wife in manner, as the Master his servant, but as the soul
doth the body, as being conjoined in like affection and good will;
just as the soul in governing the body tendeth to the benefit and com-
modity of the same, so ought the dominion and commandment of
the husband over his wife . . . tend to rejoice and content her."¹³
His guideline for husbands: "Often admonish; seldom reprove; and
never smite [your wife]."¹⁴ William Gouge described husbands and
wives as "near equals": "for of all degrees wherein there is any difference betwixt person and person, there is least disparity betwixt
man and wife. Though the man be as the head, yet is the woman as
the heart . . . Can it then be thought reasonable that she who is the
man's perpetual bedfellow, who hath power over his body, who is a
joint parent of the children, a joint govenour [sic] of the family,
should be beaten by his hands? . . . The wife is as a man self [for]

'the two are one flesh.' No man but a frantic, furious, desperate wretch will beat himself."[15]

Although the historian can never know for sure the degree to which such advice was regularly translated into practice, it would defy experience to believe that an age that wrote and taught so much about companionable marriage and the sharing of domestic responsibility utterly failed to practice what it preached. I suspect that Hermann von Weinsberg's description of his father's "rule" in his home, a Catholic, burgher household in sixteenth-century Cologne, attested a typical urban household in early modern Europe. Hermann recalled that his parents, like other married couples, were human, not angelic. In running the household, one parent would attempt to establish his or her opinion as best, and when the other refused to yield, quarreling would ensue. According to Hermann, his father, generally a patient and yielding man, although not gladly so, often would say to Hermann's mother: "Wife, let's make a deal: one week you rule over the house and hold authority, and the next week I will rule and hold authority." If a conflict arose thereafter, his father would then say to his mother: "Housewife, whose week is it to rule today?" If his mother persisted in her opinion and refused to submit to his father, his father would then say: "Well, you rule today and this week, and I will rule next week." Hermann said his father often "amused" himself in this way.[16] On more than one public occasion, Luther said of his wife Katherine: "I am an inferior lord, she the superior; I am Aaron, she is my Moses," and he freely accepted her criticism and wrath.[17]

A husband also owed his wife *fidelity*. On this subject pamphleteers and tractarians universally rejected a double standard of sexual behavior, endorsing Albrecht von Eyb's sentiments on promiscuous husbands: "If your wife becomes unchaste and breaks faith with you, consider whether you have also been unfaithful to her; those husbands are completely unfair judges who demand that their wives be chaste, while they are not, and excuse their own promiscuity with fine words, while severely damning and punishing that of their wives, as if it were right for them to have every freedom and their wives no faults at all."[18] Nor did Corvinus mince words in his moral instruction to Saxon noblemen: "The Bible teaches that a man should leave father and mother and cleave to his wife; it does not say that he should cleave to *other* men's wives, only to his own."[19]

Such sentiments fueled the Protestant assault on whorehouses, which the government in Lutheran territories successfully restricted in the name of sexual fidelity and family unity. The case against

prostitution was brought together by Melchior Ambach, the editor
of a medley of biblical, patristic, and contemporary writings against
whoring and adultery, accompanied by his own gloomy commentary. According to Ambach, sexual misconduct was taken far too
lightly by his contemporaries.

> Unfortunately today all sins and outrages, but especially
> adultery and whoring, are committed without a sense of
> shame; indeed, adultery and whoring are treated as very
> minor sins, even as no sins at all. One *jokes* about them!
> How many cuckolded husbands are there? How many wives
> justifiably enraged at unfaithful husbands? How many
> respectable young girls go about with their bellies swollen
> by unroasted bratwursts?[20]

Against the popular argument that whorehouses prevented still
greater social evils, Ambach and the magisterial Lutheran apologist,
Johannes Brenz, whose sermon on the subject Ambach included in
his collection, condemned whorehouses as "schools that teach more
shameful things than they prevent," their very existence "an induce-
ment to infidelities that would otherwise not occur to the mind."[21]
Sensitive to the criticism that Protestants were here pursuing an
unrealistic ideal of human perfection, indeed, that they "wanted to
make monks and nuns out of people" and in their social policies
followed "the same logic that created the Münsterite kingdom,
which also wanted to root out all godless behavior,"[22] Ambach made
what must have been an astonishing proposal for his sixteenth-
century readers: if we can have a "house of women" for single and
married men to frequent without sin, let us also provide a "house of
boys" (*Bubenhaus*) for our womenfolk, especially for those who are
old and poor and have no husband to service them. "Would whoring
be any worse for the poor, needy female sex?"[23] Ambach was not
serious, of course. But by approaching the problem of infidelity from
the perspective of male rather than female prostitutes, he drove
home how disruptive it was of family and society. The proposal
could only have served a didactic purpose in a society newly sensitive to the mutual responsibility of marriage.

Protestants logically extended their concept of marriage as companionship based on mutual respect and love when they secured for
both men and women the legal right to divorce and remarry. The
records of marriage courts provide evidence of a campaign against
male adultery and deceitful seduction that went beyond the writings
of moralists and social critics. Over 40 percent of Zurich's divorce

cases in the late 1520s involved the suits of wives against adulterous husbands.[24] In recatholicized Constance, two-thirds of the court cases heard between 1551 and 1620 concerned petitions by single women to have promises of marriage (half with alleged sexual consummation) declared valid.[25] Although the Protestant courts were reluctant to grant divorce and the Catholic courts equally hesitant to enforce promises of marriage acknowledged by only one party, the persistence of such suits suggests widespread impatience with male infidelity and deceit.

Contemporary wisdom held it not only a husband's moral and religious duty to treat his wife honorably, but also very much in his own best interest. The man who mistreated his wife, warned Johannes Coler, undermined his entire household, for an insulted and beaten wife would not be able to maintain the respect of her servants, who were perceived as a low breed ready to take advantage even without provocation;[26] with the loss of a wife's respect within a household went also the good order of the household.[27]

A wife required proper deference also because of her perceived physical and temperamental weakness, compared to men; magnanimity, patience, and forbearance befitted the superior nature and position of a man. Commented Justus Menius:

> Just as a woman's body does not permit her to do the same physical labor as a man, neither does a woman have it in her heart to be as patient and long-suffering when adversity strikes. One says, and I observe it to be close to the truth, that women wear long dresses, but have short dispositions. Therefore, let the husband be [the voice of] reason and wisely spare his wife punishment, willingly bearing what fortune brings so that they may live together in peace.[28]

The Puritan Cleaver made apparent the biblical basis for such charity ("Woman is the weaker vessel" — 1 Peter 3:7): "Like as a vessel, the weaker it is, the more it is to be favored and spared, if we will have it continue, even so a wife."[29]

Despite such "sexist" views, which the women of the age appear fully to have shared,[30] both sexes were encouraged to approach marriage as a rational decision, not — at least initially — simply as the fulfillment of the heart's desire. "At first," Luther warned, "love is glowing hot (*fervidus*), an intoxicating love by which we are blinded and rush forth"; but once married, couples soon grow tired of one another, confirming the saying of Ovid: "praesentia odimus, absentia amamus."

A wife is easily taken, but to have abiding love, that is the challenge. One who finds it in his marriage should thank the Lord God for it. Therefore approach marriage earnestly, asking God to give you a good, pious girl, with whom you can spend your life in mutual love. For sex [alone] accomplishes nothing in this regard; there must also be agreement in values and character (*ut conveniant mores et ingenium*).[31]

Another author, following the advice of the Roman philosopher and satirist Apuleius, suggested that a man should select a wife in the same deliberate way he would buy a horse. One does not, he pointed out, buy a horse because he fancies its saddle and bridle, its harnass, or its gait, and neither should one choose a wife because she has a striking appearance and dress. One should rather search out inner strengths and weaknesses. Is she virtuous, pious, and honorable, a woman readily respected, a person with companionable qualities?[32] To approach marriage with such questions in mind was to court lasting success.

A wife was also to be chosen for her maturity, so she would be able to manage the household economy. It was suggested that a woman be between twenty and twenty-four years, and her husband between twenty-four and thirty, roughly the ages at which, according to modern demographers, most people tended to marry in early modern Europe.[33] These were the perceived ages of emotional and vocational maturity, when men and women had completed their educations and/or mastered the skills necessary to support a household. A ready inheritance alone did not suffice; a successful marriage required mature judgment and the ability to perform useful, rewarding work. Genevan officials opposed marriages between young women and vastly older men (one example was a sixty-year-old man and a twenty-year-old woman).[34] Hermann von Weinsberg wondered whether his physician, Dr. Cronenberg, who at age sixty had taken a young wife, had acted foolishly out of blind passion, that is, for sex, or had done so wisely, to gain a housekeeper and companionship, "so that he might have a more pleasant death than Seneca" (who had died unconsoled, a forced suicide).[35]

Many moralists considered marriage to an older woman as risky as one to an immature girl; they feared that an older woman, especially if she were wealthy and experienced (a rich widow), would not be properly subservient to a younger and less affluent mate. A great dowry, regardless of a wife's age, could also doom a marriage by threatening the husband's confidence. According to the humanist von Eyb, wives who brought great wealth into a marriage tended to be demanding and haughty; they neither feared nor looked after their husbands properly and believed they could do wrong with impunity. The poorer husband, humiliated by the fact that his wife's wealth had made him more important than he otherwise would have been, tended to tolerate such abusive behavior. Such women, von Eyb concluded, were "wives," but not "companions" (*gesellin*); by contrast, a wife with little or no dowry could be expected to obey her husband willingly and serve him diligently.[36] In this same vein the Lutheran Eberlin von Günzburg bragged that his wife was "of noble blood, but right poor (*blut edel und gut arm*), judged by all to be prudent, self-disciplined and pretty; . . . she could have married a much richer man, had she not preferred a husband who loved God's word more than riches."[37] Despite such fears and suspicions, successful marriages between younger men and older, wealthier women were eagerly pursued in the sixteenth century.

Marriages that were considered to work best were those in which a couple shared the same religious beliefs, were of the same generation, had similar economic positions and social backgrounds, and entered marriage with the approval and support of both family and friends. This last consideration was as important in "arranged" marriages as were purely economic considerations of patrimonial inheritance, for a marriage blessed by parents and friends was far more likely to succeed and prosper than one that was not.[38] The most important thing, all authorities agreed, was that the spouses themselves be worthy of respect, people who could be trusted to do what was expected and depended upon in time of trial or need. Then a couple would find the duty of love a light yoke and would grow in affection for one another.

Here we find a distinctive feature of early modern marriage that distinguishes it from much modern practice. Physical attraction and emotional love were not viewed as essential conditions for marriage, although few doubted that they played a role; the love that drew husband and wife together was a mutual willingness to make sacrifices for one another, hence, a duty that developed within marriage. Such love emerged most readily between spouses who at the outset found one another worthy of respect and trust.[39] Not "Do I desire and want this person?" but "Do I find this person honorable and companionable?" — that was the central question for a successful marriage. For how could one make sacrifices for or become affectionately attached to a person one did not first respect and trust? Unlike the modern romantic approach to marriage, in which

Der Jung Gesell.

Ein jung Gesell gerad von leyb
Der bulet vmb ein altes weyb
Geruntzelt dürr waß jr die haut
Allein er auff die gülden schaut
Nach dem selben er schnappen thet
Vil süsser wort er mit jr redt
Verhieß gar vil der guten alten
Er wolt sy schön vnd ehrlich halten
Gedacht heimlich die sach wer schlecht
Wan er jen strick ant hörner brecht
Dan wolt er das gelt verzeren
Vnd jr die alten haut erberen
Ein jünge halten frü vnd spat
Ließ darnach den alten vnflat
Vmb gon an einer Hennen stat

Das Alt Weib.

Die alt die sach den Jüngling an
Der waß schön glat vnd wol gethan
Sy sprach ich sorg jr seyt z frech
Vnd mir wie mancher alten gschech
Die jr erst zu richtet vnthu
Iedoch traw ich euch bessers zu
Jr wert an mir nit vbelo than
Sunder euch wie eir bider man
Gen mir halten in allen sachen
Ich wil euch zu eim herren machen
Mein gut euch machen vnterthan
Waß vor erspart mein alter man
Wo jr euch halt wie ich euch bit
Die heyrath wardt beschlossen mit
Nit weyß ich wie die Ehe geriet.
Bey Hanns Adam.

The Young Man and the Old Widow

The importance of companionship in marriage was also attested by criticism of marriage between partners of vastly different ages. Such a marriage was considered to be made for selfish gain rather than out of sincere respect and affection.

The young man

A young man, fine of body,
Made love to an old widow,
Whose skin was wrinkled and hard.
He thought only of her money.
Afterward he conversed idly,
Plying her with sweet words and
　promising many things,
Saying how he wanted to support her
　honorably,
While all the while thinking to himself
Of the time when he would dominate
　her.
Then he would spend all her money
And thrash that old hide soundly.
　Restrain a young man both day and
　　night,
　For he will flee an old creature
　And visit the chicken coop.

The old widow

The old widow looked on the young
　man,
Who was beautifully smooth and well-
　shapen,
And said: I worry that you are too rude
And that what has happened to so
　many other widows
Will also happen to me after our first
　quarrel.
Still, I will hope better of you,
That you will do me no harm,
And treat me with honor in all things.
I will make you a lord
And give you the property
Amassed by my first husband,
If only you will do as I bid.

　The marriage occurred;
　I do not know how it turned out.

---

one "loves" another in spite of irreconcilable personal, religious, and/or social differences, the marriage counselors of Reformation Europe urged people to seek mates they believed they could *learn to love* because they *first* respected their persons and shared common values. The argument of Cornelius Agrippa of Nettisheim, often cited as transcending the sixteenth century — that marriages based on mutual affection and companionship rather than on procreation and family self-interest would put an end to adultery and divorce — was the commonplace opinion of the moralists of the age.[40]

Among Protestant groups the Hutterites carried opposition to marriages based on passion and self-will to an extreme by making the choice of a spouse completely impersonal. The elders of the community, who were thought best able to weigh God's will in such matters, paired young people for marriage without consultation. This practice was tempered only slightly in certain Moravian communities, which permitted a young man to choose among three preselected girls.[41]

Despite general opposition to purely emotional marriages, Protestants and Catholics did not encourage impersonal, loveless matches. Protestants believed they had opposed the very possibility of loveless marriages when they rejected clandestine marriages based on the mere verbal exchange of vows, something Catholics too

Der alt Man

Eins mals ein gar ꝛalter man
Ein iunges meydlein lieb gewan
Dem thet er lange zeyt hoffiren
Thet sich fast schmücken vnde ziren
Vnd sprach / wann yhr wolt willig sein
Vnd euch in dꝛewen halten mein
Mich ehꝛlich halten spat vnd frü
Wan mir geht ab so get euch zü
So wolt ich euch des wol ergetzen
In ehꝛ vnd grossen reichtum setzen
Kauffen was ewer hertz begert
Euch halten freüntlich lieb vnd werdt
Kleckt ein magt nit ich halt euch zwü
Halt yhr euch freündlich spat vnd frü
Wolt yht das thun so sagt mirs zü.

Die Jung Magot

Die Jung die was der sach geschickt
Den alten sie freündlich an plickt
Vei hieß yhm als was er begert
Sie wolt yhn halten lieb vnd wert
Sie maint aber sein bares gelt
Mit süssen wozten sie yhm strelt
Damit sy auch den alten lapen
An den hals streyfft die naren kapen
Darnach als sie sich dozfft gerüren
Thet sie am naren seyl yhn füren
Als manchem alten noch geschicht
Alt vnd iung zu sam sich reimet nicht
Sonder geleich mit seinem gleich
Das ist lieblich vnd freüdenreich
Wie man es spüret tegeleich.

Getruckt Bey hanns Adam

The Old Man and the Young Girl

The old man

Once upon a time a very old man
Became enamored of a young girl.
He courted her for a long time,
Grooming himself from head to toe.
Finally, he said: if you are willing
to pledge your troth to me
And hold me always in honor,
When I die, you will increase,
I will see that you are well
compensated,
Held in honor, and given great riches.
You may buy whatever your heart
desires,
Only show me friendly love and honor.
If one servant does not please you, I
will get you two,
Only always be friendly to me.
If this pleases you, tell me so.

The young girl

The girl understood the situation well;
She gave the old man a friendly stare
And promised what he desired:
She would hold him in love and honor.
She thought, however, only of cold
cash.
Stroking him with sweet words,
She draped a fool's cape
About the old dandy's neck,
And taking him in tow,
She led him away on a fool's rope,
As happens still to many an old man.

Old and young do not go together,
Like belongs with like.
Here love and joy abound,
As one observes all around.

---

came to reject in the course of the sixteenth century under the pressure of internal critics and secular rulers. Martin Bucer defined a "fully confirmed" marriage as one that had celebrated a wedding feast and enjoyed "plenty of carnal intercourse," and he deemed no true marriage to exist where there was not "a true assent of hearts between those who made the agreement."[42] For this reason he also sympathized with the Israelite practice of permitting a marriage to be dissolved even after sexual intercourse and long cohabitation, if true love and all pleasure had manifestly left it.[43] This was not far from John Milton's later sanctioning of the absence of "true companionship" as a legitimate ground for divorce—no doubt the reason for Milton's high regard for Bucer. Consent, respect, and companionship: these were the glue of marriage. The Lutheran catechist Cyriakus Spangenberg defined a proper marriage as "the joining together of two people by common consent, who wish to live together until death in friendship and honor, avoiding sin [infidelity], and bringing forth offspring."[44]

What of the specific duties of a wife? Her first responsibility in marriage was to be faithfully at her husband's side. Drawing on an image that originated in the Middle Ages with Peter Lombard, sixteenth-century writers were fond of pointing out that woman was created neither from Adam's head nor from his foot, but rather from his "middle" or "side."[45] She had not been set above him to rule over him as his lord, nor was she placed beneath him as a "footstool" or "footrag" for him to abuse as he pleased; rather she had been created to be his "co-worker" and "companion" (*mitgeselle, mithelffer, gehilfin, mitgehulffyn.*)[46] "The office of wife is one of brief joy and much unpleasantness," wrote the author of *Wife's Work* (1553), "because she is not permitted to sit around with her hands in her lap, while good Adam toils and groans alone at his work; she too must take hold at his side."[47] As "bone of his bone," she must "walk jointly" with her husband.[48] It was *her* responsibility to feed and discipline the servants and the children; guard the stores from pilfering and the stock from theft; feed and care for the animals; and conduct herself so as to maintain the respect and good opinion of those around her. For she too "rules over the entire household and owns the entire house" (*eine Domina und Besitzerin dess gantzen Hauses*).[49] Her ability to lead and make sacrifices is especially tested when her husband becomes ill and they fall on hard times. The author of *Wife's Work* declared:

> It is no test of a wife when her man is healthy . . . and all is going well. The test comes when he is ill and impoverished and lies distressed and dependent upon her to wash and clean him and to help him stand and sit. Then may such a crippled patient truthfully say, "I entrust my life to my wife" (Prov. 31). A husband who can say this is truly blessed, for here is the true work of marriage, the sacrifice that gives it its dignity. The other things in marriage can be done as well by whores and scamps, but only an honorable Christian heart and mind can make this sacrifice.[50]

One is here reminded of John Calvin's description of the "beauty" that attracted him to a potential wife: "If she is chaste, if not too nice or fastidious, if economical, if patient, if there is hope that she will be interested about my health."[51]

Some writers depicted the good wife as near heroic. Von Eyb, for example, admiringly cited exemplary women from antiquity so totally devoted to their men that they preferred death to life without them. He singled out Portia, the wife of Brutus, who, denied a knife after her husband's murder, still joined him in death by swallowing hot coals, and Dido, who chose a fiery suicide rather than become unchaste or remarry after her husband's death. Von Eyb found especially inspiring the reported custom in contemporary India of the most favored wife's joining her deceased husband on his funeral pyre.[52] Another heroic woman held up as a model for wives in Reformation Europe was St. Elizabeth of Thuringia (1207–1231), who reportedly never left her husband's side willingly and when forced by circumstances to be apart from him always refused to dress up or in any way groom herself, choosing a solitary ascetic life until his return (she joined the Franciscans after her husband's death).[53] A much admired contemporary woman was Isabella, sister of Emperor Charles V and wife of the Danish king Christian II, a man reportedly given to extremely dark moods. Isabella, a staunch Lutheran, won the praise of Protestant moralists for what one described as her "exceptional ability to bear her lord and master's harsh temperament and manner and remain through all his misfortune an honorable, firm, friendly, and constant presence."[54] According to Luther, women had been created by God to be by nature compassionate, "so that by their acts of compassion they might move men to become compassionate also."[55]

Depictions of heroic wives may reflect the persistence of a Griselda or a Madonna complex, or even the traditional view of women as temptresses ("Women are still Eve," warned Conrad Sam, the Lutheran pastor of Ulm; "they still hold the apple in their hand").[56] It was certainly widely believed that the good wife far transcended ordinary human nature. On the other hand, despite apprehensions about womankind imparted by their theological beliefs, men of that age remained manifestly fond of their wives. The fifteenth-century Augsburg merchant Burkard Zink wrote of "loving" and "liking" his wife and their "helping one another."[57] Ludwig von Diesbach, a nobleman, commented on the death of his wife of ten years in 1487 after the birth of a premature child: "It is impossible to describe my heartbreak (*herzleid*); only one who has experienced it can believe it. I will now risk the damnation of my soul and say that if it were not against God's will and the salvation of our souls, I would give Almighty God a hand and a foot from my body, if He would let me have my wife back in joy and health until we both grow old. God knows such a sacrifice would also be a great pain for me."[58] When Thomas Platter became a research assistant to the Basel publisher Johannes Oporinus, he and his wife, the mother of a newborn daughter, celebrated with an *angster* of wine (a long-necked bottle). Drinking directly from the bottle, they toasted one another: "Drink up," Thomas said to his wife, "for you must nurse [our child]. "Drink up," she replied, "for you must study and work hard at school."[59] When in 1553 Hermann von Weinsberg's sister-in-law died of a sud-

A Wise Woman

This is a traditional Catholic portrayal of the good wife, as evidenced by the association of good works with gaining eternal life. However, her virtues of perceptiveness, piety, discretion, fidelity, charity, and steadfastness were those desired in women by moralists of every religious persuasion.

Look at this figure, which signifies
a wise woman; any woman who does as
she instructs protects her honor well.

(Eyes)

I see as keenly as the hawk
And discern the honest from the false.
I guard myself both day and night
From one who against my honor plots.

(Ears)

I shall not be discouraged
From opening my ears
So that they can hear God's word,
Which keeps the pious on their guard.

(Right hand)

I will despise pride
And behold myself in the mirror of
   Christ,
Through whom God has redeemed us.

(Mouth)

Every hour, day and night,
I wear a golden lock upon my lips
So that they say no harmful words
Or wound another's honor.

(Breast)

Like the turtle dove,
I have a steadfast heart,
Faithful to him who will be my
   husband.
No fault of his will break my loyalty.

(Waist)

My waist is girded with serpents,
As should that of every honest woman
Who wants protection from the poison
   of scandal,
From evil love, and shameful play.

(Left hand)

I shall serve the aged freely
And thereby gain eternal life.
No other thing that I can do
Will bring this end about.

(Feet)

I shall go about on horses' hoofs
And be steadfast in honor.
And not fall into sin,
Which, while sweet at first, turns bitter
   as gall.

Any woman who has such traits
Will maintain her honor undiminished.
And surely earn from God above
An eternal kingdom in heaven.

den illness at twenty-one, he recorded in his chronicle how his brother, her husband, kneeled at the bedside of "this young, beautiful, and intelligent woman", raised her in his arms, kissed her, and then exchanged "good nights" as she fell limp.[60] To the seventeenth-century Puritan clergyman Ralph Josselin, his marriage was the most important thing in his life; he repeatedly expressed affection for his wife (especially during periods of her illness) and respect for her counsel.[61]

According to most commentators, a woman's obedience and self-sacrifice to a husband was made easier by her assumed "more pliant" (*waicher*) nature, although it was also observed that some women, especially as they grew older or became richer, developed inflexible "devil's hide."[62] The yielding nature of women had clear disadvantages in the face of temptation, as the witch-hunters were always quick to point out, but it was also seen to make women more generous and charitable than men.[63] We find the argument, highly flattering to women and perhaps equally self-deluding on the part of the men who make it, that once a woman has sincerely given her love, she remains less inclined to infidelity than a man; whereas men boast pridefully of their adulterous sexual conquests, women consider it shameful to share their love with another after having pledged it to one.[64]

The good wife was also portrayed as always friendly and helpful (*gutwillig*), modest and civil (*sittig*), never given to excess in food, dress, speech, or, especially, in drink. "Can one witness a more horrifying sight than a falling-down-drunk wife?" asked the Lutheran Caspar Cruciger.[65] The good wife was "forbearing of her husband's weaknesses and faults and does not respond with hate and malice when he has sinned or done wrong."[66] Ever a comforting, consoling, and supportive presence in the home,[67] she would permit nothing to come between herself and her domestic duties. In this sense she was said to be "homely" (*hausslich*).[68] The good wife is "never without her home; that is why the Greek artist Apelles painted Venus standing in a snailshell — to show that a wife and homemaker should be constantly with her house, like the snail that carries its little home with it wherever it goes."[69] It was inappropriate for a wife to be involved in external social and political issues because they would distract her from her primary household responsibilities. There was no objection to her employment outside the home in her own or her husband's business, or in volunteer charitable work, but her household remained her first priority, a divinely ordained discipline through which women exercised their faith and worked out their salvation;[70] neglect of the household betrayed a woman's reason for existing. The thing that most impressed Hermann von Weinsberg about his seventy-seven-year-old mother as she lay bed-ridden and dying in 1575 was that "she still ruled the house in all necessary matters from her bed."[71] Respect for women was closely tied to their devotion to homemaking; where women were "constantly present and vitally important to the family's continuity and well-being," antifeminism seems to have been greatly reduced.[72]

Here was a demanding ideal, one that was certainly not attained by all and clearly spurned by some. The author of *Wife's Work* described "young wives" he had observed who retaliated at the first insult and shamelessly complained in public about faults in their husbands that "pious women" did not even notice or, if they did, had the good will to ignore. These same young women were observed to prefer idle pleasure to housework, "their heads hanging out of the window, their backsides turned to the stove."[73] In his popular guide to household management, Johannes Coler also criticized women who "all the time have the window on their neck," chatting with passersby.[74] It was to rescue women from such laziness and self-indulgence, the authorities agreed, that God had given them so many good and necessary household chores: embroidery, knitting, sewing, spinning, weaving, cooking, gardening, and marketing the family's produce and wares.[75]

For women who chafed under a husband's yoke, the moralists explained that submission was part of the punishment women justly inherited from Eve, like the pain of childbearing, a labor in penance for mankind's fall — but that their task was no more severe than that of their poor husbands as they bent their backs to earn the family's bread by the sweat of their brows. The wife's submission to a husband was viewed as no more an indignity than the husband's caring for his wife. When Martin Bucer compared the relationship of husband and wife to that of shepherd and sheep,[76] or when the housefather books described the good wife as an "echo" and "mirror" of her husband,[77] the intention was to remind *both* of their high responsibilities to one another as companions in marriage, not to demean women.

A wife had the right to disagree with her husband and oppose his decisions when she felt she must. In doing so, however, she was urged by marriage counselors to make clear her abiding respect for her husband's authority. One author suggests the following (extreme) approach:

> [Let her speak to him] in a modest tone, choosing a pleasant time and occasion so that all is said in strictest privacy, and let her words be chosen with such care that he will recognize

that her action is no impertinent attempt to control him or
any presumption to power over him, but rather an expression of her love and concern for his own best interest. For
this reason, it is better that such a conversation proceed
with demonstrative entreaty and pleading on the part of the
wife — if the circumstances require, even with tears — than
that a wife give the impression of asserting authority or
severity against her husband.[78]

The intention of such advice was to preserve the husband's authority
over his household at the point of greatest possible conflict with his
wife, namely, a challenge to his rule. The "cunning" urged upon
women to this end reveals how important male self-confidence was
believed to be for the maintenance of family solidarity and social
stability. Many today find it unfair and even cruel that a woman
could be more severely punished for the allegedly "unnatural act" of
striking her husband than a husband for beating his wife (although
sixteenth-century wife-beaters hardly went scot-free).[79] In the communities of Reformation Europe, however, it was believed that
marriage, family, and society could not long survive if the "fathers
of the house" lost their nerve. The consequences of men doubting
their abilities and fearing their responsibilities were all too clear in
fragile premodern society. In their strength and self-respect lay also
the well-being of all around them. For this reason wives were urged
to humor and console them in their darkest moods, and children and
servants to jump at their sternest commands, while pastors and
moralists never let the fathers of the house forget that God watched
and weighed their every act. All conspired to tame the "lion"; none,
however, dared to go too far in the process, lest his pride be
altogether lost.

The advice of moralists may not have been so far from people's actual practice as modern historians have tended to believe. The way
life *should* be lived and the way it *is* lived, the ideal and the fact of
existence, have a certain reciprocity. Life is both creative and adaptable; ideals evolve from experience and, in such forms as parable,
exhortation, and law, return to shape it. On the other hand, the
range for innovation in life's most basic relationships is probably not
large. Left to themselves day after day in the quiet of a small house,
a husband and a wife have limited options as to what they will do
with one another, and these are probably determined as much by set
routine and natural need as by world view and ideals. It is doubtful,
I believe, that different religious allegiances influenced the basic re-

Taming the Lion

A No man is ever so high or good
That he cannot be managed by a
woman
Who does his will
In friendly love and service.

B Although he is tyrannical wild,
He is soon calmed by a woman.
She boldly strokes his open mouth,
His anger fades, he does not bite.

C The lion, most lordly of beasts,
Famous for his strength and
nobility,
Favors us women with heartfelt
gifts
And good humor accompanies his
kindness.

D How wonderfully you reflect
Your taming at woman's hand,
Bearing patiently what another
Does to you against your will.

E O powerful king and greatest lord
Your equal is neither near nor far.
Excelling all, both large and small,
Upon your head should lie a
crown.

F Lord lion, although you are feared
by all,
A woman knows how to saddle
you,
Bending you to her will by love.
True love finds a home with a
good man.

G How well you have been groomed!
Now how lively and cheerful!
One so spirited
May have the company of women.

H Lord lion, you may have your
every wish.
Cover your trail with your tail
And you will not be tracked down.
Those who love in secret know this
well.

Lion I let the women amuse themselves
by serving me.
What harm can they possibly do
me?
If I want, I can suddenly turn
fierce again.
He is a fool who lets himself be
taught by women.

lationships between spouses in Reformation Europe in significantly different ways. To be sure, different religious systems provided for very different *public* expressions of personal feeling, and, as was shown in chapter 1, the new Protestant institutions did make important alterations in the *external* requirements for marriage and in the communal disciplining of both spouses. But it would be difficult to argue that Protestant marriages were more egalitarian or that the spouses loved one another any more intensely than did Catholic spouses. Wife-beating and cuckolding certainly knew no religious confession, and pagans and heretics surely appreciated companionable marriages as much as orthodox Christians. And who can doubt that while the public response to the death of a spouse might vary from one religious confession to another, the sense of personal loss for the individuals involved remained equally great? In a word, the most intimate domestic relationships — those between spouses and between parents and children — possess from age to age and from culture to culture a certain internal force and life of their own.

The Wives of Hermann von Weinsberg

Hermann von Weinsberg of Cologne was a slightly eccentric lawyer, councilman, and petty wine merchant and a Catholic layman who admired Erasmus. He could on occasion be outspoken in criticizing the greed and deceit of the local clergy, and he sympathized with certain goals of the Protestant reformers. On one occasion he paired at dinner, somewhat to his regret, a Calvinist pastor and a "Jesuitical" niece.[80] On the other hand, throughout his life Hermann held firmly to traditional religious beliefs and practices, endowing local cloisters and supporting local churches, celebrating his private joy and consoling his private grief through traditional religious institutions. He was married twice, to two very different women. His extremely frank accounts of both relationships, recorded in his family chronicle, provide as rich a commentary on sixteenth-century marriage from the point of view of the participants as the historian could hope to find.

In 1544 Hermann's father tried unsuccessfully to join his twenty-six-year-old son with a widow of means who was twenty-two years older.[81] Hermann continued to search for a proper mate for four more years. On January 7, 1548, his parents suggested he consider marrying his neighbor Weisgin Ripgin, the proprietor of a wool and yarn shop, recently widowed (August 1547) after sixteen years of marriage. His parents explained why they wanted the match and

asked Hermann whether it also pleased him. Hermann, who knew
Weisgin well, was indeed pleased by the prospect and urged his
parents to pursue it. "Because you and my mother so advise me," he
responded to his father, "and because I know her well and trust God
[whom all assumed to be behind this new state of affairs], I shall be a
happy man if the woman also desires me." When Hermann's father
approached Weisgin the next day as she was leaving church, she
acknowledged having heard rumors of an impending "proposal,"
evidence that the family had been at work on the union for awhile.
"If this has indeed been arranged by God and my family approves
it," she responded, then she too would welcome the match.[82]

Before formal marriage negotiations began, Weisgin took
counsel with both her own and her deceased husband's family. Like
Hermann, she took the advice and consent of family and friends very
seriously. A meeting was then arranged among Weisgin's brother-in-
law and his wife, Hermann's parents, and Hermann and Weisgin.
This meeting ended with friendly handshakes and Hermann's
presentation of gold coins to Weisgin as a pledge.[83] On January 12
Weisgin's brother, the burghermeister of neighboring Neus, met
with Hermann and his father to work out a marriage contract. They
agreed that any children of the union would inherit from Hermann
what he received from his father and would inherit from Weisgin
the same amount her two children from her previous marriage
received from their father — equal shares of the paternal inheritance
all around. If the marriage remained barren and Weisgin survived
Hermann, she would retain what Hermann brought into the marriage as the property of the marriage (*heilichsgut*) and would have
the use and enjoyment of his patrimonial inheritance (*die leibzucht
mines patrimonii*) so long as she lived. If Weisgin died first, Hermann was to share her possessions equally with her two children (*ein
kintteil*). When both spouses were dead, all possessions and proper-
ties were to revert to the nearest blood relatives (*Leibeserben*).[84]

The following day Weisgin and Hermann met in church, exchanged gifts (further pledges of the marriage), and confronted the
issue of possible impediments to the marriage. Two years earlier
Hermann had been intimate with his parents' serving girl, Greitgin
Olup. In November 1546 she had borne a daughter whom Hermann
presently supported as his own. Greitgin's father now visited the
pastor and urged him to prevent the planned marriage with
Weisgin, alleging an impediment, the existence of a "prior engagement" between Hermann and Greitgin. Hermann vigorously denied
such an engagement, and when the priest examined Greitgin on the
the matter, she could not swear to an exchange of private vows be-

tween them. After a visit to the aggrieved father by a delegation led by Hermann's father, the objection to the marriage was withdrawn.[85] On Sunday, January 14, only a week after Hermann's parents set it in motion, the marriage was proclaimed in church. Hermann's father stood guard under the church tower to prevent Greitgin's father, or any other detractor, from disrupting the proceedings. The following day Hermann entered Weisgin's house for the first time to celebrate the wedding feast.[86]

Reflecting on his wedding day, Hermann described Weisgin as "beautiful of face, rather tall and large of body, god-fearing, virtuous, busy (narhaftich), cheerful, and a peace-maker." These personal traits, apart from familial and economic considerations, moved him to marry her. The fact that she was older he considered a distinct advantage—an exceptional point of view in the sixteenth century: "I thought it would make for a better marriage, if the husband was younger than the wife, a conclusion to which I was drawn by personal circumstances and by the wisdom of the proverb: 'one should marry the experienced in the neighborhood.' "[87] The "personal circumstances" he alluded to concerned a childhood hernia, which had rendered him shy and withdrawn as a youth. Hermann also worried that the injury might pose an obstacle to his ability to father children and for this reason had been reluctant to take a young wife.[88] That Weisgin had children of her own was a fact he accepted. ("Who," he asks, repeating a favorite saying of his father, "can avoid all hedges?") He was much consoled by her income-producing business and a thriving household (they resided in Weisgin's house after the marriage).[89]

There is every indication that the marriage was companionable and egalitarian, no doubt in part because of Weisgin's seniority and economic independence. Hermann frequently sought her counsel on matters affecting his modest political career. Before successfully standing for election as Hausmeister in the city council in 1549, a post for which he was far less qualified than the other candidates, he discussed the wisdom of the move not only with Weisgin but also with his mother and sister Catherine.[90] He described assisting Weisgin in making cherry jam, carefully recording every step in the process for future use (he provided the recipe for the reader).[91] In 1554 Hermann and Weisgin quarreled over the writing of their last will and testament. One of Weisgin's two sons from her first marriage had died, and she did not want to write a will because (irrationally, according to Hermann) she feared it might in some way disadvantage her surviving son. Since Hermann had no children, he worried that his death without a will would disadvantage his relatives, and that if Weisgin died before him he might be left disadvantaged. Assuring Weisgin that a will was in everyone's interest, he discussed the provisions point by point, weighing everything to Weisgin's satisfaction, "for Weisgin was clever and understanding enough" (*kloik und verstendich genoig*). He gave her a draft to scrutinize at her leisure "so that she could question and consider every point with mature counsel" (*mit reifem rait*). Weisgin struck certain things out and added others until, after many discussions, both were satisfied that the will fulfilled their desires.[92] The will was notarized in October, at least four months after the discussion had begun. Highly detailed, it ensured that the property and goods common to the marriage would be divided equally among the nearest relatives on both sides at the death of the surviving spouse. It also provided that Hermann would receive the deceased son's inheritance if he outlived Weisgin, although at his death this portion was to be divided equally among the relatives on both sides.[93]

As it worked out, Hermann did benefit from the will, but not excessively. Weisgin died on May 28, 1557, after a painful illness that her physicians diagnosed as a uterine infection (*gebrech an der moder*). Hermann recorded the event: "So died a pious, god-fearing, understanding, and friendly wife; as she was in life, so she remained in death . . . May God be gracious and merciful to her; I hope she may be a child of eternal life and beseech God on our behalf."[94] Thereafter Hermann regularly visited her grave on All Saints' Day, placing candles and saying prayers.[95] Many years after her death, on May 13, 1575, a Friday, when he was ill with chills and a fever , he recalled that Weisgin had died on a Friday (as his second wife did later); the memory of it depressed him.[96]

By October 1557, a scant four months after Weisgin's death, Hermann had received no fewer than three offers of marriage and had had an affair with a young widow. In February 1558 he married Drutgin Bars,[97] a rich widow with several children, who was ten years his senior. The match had been encouraged by his sister, who made the initial contacts with Drutgin, another indication of the extent to which marriage was a family affair.

The editors of Hermann's chronicle have described his new wife as a "true Xanthippe."[98] The marriage was unquestionably conflict-laden. On July 18, 1558, Hermann recorded the first of many violent quarrels. Having learned of his intimacy with another woman while a widower, Drutgin, an extremely jealous wife, raged against him and attempted to flee the house. Fearing a public scandal, Hermann forcibly restrained her, and when she taunted him, he violently beat and cursed her (*ir hart zugekrischen hab und ir hesslich*

Die Meünerley bewt einer bösen Frawen/sampt jren neün aygenschafften.

The Nine Lives of a Bad Wife

While strolling one evening, a man met a recently married friend who was scratched and bruised, and he asked him if he had been attacked by cats. The friend replied that his marks were the result of a brawl with his wife, who, unlike other women, had "nine lives or natures." Urged on, he elaborated. Returning home from the pub last Monday, he greeted his wife but received not a word in reply; she was like a codfish. So he struck her a good blow, whereupon he encountered a raging bear, pawing at him. So he struck her again and this time he met a hissing goose. Then she was a dog, snarling and barking epithets at him: "Ass, fool, simpleton." Struck still again, she became a rabbit on the run, bounding about, and cursing him as she ran: "Scoundrel, whoremonger, adulterer, gambler, drunkard." He ran her down and beat her about the head, now to find himself astraddle a wild, kicking horse. Then she was a cat, pouncing on him in full cry, scratching and clawing him mercilessly. At this point he grabbed a club and beat her incessantly until she became a pig, squealing and bawling. Finally, she crumpled into human form at his feet, threw her arms around him, and begged for mercy. He now learned that a neighbor had led her astray, teaching her to behave in these ways so unbecoming to a woman. She promised never again to forget her place and challenge her husband. After this display of contrition he forgave her, but with the warning "never again to rise up against me." Although they have made their peace, it remains tenuous.

Having listened intently to this story, the man offered his friend the following advice:

My good fellow, mark well what I say.
You young husbands are too ill-
tempered,
Petulant, mad, stupid, and shameless.
When your wife displeases you,
Or fails to agree with your point of
view,
Or overrides your wishes on a matter,
Or has not yet learned to make a proper
home,
You want to correct everything with
blows.
No honorable man would ever behave
this way.
The result of such behavior is a mismar-
riage.
One does not keep house by war,
But by peace and friendship.
St. Paul has taught us men
To rule our wives with understanding
Not by harassment and crude tyranny,
Because wives are the weaker sex.
Therefore, punish your wife
Only with kind and understanding
words,
Spoken together in private.
[Say to her]: "My dear wife, this you
should not do.
It is not fitting for you,
And it is shameful and harmful.
If you want my favor and good will
You must learn to obey me.
In return I will obey you
By not doing those things that ill befit
me
And conduct myself as an honest man.
I will speak no more unkind words to
you.
We shall live well together as friends.
On your life let no one incite you

To rebel against me;
And I shall not let any lead me astray
To act improperly against you.
When something disturbs you, bring
your complaint directly to me,
And when something bothers me, I
shall speak directly to you.
I forbid you to stand before me in fear.
There is no one else we can trust com-
pletely.
Since we belong together with each
other,
Why should we quarrel and bare our
teeth
And lead so devilish a life
That our reputation
Brings us only disrespect?"
So punish your wife modestly,
And if there is any honor in her,
She will become an obedient wife.
As one says, "A devoted husband
Can bring forth a devoted wife."
But if she remains self-willed,
And refuses what is fair and reasonable,
And opposes you in all you request,
Ever disobedient and rebellious,
On those occasions when she spurns
cooperation,
You may punish her with blows —
Yet do so still with reason and
modestly,
So that no harm is done to either of
you.
Use both a carrot and a stick
To bring about companionship,
As befits an honorable man.
Herewith Hans Sachs wishes that you
May in time find here on earth
Peace, joy, and friendship in marriage.

gefloigt), something he claimed he had never done with his first wife. Drutgin apparently took her revenge two days later. Early in the morning she awakened Hermann with the news that she had aborted a fetus in her chamberpot, which she showed to him. He was shocked because Drutgin had long maintained that she could no longer bear children. Upon reflection, however, he suspected that what he had seen in the chamberpot had been only wet paper in the outline of a fetus. He concluded that Drutgin had concocted the entire episode so he would never strike her again, although he conceded that only God knew for sure whether a fetus had been aborted. The following year, on June 24, Drutgin again claimed to have passed "aborted matter" into her chamberpot.[99]

The marriage continued to be afflicted by jealousy. In 1559 and 1560 the couple separated, and Drutgin made charges — unfounded, according to Hermann — of his adultery and whoring, which she publicized to their priest, friends, and her children and relatives.[100] On one occasion Drutgin complained that Hermann treated her with less respect than a housemaid, "like a dustrag"; she especially resented having to go to market and plan daily meals. After arguing in vain with her that these were not unreasonable chores, Hermann performed them himself for two weeks before Drutgin again resumed them.[101] A bitter fight occurred on their first anniversary, with Drutgin threatening to kill herself and Hermann to expose her insane jealousy to her children. At the end of their first year of marriage, Hermann described her as "the kind of person who can at times be so completely good, yet at other times be as bad as rat poison, frequently seized by fits (*stupen*) that throw her into a violent temper."[102] Hermann reported their priest's concurrence that Drutgin suffered from "the evil of jealousy and an infirmity of the mind" (*zelotypiae malum et infirmitas capitis*).[103]

This, however, was only one side of their marriage. There was also accommodation and companionship, perhaps even a special underlying excitement that was both belied and revealed by the surface hostility. Hermann surrendered, gradually and grudgingly, to Drutgin's request that he leave his office as housemaster of the city council, a position he enjoyed, even though it was largely honorific. They were required to live under the Rathaus, which for Drutgin was a distressing abode.[104] Time progressively healed their wounds; Hermann reported both "peace" and "happiness" at the celebration of their eighth, ninth, and tenth anniversaries.[105] When in 1570 he inadvertently discovered that Drutgin was secretly paying off her late husband's debts, he respected her privacy.[106] And he wrote with seeming envy of her best friend, a woman with whom

Hermann says she shared and did all, "the one person she trusted more than any other."[107]

Drutgin died of dropsy on May 1, 1573, after a painful illness, "her legs so swollen that we had to make wool tights for her wider than leather knickers."[108] Hermann described his reaction to the approach of her death: "I cried bitterly and kissed her cheeks, and she spoke to me, although not coherently, but she understood well when I spoke and communicated with gestures."[109] On May 3 Drutgin was buried beside her mother and father, her first husband, and several of their children.

Soon thereafter Hermann moved into a refurbished family house to begin his life anew. As early as July there were rumors that he would remarry, but he squelched them with the declaration that "my mother is woman enough for me" — a reference to the fact that his mother and sister Sibilla now kept house for him. He mused on his new state:

No woman would now look at me, save for the sake of gain. A young wife might flatter me, but hold nothing dearer than my death. An old wife might be vexatious and impossible to advise. And howsoever good a new wife might be, she would still bring her cares with her. I have served the world for twenty-five years as a married man; now I may, with God's grace, live alone without a wife.[110]

Despite Hermann's praise of "celibacy" and his occasional suggestion that men need wives mainly to keep house,[111] he clearly missed the stimulation of marriage. After four months of being a widower, he wrote of "a change of heart brought about by my change of dwelling, since I now had no wife, nor quarrels with stepchildren to look forward to; nonetheless I took heart and believed I would be well."[112] He did not in fact escape conflict with Drutgin's children, a resentful lot, who contested him for years over their mother's inheritance.[113] He regularly observed the anniversary of Drutgin's death and on occasion included in his chronicle itemized accounts of the sizable sums he spent in remembrance of her on vigils, masses, candles, beguines at graveside, and other commemorative objects and personnel.[114] On the tenth anniversary of her death, he pondered that he was now the same age (sixty-five) as she had been when she died. His tone was that of a man who had been fond of his wife and missed her. He wrote that she would never have believed that he could live so long after her. She had not wanted him to remarry after her death. Not only had he remained single but, he confessed, he had "not so much as touched another woman, save in public with polite kisses and dancing": "this will make Drutgin very happy, if she may know it wherever she now is, and if she still thinks and feels the way she did in life" — a reference, of course, to her uncontrollable jealousy.[115]

Divorce and Remarriage

In traditional Christian practice, divorce had been granted only on grounds of adultery; "divorce" was understood to be the separation of the adulterous spouse from the bed and table of the innocent spouse, not a definitive dissolution of their marriage bond and the right of each to remarry. Because medieval theology deemed marriage to be for eternity, the separated spouses remained husband and wife in the eyes of the church, even though all personal contact and commerce between them came to an end. Of course, numerous impediments could be invoked to annul a valid marriage even after a couple had ostensibly been properly married for years and produced several offspring. This traditional practice has been viewed as tantamount to divorce and remarriage.[116] However, an annulment did not dissolve an established bond; it rather declared that the marriage never existed because it was entered upon improperly. The system of impediments and annulments regulated marriage *at its inception*, thereby giving the church moral influence and oversight of it; it was not designed to deal with marriages after they had irretrievably broken down.[117] In the case of a breakdown, even when a court separated a couple from a common bed and table because of adultery, the turmoil of a failed marriage continued for them, since the marriage bond remained and neither was free to enter a valid relationship with another.

We find an example of traditional divorce in Cologne in the chronicle of Hermann von Weinsberg, who recorded the history of the failed marriage and divorce of his sister Sibilla. Hermann's account makes vivid the human suffering created by laws that prohibited true divorce and remarriage after a marriage had broken down both privately and publicly. Sibilla had married Conrad Eck, an occasional worker and frequent mercenary, in August 1562. Within two years the marriage had reached the breaking point, with violent quarrels over Eck's squandering of Sibilla's dowry and recurrent wife-beating.[118] In November 1565 Hermann wrote that he was unwilling to visit his sister because his brother-in-law treated her so badly.[119] By 1568 the couple had informally separated, and talk of divorce, that is, formal separation from a common bed and table, brought the intervention of even the burghermeister, who argued with Sibilla that divorce was "ungodly and caused sin."[120] In March of the same year Eck quarreled publicly with Hermann and Gotschalk (another brother), accusing the Weinsbergs of poisoning their sister's mind against him and attempting to "steal" what was his own—they wanted Eck to account for Sibilla's portion of the property of the marriage. The incident landed the three in court, where Eck was censured for disorderly conduct and slander.[121]

After an almost three-year separation, during which time Sibilla lived with her mother, the couple reconciled in August 1570 (much to the anger of Gotschalk), and they lived together for a year before Eck went to Denmark on mercenary service. When he returned in October 1572, broke and with debts still outstanding in Cologne, the marriage went on the rocks again. Sibilla moved back to her mother's house, this time taking with her Eck's clothes, which she treatened to keep until he agreed to make good on what he owed her. In December Eck smashed a window in the Weinsberg house before returning to war in Denmark.[122] Upon his return to Cologne in July 1573, a formal divorce proceeding was initiated by Sibilla but was not pursued to a conclusion.[123] In August of the following year Eck came home from still another military stint to discover in the Weinsberg family church a newly installed window that depicted him beside Sibilla. So great was his anger over the portrait, presumably because he was portrayed as a happy member of the Weinsberg family, that Sibilla had the portion of the window containing his likeness removed. Hermann's comment on the incident was: "Fools are also people."[124]

Serious litigation began again in the summer of 1576, when Eck's "maid" gave birth to a son.[125] Sibilla made a jealous search for the woman, whose relationship with Eck was a serious one. After exchanging blows with her husband, Sibilla took him to court for adultery, where he was ordered to "set the dove aside" and was fined for his behaviour.[126] These events emotionally exhausted Sibilla; by this time the marriage had also placed her in such economic difficulty that she was forced in the following year to negotiate an annuity from her brothers in exchange for her propertied inheritance.[127]

Finally, in June 1580, after almost eight years of informal separation and recurrent hostilities, a formal divorce was obtained and the status quo officially ratified. The process began in February of that year, when Eck brought suit demanding all of Sibilla's property on the ground that she had "maliciously abandoned" him.

Before a court composed of both civil and ecclesiastical officials, Sibilla explained that her separation from her husband had been an act of self-defense, and she lodged countercharges of chronic prodigality and indebtedness, whoring, absenteeisim, and having the "French pox" (syphilis). Serving as his sister's attorney, Hermann demanded that Eck pay 500 reichstaler as Sibilla's fair share of the property of the marriage plus an additional 300 reichstaler to cover a seven-year pension (alimony), legal fees, and damages to his sister. Eck paid the final settlement of 620 reichstaler after selling his house for more than twice that sum. On June 30 the two were divorced in a formal ceremony, which pronounced them "separated from bed and table" (*scheidung zu bedde und dische*). The key passage declared:

> Since it is found in truth to be the case that Conrad and Sibilla have not kept house together for almost eight years, but lived alone, so it is stipulated and agreed that Conrad and Sibilla shall henceforth live apart, each with a separate dwelling, bed, table, and goods; and that each shall behave honorably so as to be able to answer to God their Lord; and that neither shall, either by word or by deed, in person or by an agent, act against or harm the other or the other's relatives on the streets, in church, at home, or in any place within or outside Cologne; and that each shall wait patiently to see what God next has in store for both.[128]

The lives of Eck and Sibilla after their divorce suggest that the stigma of such a separation punished the man at least as severely as the woman. In mid-July 1580 Eck became a minor civil official (*hauptman*); Hermann wondered "how one who had not yet proved to be of any use to himself could be expected to be such to the city," and he concluded that Eck's character must have changed.[129] In September 1581 Eck was dismissed from his post, in part because he "now lived openly with a whore outside the bond of marriage" (*baussen der ehe mit einer dirnen hausgehalten*), and in part because illness (apparently complications of syphilis) had prevented him from fulfilling his responsibilities on a regular basis.[130] In October 1582 Hermann reported that Eck had moved to a nearby village and now made his living bottling wine. He still had his "maid" with him, whom he introduced to others as his "true wife" (*getrewete ehefraw*). This outraged Hermann, who agreed with "others [who] say she is an adulterous whore and their [two] children bastards; what shameful, wanton evil to live openly with a

whore before the eyes of my sister Sibilla, his lawfully wedded
wife!"[131] Hermann wondered how the clergy and magistrates of Cologne could allow him to go unpunished.[132] By the end of 1582 Eck
had gone through two new jobs, those of cooper and weightmaster.
Hermann now expressed the wish that "Eck and his new wife or
whore and bastards" would move to another city so that his sister
would not have to see them.[133] In May 1583 Eck was imprisoned for
unruly behavior and interrogated about living openly with another
woman, "while still married to the daughter of a respected
burgher." Eck reportedly responded that the woman with whom he
now lived *was* his true wife "although not in the papal manner" (*das
were sin ehefrawe, aber nit uff die pabstische weise getrawet*).[134]
Eck had further brushes with the law and apparently suffered
severely from syphilis before dying outside Cologne in March 1587.
Afterward his "maid" settled in Cologne with their two sons.[135]

As for Sibilla, she maintained the expected propriety of a
sixteenth-century divorcée. She was tempted in 1587 to become
housekeeper for a clerical scholar, but Hermann was opposed to her
"living in a priest's house" and kept her home.[136] In August 1588,
now fifty-one years old, Sibilla caught the eye of a widower, a successful brewer. Pointing out that her husband was now dead, she expressed to the family her wish to remarry and recited to Hermann
the assets and qualities that would make the brewer a good husband.
He had property and money and owned his own house; although
"rather old," he was modest, earnest, experienced, thrifty, diligent,
and understanding; although "rather heavy," he remained "well-
formed about the face" and had "good manners"; and although he
could neither read nor write, he was very pleased that Sibilla could;
finally, Sibilla did not mind that he did heavy physical labor.[137]
They were married August 6 in the Weinsberg house.

From Martin Luther to John Milton, Protestant thinkers found it in-
creasingly difficult to recognize the validity of a marriage in which
the husband and wife no longer slept or ate together, and they
challenged laws that deemed otherwise. Protestants rejected the
sacramental status of marriage and refused to view it as a once-and-
for-all state. If marriages were made in heaven, they were also
dissolved there. A marriage could definitively end this side of
eternity and a new one begin for the separated spouses. In his
earliest writings on social issues, Luther expressed "great wonder"
that people divorced on grounds of adultery were not permitted to
remarry, since in the Bible "Christ permits divorce on the ground of
unchastity and compels none to remain unmarried, and St. Paul

would rather have us marry than burn."[138] When the Protestant marriage board of Zurich confronted the traditional view of divorce as separation from bed and table without dissolution of the marriage bond, it commented, disarmingly: "To separate spouses from a common bed and table while still having the marriage bond hold makes no sense; the major reason people get married is to share a common bed and table."[139] No one was more forceful on this subject than Martin Bucer, by all accounts the most "liberal" sixteenth-century Protestant on the subject of divorce.[140] Bucer considered a sentence of divorce and the right to a new marriage to be "one and the same,"[141] and he refused to recognize a valid marriage bond where there was not "continual cohabitation and living together" with "benevolence and affection."

> The Papists . . . oppose themselves to God when they separate [couples] for many causes from bed and board and yet have the bond of matrimony remain, as if this covenant [of marriage] could be other than the conjunction and communion not only of bed and board, but of all other loving and helpful duties . . . God requires of [both spouses] so to live together and to be united in body and in mind with such an affection as none may be dearer and more ardent among all the relations of mankind . . . The proper and ultimate end of marriage is not copulation or children . . . but . . . the communicating of all duties, both divine and humane, each to the other with utmost benevolence and affection.[142]

The popular impact of such teaching in the early years of the Reformation was attested by the Catholic apologist Caspar Schatzgeyer. In 1524 he published a vernacular pamphlet condemning five "Lutheran" errors on divorce and marriage that were being preached to ordinary people. According to Schatzgeyer, these threatened social order by encouraging "many serious frantic acts" in a rush for the divorce courts. The errors being preached by Lutherans were: (1) that the guiltless party in a divorce may remarry; (2) that a Christian spouse may remarry if deserted by an unbelieving spouse (the so-called "ordinance of St. Paul," *privilegium Pauli*); (3) that St. Paul permitted divorce on grounds of chronic anger and disunity between spouses; (4) that the guilty party (the adulterer) in a divorce case may remarry if the innocent spouse refuses to reconcile; and (5) that, according to the Bible, it is also better to remarry than to burn, if one spouse forces the other into sin by denying the marital duty.[143]

What precisely were the Protestants teaching? Lutheran beliefs about divorce were explained and justified in large vernacular tracts by Johannes Brenz (1531) and Johannes Bugenhagen (1540), who were, with Luther, the most influential Lutheran catechists of the sixteenth century. Bugenhagen wrote his magisterial work on the subject as a summary of Lutheran practice for King Christian III of Denmark who reigned from 1536 to 1559, to guide the reorganization of the Danish church, which was Lutheran after 1536. In 1537 Bugenhagen, assuming a prerogative formerly exercised by the Catholic archbishop of Lund, crowned Christian king in Copenhagen. Both Bugenhagen's and Brenz's works reflected the conservative bent of Lutherans, in distinction to the Zwinglian Protestants, in their teaching that adultery was the only legitimate biblical ground for divorce and remarriage. However, both Brenz and Bugenhagen found ways to acknowledge the propriety of other grounds for divorce.

For Bugenhagen, adultery, by its very occurrence, dissolved a marriage bond. An understanding of this fact, he argued, was necessary both to distinguish Lutheran teaching from traditional Catholic teaching and to counteract the contemporary fashion of treating adultery lightly. ("Have you not observed," he complained, "how people today find adultery amusing? One is heard to say of another, 'He has great luck with the ladies,' when what the man in question has really done is to commit the most shameful act of betrayal.")[144] After committing an adulterous act, Bugenhagen maintained, a husband was no more a husband, nor a wife a wife, than a virgin was a virgin after fornication; something irretrievable left a marriage the moment one of the partners became unfaithful. For this reason Bugenhagen viewed an adulterous act by a spouse as more lamentable than the death of a pious spouse, since the finality of the loss was so much greater (the apparent assumption being that a pious couple would be reunited in eternity, while a couple separated by adultery remained apart forever.)[145]

When a couple became estranged because of adultery, the first duty of the pastor was to seek their reconciliation and reunion, the best solution both in the eyes of God and for the moral health of the community. Just as any husband or wife would bring back to life a spouse who had died prematurely if he or she had the power to do so, Bugenhagen argued, so should each attempt to "resurrect" a spouse stricken by the greater tragedy of unfaithfulness. True to the logic of his argument, Bugenhagen considered a reconciliation to be a *new* marriage, not a continuation of the old, which had ended in the act of infidelity. Like other moralists who addressed the subject of divorce and remarriage, Bugenhagen much preferred that the first wife become also the "new" wife.

In practice the pastor visited both parties, urging the guilty to be humble and beg forgiveness, the betrayed to be forgiving and seek reconciliation. The extreme penalties of exile and execution, which the Bible urged and magistrates applied in rare cases as a last resort to hardened, repeat adulterers (usually after the fourth offense),[146] were seen to work against the pastoral and communal goals of reconciliation. Indeed, exiling a husband for other crimes often established the conditions for adultery and a permanent divorce. In a significant number of divorces filed in Zurich because of desertion, the city's punishment of criminal behavior by exile was a factor.[147] This circumstance lay behind the pastor's insistence that a wife had an obligation to follow an exiled husband.[148] The pastor also besought the magistrates not to foreclose the possibility of reconciliation between a couple separated by adultery by fining the guilty party beyond his means to pay, thereby creating a financial crisis that an estranged spouse might be unwilling to share.[149] All agreed that swift official punishment of flagrant adultery and support of the innocent party were essential to the social order,[150] but despite lip service to the stiffest penalties,[151] everyone preferred lesser penalties that allowed for the possibility of reunion. When a table companion of Luther's expressed the belief that adulterers should be summarily executed, Luther rebuked him with a local example of harsh punishment gone astray. A pious wife, who had borne her husband four children and had never been unfaithful, one day committed adultery. The husband had her publicly flogged for the transgression. Afterward Luther, Bugenhagen, and Melanchthon tried to persuade the couple to reconcile, and the husband was willing to take her back. However, the wife had been so humiliated by the public flogging and resulting scandal that she abandoned her children to her husband and wandered away. "Here," Luther comments, "one should have pursued reconciliation before punishment."[152] In Württemberg in 1571, long after Anabaptism had become a capital offense, the practice of exiling women who converted to Anabaptism ended because of the turmoil it brought upon their families; the city even permitted Lutheran husbands to prevent zealous Anabaptist wives from taking flight by "chaining them in the house."[153]

The immediate obstacle to reconciliation was usually the spouses themselves. Bugenhagen reported encountering wives with "hearts turned harder than stone" by philandering husbands. His own approach was to deny the sacrament to any man or woman who refused to take back a sincerely penitent spouse who begged forgiveness and promised reform. Obstinacy, however, often prevailed, and permanent separation became the only recourse. If, after a year, all efforts at reconciliation by clergy and friends proved fruitless, and there was reason to fear for the safety of one or the other spouse (because of the possibility of physical assault or poisoning) if they continued to live under the same roof, then it became the duty of the authorities to separate them physically and proceed with a divorce.[154]

The Catholic argument against remarriage was that so long as an adulterous spouse lived, even though separated from the bed and table of his or her mate, a valid marriage still existed since "what God has joined together, no man may put asunder" (Matt. 19:6). But Bugenhagen deemed that the adulterous spouse was no longer a husband or a wife but only a "scoundrel" in the eyes of God, who Himself dissolved the marriage at the moment of infidelity and set the innocent party free to remarry.[155] Johannes Brenz made a similar case for remarriage, arguing that the New Testament forbade remarriage only to couples separated by transient anger, not to those properly divorced because of adultery.[156] Declaring that a marriage plagued by hostility and infidelity was manifestly not a work of God, Bucer inverted Matthew 19:6: "What God has not joined together, man may put asunder."[157]

According to Bugenhagen, the Protestant practice of permitting divorced spouses to remarry was not new. He claimed that certain "learned and understanding Catholic officials and bishops," both in the present and in the past, had followed natural law rather than papal law to help spouses caught in "emergency situations," that is, trapped in hopelessly broken marriages yet unable to restrain their sexual and emotional needs for companionship with the opposite sex. Declaring such dispensations (*ein Permittimus*) easier to grant "on the basis of our doctrine," Bugenhagen pointed to the recent case of Philip of Hesse who, long unhappily married, received in 1539 the grudging permission of leading Protestant reformers to enter a secret, bigamous marriage with one Fräulein von der Sale.[158]

Luther had actually sanctioned bigamous marriages as early as 1521, albeit under circumstances far more extreme than those surrounding the case of Philip of Hesse. In his popular treatise *On the Babylonian Captivity of the Church* (1521), he counseled a woman living with an impotent husband, and either unable or unwilling to prove her case in court because of the evidence required or fear of notoriety, to enter, with her husband's consent, a secret marriage with his brother or another mutually satisfactory person and raise the children of this second union as those of the impotent husband. Luther preferred such private bigamy to outright divorce because he believed it kept the first marriage intact and prevented whoring and adultery. If, however, a husband refused such an arrangement and a wife's sexual desires remained overpowering, then Luther instructed her to take a second husband and flee to another land where they could live together without prosecution for bigamy. The same counsel was here extended to a husband with a sexually incapable or unwilling wife.[159]

To Luther's critics, such advice did not seem sage. Jaspar Gennep, a Cologne bookdealer and Catholic "counter-catechist" active in the second half of the century, appealed to this very passage to support the charge that moral life had deteriorated with the success of the Reformation. The Protestant denial that it was possible to live a chaste life not only placed temptation before pious merchants and their wives who had previously managed to remain virtuous during long periods of separation, but it also weakened the resolve of the young to maintain sexually pure lives.[160]

In Lutheran lands those who chose to remarry after divorce were expected to wait at least a year, just as after the death of a spouse. In fact remarriage after a death often occurred sooner, with apparently little public criticism.[161] The remarriage of a divorced person, however, was very discreet. Because of traditional opposition to such marriages, a stigma remained even after they were recognized in law. A parallel may be drawn with clerical marriages, which were also looked on with distress after their legality had been ensured.[162] When a divorced person remarried, Lutherans denied the couple a public church ceremony and other public celebrations. The couple would appear before the appropriate civil authorities, make their pledges, and then meet on a prearranged date at home in the evening with friends and the pastor, at which time the marriage was concluded.[163] The marriage of a widow also was undertaken with a certain restraint, though greater acceptance, as if a second marriage were always a lesser marriage. Hermann von Weinsberg, for example, reported that his second marriage occurred without fanfare and celebration (*on grossen pracht*) "because we were both widows."[164]

Lutherans recognized that marriages broke down for reasons other than adultery and that precedents existed for awarding divorce on other grounds. On this subject Brenz could write as perceptively as any modern marriage counselor.

Because people who marry remain different, and some totally lack the will to agree and cooperate, in time obstinacy and hatred overwhelm some marriages. For this reason, and in order to protect such couples from greater harm and unhappiness, Moses in the Old Testament favored their divorce, reasoning that while it did not accomplish anything positive, it at least prevented further and greater evil.[165]

Christians like Brenz and Bugenhagen, however, found themselves bound by the teaching of Jesus in the New Testament (Matt. 5, 19), which recognized only adultery, not chronic anger and hatred, as ground for divorce.[166] Both writers, nonetheless, did consider other grounds. Brenz, for example, called attention to a variety of reasons a husband might divorce a wife (and a wife a husband) in imperial law: if she plotted a liaison or did things that indicated infidelity, if she frequented "public games" against his wishes and command, if she threatened to poison or stab him, or if it was discovered that she practiced harmful magic against the state.[167]

Although Brenz could not personally endorse such reasons as legitimate grounds for divorce from a purely Christian point of view, he sympathized with the necessity of such laws for the good of society. Here he gained perspective from Luther's doctrine of the "two kingdoms," the theological distinction that gave Lutherans the flexibility needed to deal realistically with the world while espousing high Christian ideals. God's word, Brenz pointed out, always teaches what is absolutely right, that is, what *should be* in a kingdom of perfect Christians. Worldly magistrates like Moses and the emperor, however, do not rule over such a kingdom. Because secular rulers govern non-Christians and imperfect Christians, their first concern must be to maintain a peaceful and viable society. Hence they often permit lesser wrongs or evils to occur so that society might be protected from greater ones. When rulers make such compromises, Brenz concluded, God forgives them; the magistrate who permits de facto bigamy on the ground of emotional incompatibility has, by absolute Christian standards, sanctioned adultery, yet he has not acted irresponsibly in light of his mandate to maintain worldly peace and order.[168] In this sense God has exempted secular rulers from absolute Christian standards. As Bugenhagen pointed out, just as magistrates may execute criminals without transgressing God's commandment against killing, so they can permit divorce on grounds other than that approved by Jesus in the New Testament without necessarily putting asunder what God has joined together.[169]

When Lutheran theologians attempted to follow the strict logic of their Christian ideals, the conclusions they drew about marriage appear cruelly inappropriate to a modern reader. Brenz, for example, denied that leprosy might be a ground for divorce, since Christ had recognized only adultery. To emphasize that a marriage remained intact despite the presence of this dread disease, Brenz insisted that the healthy partner was still obliged to perform the marital duty if the stricken spouse requested. Brenz did advise any couple in this predicament to avoid "the many disadvantages of sex and remain chaste."[170] In their arguments against monasticism, Lutherans had proclaimed humankind's inability to suppress sexual desire, but in counseling a man or woman suddenly burdened with a spouse rendered sexually incapable or undesirable by physical or mental illness, they reminded the person of the extrasexual companionship of marriage and assured that God would provide the strength to subdue carnal desire.[171] Marriage had obviously created a new basis for self-sacrifice. The only marital incompatibility of a personal nature generally recognized by Lutherans as justifying divorce and remarriage was impotence, and that, according to Brenz, only after a marriage was still sexually unconsummated after three years.[172]

As one might expect from men who stressed the importance of companionship in marriage, desertion by a spouse received a great deal of sympathetic support as a ground for divorce. Bugenhagen distinguished three basic types of abandonment. The first he described as "friendly," when a husband left a wife with her knowledge and consent to go away on business or on a trapping expedition to fill the family larder. Such separations, though often prolonged, raised no moral or legal problems affecting a marriage unless the absent spouse failed to return at the expected time. More serious was desertion occasioned by anger, the most frequent example of which was the runaway wife who "abandoned" her husband because of his bad behavior or harsh treatment of her and fled to the home of her parents or of a friend. Moral and legal problems arose here only if the estranged wife rejected a penitent husband's friendly overtures to return. To Bugenhagen, such rejection transgressed the Bible's command to leave mother and father and cleave to one's spouse, and for this reason he supported forced reconciliations, provided the hostility between a couple seemed to be transient and not life-threatening.[173] So long as adultery did not occur during such a separation, no basis existed for pursuing a divorce.

Another species of desertion occasioned by anger involved partners with different religious convictions, a problem that had again arisen among Christians in the sixteenth century with the widespread success of the Reformation. In the New Testament St. Paul had permitted Christians to remarry if their non-Christian spouses had abandoned them on religious grounds (1 Cor. 7). Lutherans agreed with this judgment only in cases of *willful* abandonment (see below); religious incompatibility alone did not constitute a legitimate ground for divorce but was one of many crosses a Christian spouse must bear patiently.[174] Bugenhagen, however, was sympathetic to the secular judicial practice of permitting a husband and wife with strong religious differences to live apart by mutual consent in the expectation that time would moderate their differences. Couples so separated were expected to live chaste lives; the separation was not tantamount to divorce, and neither party was free to "date," much less to remarry. The arrangement could be upset, however, if a husband decided that he could not keep house by himself and demanded in court that his wife be made to return. Since no adultery or other grave offense was involved in such a separation, a new marriage for the abandoned husband was out of the question; "how intolerable," Bugenhagen observed, "that a man should take another wife in order to gain a housekeeper when his first wife goes back and forth under his nose." Judges treated such cases exactly as they did that of a runaway wife and, according to Bugenhagen, the results of court-ordered reconciliations were often happy.[175]

Radical Protestant sects took religious differences between spouses much more seriously. Anabaptists, for whom the believer's union with Christ was more important than any earthly marriage, required true believers to separate from non-Christian (that is, non-Anabaptist) spouses.[176] This was far more extreme than the trial separations described by Bugenhagen. However, Anabaptists did not, as Lutheran apologists frequently charged,[177] treat religious incompatibility as a ground for divorce and remarriage. Anabaptists were more stringent than Lutherans in permitting divorce and remarriage only for adultery.[178] In Hutterite communities the church banned nonconforming spouses and required their orthodox partners to join the community at large in avoiding all contact and communication with them until the wayward spouses repented their errors. As in Lutheran lands, couples so separated from one another because of religious differences could not remarry so long as both lived. If and when religious conformity made possible the return of an estranged and banned spouse, the community sometimes celebrated a new marriage to indicate the momentousness of the event.[179]

Separation because of anger or religious differences did not constitute willful desertion, and most such cases appear to have been managed successfully by communal persuasion or coercion short of a divorce suit. Spouses who intentionally deserted their mates, never to return again, were another matter.[180] Lutheran consistories permitted abandoned spouses, whose mates had disappeared without their knowledge and consent, to remarry after a year.[181] This was allowed on the basis of natural and imperial law, contrary to traditional church teaching and practice. In such cases Bugenhagen declared natural and imperial law higher than the "foolishness of the pope and the common man," who believed that only the death of a spouse could set free a married person.[182] Bugenhagen deeply sympathized with deserted women. He raged against what he described as sophistical and cruel pretense by popes who deemed abandoned wives, like the wives of adulterous husbands, to be lawfully married for life. Did not such traditional practice encourage immoral behavior (*buberey*) by foreclosing any honorable way out of an impossible marriage? Popes themselves, Bugenhagen hastened to add, had none too good a record of fidelity to their "covenants," that is, their political pacts with kings and emperors; those who so sternly condemned divorce under any circumstances had throughout history routinely reneged on their own solemn vows and promises.[183]

To Bugenhagen, willful desertion did far more harm to marriage and family than any act of adultery. Whereas an adulterer might be reformed and reunited with his family, a husband who deserted placed his wife and children in a hopeless situation.[184] He forced an innocent wife to suffer in celibacy and poverty for a crime uniquely his own, and if she succumbed to sexual temptation in his absence, as many such unhappy women understandably did, she and her children were often mercilessly ridiculed by their neighbors.[185]

Despite the fundamental and lasting changes that Lutheran reformers and magistrates brought about in marriage law and practice, they generally remained conservative in domestic matters, hardly going so far as Luther's original teaching suggested they might.[186] An extreme example was staunchly Lutheran Nuremberg. There the city council very much feared a right to divorce and remarriage, envisioning both wanton abandonment of spouses and the eternal enmity of the Catholic emperor. The council resisted the urgings of its clergy until the second half of the sixteenth century, when it first recognized the right to divorce and remarry on grounds of adultery and desertion.[187] Reformers also shared this fear. In Basel Johannes Oecolampadius foresaw uncontrollable lust and serial polygamy if the "door to divorce" was flung wide. He proposed that only adultery be recognized as a ground for divorce; impotence, desertion, and leprosy were to be borne by married Christians with "true conjugal affection," in patience and continence.[188] Oecolampadius nonetheless went along with the more liberal Zwinglian divorce laws adopted by the city.

An exception to the Lutherans' general conservatism was Bucer. Believing no true marriage could exist where the sharing of affection and conversation had ceased, Bucer recognized, in addition to impotence and willful desertion, leprosy and madness as grounds for divorce if the afflicted spouse was sexually incapable and the healthy spouse could not remain continent.[189] Bucer cited approvingly the many grounds for divorce contained in the Roman civil code, and he searched Justinian for such additional grounds as a woman's right to divorce a husband who refused to defend her against malicious gossip or falsely accused her of adultery, and a husband's right to divorce a wife who procured an abortion or committed bigamy.[190]

The Reformation's impact on marriage and divorce in actual practice can be seen in the records of the marriage courts of Zurich and Basel. In Zurich four laymen from the city councils served with two clergy, in Basel five laymen with two clergy. As their composition suggests, both courts were firmly controlled by secular authority. These Zwinglian cities took a more flexible approach to defining grounds for divorce than their counterparts in Lutheran lands. On the other hand, their "theocratic" impulses led them to enforce new moral and domestic laws more stringently, especially in Zurich.[191]

The Zurich court recognized six basic grounds for divorce — adultery, impotence, willful desertion, grave incompatibility, sexually incapacitating illness, and deception. The court in Basel recognized adultery, impotence, willful desertion, capital crimes, leprosy, and a serious threat to life. Between 1525 and 1531 the Zurich court heard seventy-two cases of adultery, in forty-two of which the wife was proved the guilty party, in thirty-three the husband, and in three, both husband and wife.[192] Zurich sentenced convicted adulterers to three days in jail on bread and water, a penalty doubled at the second offense and tripled at the third. The fourth offense could bring exile, and the fifth possible execution by drowning in the Limmat.[193] Basel fined a convicted adulterer five pounds (double that for a councilman or a pastor); a second offense brought six days in jail and a ten-pound fine; a third, nine days in jail and fifteen pounds, while a fourth offense could bring exile, and a fifth, execution.[194] Zurich banned the guilty party from church, stripped him of his right to hold public office, and removed him from any official positions and from membership in city guilds and societies. Such ostracism remained in force until he had demonstrated satisfactory moral improvement, and a fitting period of penance had passed.[195]

Barring reconciliation, the innocent spouse in a divorce for adultery received damages in the form of cash, as well as a property settlement, and was free to remarry six months after the divorce. No set rule existed for the remarriage of the guilty party; this privilege depended on whether he or she actually reformed, as judged by the court. The Zurich court did recommend a one-year probationary period for adulterous males and a three-year period for adulterous females — a double standard that suggests both greater outrage over female adultery and greater anxiety about unsatisfied male sexuality. In practice, however, the probationary period for both men and women varied from one to five years. The court firmly denied remarriage to second-marriage adulterers of both sexes.[196]

Basel's practice in a divorce for adultery was more conservative than Zurich's. There the innocent party had to wait a full year before remarrying, although the court could intervene to shorten this period if circumstances justified it. In one case a respected abandoned wife remarried within two months of her divorce from an adulterous husband because carnal temptation was threatening to undo her (apparently a budding relationship with another man.)[197] Generally, good behavior and reputation ("piety and honesty of life") were the basic requirements for the court's permitting the innocent party in a divorce to remarry. Unlike Zurich, but like Lutheran cities, Basel as a rule denied remarriage to the guilty party. The judges had a certain discretion in complicated cases and were apparently inclined to waive the letter of the law if the innocent spouse had remarried and moved away.[198] Everywhere there existed a strong conviction that it was improper to allow a guilty spouse to remarry while the innocent spouse was present and unmarried. A convicted adulterer who defiantly remarried anyway found the new marriage treated as null and void. The intention of laws forbidding adulterers to remarry seems to have been twofold: on the one hand, to encourage couples to remain together even under the most trying of circumstances, and on the other, to force the guilty party in a divorce either to reform and possibly even reconcile with the former spouse or to go into exile and oblivion. In Lutheran lands clergy often requested that the adulterous spouse be exiled once a divorce had become final and there was no hope of reconciliation.[199]

Between 1525 and 1531 the Zurich court heard twenty-eight

petitions for divorce on grounds of impotence. The court carefully examined each case, taking testimony where necessary from midwives and physicians to make sure that impotence was not being alleged falsely to escape an unhappy marriage. Once convinced that the problem was real, the court nonetheless required a waiting period of up to one year and the consent of *both* spouses before granting a divorce, in the hope that the problem still might resolve itself naturally.[200] Both the Zurich and Basel courts recognized that chronic impotence could develop after marriage either for physical reasons or from growing hostility and repulsion between spouses. This was *impotentia superveniens*, impotence relative to circumstances created by the marriage, as distinguished from *impotentia antecedens* or impotence that existed before a marriage and prevented its consummation. Whereas Luther followed canon law in recognizing only *impotentia antecedens* as a valid ground for divorce, Bucer and Zwingli sanctioned both types.[201] Men and women in Basel filed successful divorce petitions on such grounds as physical and psychological impairment of a man's sexual ability; natural and accidental deformation of male or female genitalia, rendering sexual intercourse physically impossible; and deformation of female organs consequent upon the trauma of giving birth, making coitus either impossible or too painful for the wife.[202]

The courts as a rule forced couples seeking a divorce on the ground of impotence to work very hard to obtain it. A perhaps not atypical example was the Basel court's handling of a divorce petition initially filed on the grounds of impotence by one Pastor Fridlin Brombach against his wife Sibilla. When the pair approached the court in June 1543, Fridlin alleged that he had married Sibilla without knowing that she had a sexually incapacitating illness. Sibilla, a former nun, who had been married twice before, spoke in her own defense against the divorce. She explained that she had had medical problems in the past but that they had not disrupted her previous marriages. When she married Fridlin, she assumed that they had disappeared altogether. She admitted, however, that she had been ill for a long time and unable to keep house and sexually satisfy her husband on a regular basis. The judges responded by sending the couple away to pray for God's help, pointedly reminding Fridlin that marriage involved sacrifices: "The marriage bond obligates both husband and wife, as one flesh, to help one another in times of trial and suffering and bear one another's cross."[203] Six months later Fridlin returned with a new petition. Again the court urged prayer and patience and postponed the case until Shrove Tuesday. Fridlin came again on April 29, 1544, to confess that in the intervening months he had committed adultery. Sibilla, aware of the infidelity, now supported her husband's request for a divorce, perhaps convinced that her condition had contributed to his straying, and certainly persuaded that the point of no return had been reached. The court chose the less drastic option of separating the couple from the common bed and table. Six months later Fridlin petitioned the court to dissolve the marriage bond as well so that he could remarry. This was at last granted him, but with the stipulation that he not be permitted, at least in Basel, to marry the woman with whom he had earlier committed adultery.[204]

The Zurich court refused to grant divorce for what it interpreted to be bearable, transient incompatibility. "General quarrelsomeness" (*widerwillen*) was adjuged to fall into this category and to be at the root of eighty divorce petitions considered by the court during Zwingli's lifetime. The judges ruled that if a man was a slob or occasionally struck and demeaned his wife, or if a woman was eviltempered and occasionally refused the marital duty or permitted her mother to plague her husband, these were not proper grounds for divorce. (Philip of Hesse even alleged the "bad odor" of his wife as a ground for his bigamous marriage.) In reply to such complaints, the court reminded the petitioners that "there are many pains that must be endured together in a marriage."[205] Frigidity in women was treated as a tolerable, passing incompatibility. However, the court did recognize three instances of grave, life-threatening incompatibility that justified separation and divorce. These were if a husband beat a wife to the point of endangering her life; if proven *impotentia superveniens* resulted from physical injuries inflicted by marital fighting; and if an older spouse became ill and his or her mate refused to provide the necessary care because of enmity between them.[206]

The Basel court was even more reluctant to grant a full divorce for alleged threats to life (*do eins von dem anderen sins libs und lebens nit sicher*), although it recognized such threats as a legitimate ground. It preferred to dismiss hateful spouses and wife-beaters with warnings. Men who persisted in beating their wives eventually received short prison sentences to encourage them to reform, and recurrent hostility between spouses did bring about separation from bed and table and a division of property, but these solutions still fell short of divorce. Even in cases of "furious and insane" threats to life, the Basel court would tell the couple to separate for a time before granting an actual divorce, clinging as long as possible to the slimmest hope of reconciliation.[207]

The Zurich court heard 107 cases of desertion; in 44 the wife had abandoned her husband, in 63 the husband had left his wife. To obtain a divorce on this ground the deserted spouse had to have a good reputation and the mate had to be absent without leave and communication. In addition, the abandoned spouse was required to make every effort to confirm the absent mate's whereabouts and his or her possible death or refusal to return. If the court received proof of willful desertion from credible witnesses, a divorce could be granted without confirmation of the deserter's present whereabouts — the apparent assumption being that a spouse who had freely fled and bragged about it to others had no intention of returning. Remarriage was possible for the abandoned spouse after a year (in Basel the waiting period was up to three years). [208] If a spouse was away with the knowledge and consent of his or her mate and had departed without any ill will, then the spouse left behind had to wait three years before divorce and remarriage, unless the death of the absent spouse was confirmed. In cases where a woman had remarried in the false belief that her husband had died while away on "honest" business (in Switzerland, this often meant that he had gone to war as a mercenary), the second marriage was voided if the husband who was presumed dead returned. In cases where a deserting husband returned after his wife's divorce and remarriage to another, the new marriage remained valid and the first husband lost all claim to his former wife. [209] Finally, if a spouse converted to Anabaptism and also deserted, divorce for willful abandonment could be granted. In Basel conversion, as a capital crime, also justified divorce; a fled, exiled, or imprisoned Anabaptist spouse was considered as dead. [210]

More readily than Lutherans, Zwinglians granted divorce for various physical illnesses and handicaps that affected sexual fulfillment, especially when a wife's illness or handicap prevented sexual relations. While it expected a wife to remain with and care for a crippled husband, the Zurich court would grant a healthy husband divorce from a sickly wife who was incapable of sex if the wife concurred and the husband agreed to continue to care for her material needs. [211] Whereas Lutherans rejected leprosy as a legitimate ground for divorce, both Zurich and Basel recognized it. Zurich required the consent of the stricken spouse (Basel did not), and both cities held the healthy spouse responsible for the continuing care and support of the stricken one. [212] After 1548 Basel allowed only separation from bed and table for leprosy, tightening its laws under the dual influence of its theologians (in the 1520s Oecolampadius had opposed divorce on grounds of leprosy as unbiblical) and the experience that some divorced spouses simply abandoned their leprous mates to the charity of the city. [213]

Unlike Lutheran courts, the Zurich court recognized incurable insanity and epilepsy as grounds for divorce.[214] Like Lutheran courts, Zwinglian courts also occasionally permitted de facto bigamous arrangements if a spouse was sexually incapacitated by illness. In one case involving a woman unable to have sex because of a prolapsed uterus, the Zurich court initially urged the couple to give the malady a chance to improve naturally; when time failed to bring about the hoped-for improvement, the court, with the wife's concurrence, permitted a discreet sexual relationship between the husband and a consenting servant girl.[215] In a similar case the Basel court permitted a husband, again with the wife's consent, to satisfy his sexual needs as required, but outside the city,[216] ostensibly with prostitutes or acquaintances in neighboring villages. Such arrangements were made to protect a stricken wife who required care and support from her husband, while giving the husband the sexual release necessary to his physical and mental well-being. Courts were generally disinclined to grant divorce for a wife's sexually incapacitating illness if a couple had been married a long time. In such cases the court again reminded petitioners that "the marriage bond obligates both husband and wife, as one flesh, to help one another in time of trial and suffering and bear the other's cross."[217]

In Zurich, if a wife pretended to be a virgin when she married or willfully deceived her husband, this was a ground for divorce. The court granted divorce in six cases where a wife had been presumed a virgin before marriage only to have it discovered afterward that she had either previously given birth to an illegitimate child or was pregnant by another man. Once identified, the true father was required to provide support for the woman and her offspring.[218] Also in Lutheran lands "errors" about virginity could dissolve a marriage if the deception was proved incontestably and if the husband could not be reconciled to his wife.[219] Deceit, especially at the outset of marriage, struck at what all deemed its indispensable foundation; a proper companion in marriage was above all one who was worthy of respect and in whom trust could be placed.

In evaluating the relationship between spouses in Reformation Europe, present-day scholars have had few kind words to say, and these have been grudging.[220] Ian Maclean notes that Luther persistently condemned Aristotle and Aquinas as "monsters" for describing women as botched males (that is, as products of a generative act not carried to completion to produce a male offspring). Yet Maclean cannot place Luther on the side of the angels because Luther viewed the greater width of a woman's hips as a sign that God had created her to stay home and have babies.[221] Maclean concludes that

Renaissance humanists and theologians generally "modified only slightly" the negative image of women held by their medieval predecessors.[222] Natalie Davis finds that the French Reformed Protestants not only advocated sexual and spiritual equality, friendship and companionship in marriage, but also passed tough new laws against wife-beaters; yet she too concludes that the Reformation made no significant advance beyond traditional religion because neither "eliminated the subject status of women."[223] Keith Thomas discovers among English Puritans an exalted conception of family life, condemnation of wife-beating, and the rejection of a double standard of sexual morality, and among the more radical English Protestant sects he finds affirmation of woman's spiritual equality and encouragement of her spiritual self-expression. Yet Thomas too declares that Puritans did little to "raise women's status," and that the sects did not transcend the "patriarchal home."[224]

Surely, to judge the past by egalitarian standards that have yet to win a clear consensus even in the modern world is to sow disappointment wherever the historian turns. If the women of Reformation Europe could respond to its present-day critics, I suspect they would say something like the following. To be "subject to a man" in the sixteenth and seventeenth centuries did not necessarily mean either the loss of one's identity or the absence of meaningful and rewarding work. The many chores of housewifery and motherhood may have been personally fulfilling for the vast majority of women, but they hardly prevented women who were so inclined from working in addition at their own or their husband's craft; women as well as men had both household and professional duties. In the "patriarchal" home, authority was shared by husband and wife. A wife's subjection to the rule of her husband was not the subservience of a serf to a lord, or a maid to a master, or a child to a parent; despite male rule an ordered equality existed between husbands and wives. While it cannot be claimed that Protestants were unique in achieving loving marriages, their new marriage laws, especially those that recognized for the first time a mutual right to divorce and remarriage, became the most emphatic statement of the ideal of sharing, companionable marriage in the sixteenth century. The domestic legislation of the Reformation encouraged both spouses to be more sensitive to the other's personal needs and vocational responsibilities, thereby enhancing the status of both men and women.

·3·

The Bearing of Children

MARRIAGE SUBJECTED a woman not only to the labor of loving a husband, but also to that of bearing children. In the sixteenth century women became wives in order also to become mothers; the home was above all a nursery. No idea seemed more self-evident to both sexes; as St. Paul had taught, "Woman will be saved by the bearing of children in faith, love, and holiness, and with discipline" (1 Tim. 2:15). According to both Catholic and Protestant moralists, motherhood ennobled womankind. The bearing and nurture of children were a special blessing upon women, who otherwise, because of their natural weakness and the responsibility for humankind's fall, might have despaired altogether.[1] Observing that pregnant women were healthier and happier than barren women, Luther, in 1522, while still a bachelor, urged wives to be continually pregnant. "Even if they bear themselves weary or ultimately bear themselves out," he polemicized against the advocates of virginity, "this is the purpose for which they exist." In the last years of his life he praised the early marriages (at nineteen) and high fertility of the Israelites, denouncing contemporary women "who seem to detest giving birth lest the bearing and rearing of children disturb their leisure" (*otium*).[2]

Needless to say, the procreative purpose of sex was everywhere stressed. Both Catholic and Protestant moralists also recognized that sex was a natural necessity and served important nonprocreative purposes, such as promoting bodily health and "calming the mind," and a few authors opposed the traditional belief, evolved from St. Augustine, that engaging in sexual intercourse merely to satisfy lust or gain pleasure was a mortal sin.[3] However, most authorities treated sex primarily as the means by which God expected mankind to multiply. Sexual intercourse was above all a divinely ordained marital duty; moralists and medical advisors did not give extended consideration to the nonprocreative side of sex.[4] Although overcrowding could be a serious problem for individual families, and contemporary artists and writers expressed sympathy for parents with too many children under one roof,[5] the specter of overpopulation did not haunt the sixteenth century. And while it can be argued that Protestant and Catholic moralists contributed to an evolving moral climate that encouraged the use of contraception and planned parenthood beginning in the seventeenth century, in the previous century marriage counselors discussed birth control only to condemn it.[6] Marriage manuals did not elaborate on means of artificial contraception; they rather unfolded the divine plan of parenthood.

The World of the Expectant Mother

During the sixteenth and seventeenth centuries infant and child mortality was extremely high; at least one-third of *all* children appear to have died before age five.[7] The child was at risk before and during birth as well as in infancy, and new and expectant parents had constantly to be on their guard. Because information about these experiences is piecemeal and scattered, modern scholars have often given in to the temptation to impute modern reactions to families of that time. An important source that has been little used is the *Rosengarten* of Eucharius Rösslin, the first printed manual for midwives, published first in 1513.[8] Rösslin's work became the basic guide to gynecology, obstetrics, and infant and child care in much of northern Europe during the sixteenth and seventeenth centuries; when babies were delivered and nurtured according to the most up-to-date methods, they were delivered and nurtured according to Dr. Rösslin.

Surviving records identify Rösslin as the city physician in Frankfurt between 1506 and 1511 and from 1517 until his death in 1526. He also practiced medicine in Worms in 1513 and apparently spent long periods of time also in Freiburg im Breisgau, where in a list of property-owning burghers his name appears as an apothecary between 1502 and 1526.

The *Rosengarten* was a scholarly manual in that it drew on and synthesized the teaching of such classical and medieval authorities as Hippocrates, Galen, Rhazes, Averroës, Avicenna, and Albertus Magnus. Rösslin, however, was no mere litterateur who lacked experience in actual childbirth;[9] first and foremost, he was a practicing physician. If we take him at his word, he aspired to provide midwives and expectant mothers with detailed information about prenatal care and the complications attendant upon delivery so that "the curse of pain that accompanies childbirth" might be lessened.[10]

He dedicated the work in 1513 to Katherine of Saxony (1487–1561?), a noblewoman with whom he had been acquainted since 1508, apparently as a gesture in celebration of her marriage to Henry the Pious in the previous year and certainly as a guide for her personal use during the fertile years of a royal marriage.[11] Rösslin condemned in the strongest terms the "ignorance" and "negligence" (*hynlessigkeit, dummheit, negligentz, verwarrlassen*) of midwives and expectant mothers, in his opinion the major causes of infant mortality;[12] "the many deaths [from miscarriages and unskilled deliveries] that I have again and again witnessed" could be reduced only by better preparation for the hour of birth.[13]

It appears to have been unusual for a man, even a physician, to participate directly in the "woman's work" of delivery.[14] The English male translators of two seventeenth-century French obstetrical manuals apologized in the prefaces for intruding themselves into the peculiar domain of women.[15] In one extreme case in 1522 a physician in Hamburg was executed for masquerading as a woman in order to observe a birth.[16] By his own testimony Rösslin had often attended the birth of children and assisted with deliveries,[17] clear evidence that the taboo against males in delivery rooms was breaking down in the late fifteenth century and that male physicians were beginning to take a direct role in the birthing process. His descriptions are utterly frank, usually graphically realistic; the reader senses an eyewitness and practitioner. In the preface he warns the reader that pregnancy and childbirth, from beginning to end, are an ordeal for both mother and child who "will undergo much pain and suffer many grave infirmities, injuries, and accidents. The poor vulnerable infant may be rendered defective and die in the process, perhaps before it receives holy baptism, and thereby be robbed of eternal life; such are the hazards of pregnancy and childbirth."[18]

The practical nature of Rösslin's work is attested by his provision of a Latin-German lexicon, giving the lay reader exact descriptions of the prepared medicines to be obtained from an apothecary. The most striking practical feature, however, is the illustrations, showing the various positions a child can assume in the womb. These were borrowed from the ancient Greek studies of Soranos of Ephesus (fl. A.D. 100), whom Rösslin knew through the medieval translator Muscio.[19] The illustrations served to implement the *Rosengarten*'s major medical contribution, at least for western Europe in the late Middle Ages: detailed instruction on how to turn a child in the womb when it lay in a breech or other position that inhibited a safe delivery. In his own practice Rösslin had observed that such mispositioning often meant a cruel end for the infant.

Rösslin listed eighteen circumstances conducive to a hard and painful birth, and urged expectant mothers to attend to those that could be treated. These were: a small-framed and too young mother (examples of twelve-year-old mothers are cited but said to be rare); a vagina severely narrowed by nature, illness, or accident; ulcerated bladder or bowels; hemorrhoids so afflicting the mother that she cannot bear down; a weak and sickly disposition, frequently observed in women having their first child when either too young or too old and so fearful of childbirth that they cannot adapt and control themselves during labor; birth of a boy rather than a girl; a child that is too large or too small (too light) to navigate the birth canal; birth of twins, Siamese twins, or a deformed baby; breech birth ("the most serious, especially with twins"); premature and late births; stillbirth or the birth of an ailing infant; an embryonic sac that is too thick (prolonging the birth) or too thin (so that it breaks too soon); delivery in cold dry air, which constricts the birth canal, or in too hot a room, which stifles the mother and prevents her from cooperating; a mother who has been accustomed to hard, dry food and liquids that bind (especially crab apples, marjoram, dried berries, millet, and heavy red wine); a mother who has bathed regularly in water heavy with salts of iron, salt water, cold water, or water laced with seasonings that constrict; a depressed, sick, hungry, or thirsty mother or one who has been exhausted by lack of rest and sleep; strong odors in the delivery room; and finally, contractions that do not radiate downward.[20]

Rösslin distinguished three types of miscarriage. The first occurs in the first two months of pregnancy "before the creation of the child and its reception of a soul." According to Rösslin, human life does not begin at conception; during the first two months the womb contains only formless, soulless matter. The second type of miscarriage may strike between the end of the second month and the midpoint of the pregnancy, after the fetus has assumed human form but before it has become "active" in the womb. The third type occurs during the last four months of pregnancy when the child, now fully formed, remains nonetheless unable to survive for long outside the womb and if born prematurely is usually stillborn.[21]

Why do such untimely births occur? Rösslin drew explanations from classical and medieval medical authorities as well as from his own practice. Miscarriages happen when the entrance to the uterus becomes enlarged or the walls of the uterus are too smooth, softened by the "bad flow" that originates there; when the uterus is too flexible and moist to retain the man's seed or the weight of the fetus; when the uterus becomes ulcerated; when the umbilical cord is stopped up and insufficiently nourishes the child or breaks because of imperfections. Diseases in nearby organs, especially an ulcerated colon or bladder stones, may also trigger a miscarriage, as may chronic coughing and an ailment known as *tenasmon*, a constant need to evacuate the bowels but with little or no result. Thin and weak women often require so much nourishment for themselves that their fetuses do not receive the nourishment they need to survive and consequently are aborted. Still other causes of miscarriage cited by Rösslin are menstrual bleeding after the third month of pregnancy (bleeding is said to be less of a problem earlier because the fetus, being then so tiny, requires little nourishment); use of laxatives before the fourth month of pregnancy and after the seventh; dysentery and chronic diarrhea; chronic vomiting; malnutrition; gluttony, which "corrupts the mother's blood" by placing her in a constant state of indigestion; diseases both internal and external to the womb; and premature rupturing of the embryonic sac. Extreme cold and heat may also kill the infant in the womb. If the mother becomes overheated, the fetus will leave the womb in search of a cooler clime; for this reason, expectant mothers are advised to avoid long baths in hot water, which also cause the birth canal to expand and become slippery. Because the fetus is extremely sensitive to sudden changes in the weather, a rash of miscarriages can be expected when a cold, dry spring follows a warm, moist winter. Violent movements by the mother, especially jumping backward ("as is customary in wild, wanton dancing") or when doing heavy housework, will also bring on a miscarriage. Finally, a miscarriage may occur if the mother is violently pushed, struck, or knocked down (a censure of wife-beaters), is "too often unchaste" (that is, has sex too frequently during pregnancy), or is overwhelmed by anger, fear, terror, sadness or sudden unexpected good news.[22]

One warning sign of an imminent miscarriage is the withering of previously full and healthy breasts. According to Rösslin, who here drew on Hippocrates and Avicenna, a sudden deflation of the breasts indicates that miscarriage will occur on the same day. Rösslin also believed that if a woman is pregnant with twins and one of her breasts goes flat, the child on that side will be aborted (boys, we are informed, usually lie on the right, girls on the left side of the womb). Miscarriage also threatens when "a woman has sharp pains in her womb, turns red in the face, trembles throughout her body, develops a fever and severe headache, and feels weak in all her members." Still other danger signs are enlargement of the body without accompanying weight gain, and recurrent indigestion and flatulence after meals, indicating that a spontaneous abortion is likely in the second or fourth month.[23]

Rösslin believed that much could be done to prevent miscarriages. He advised women to take natural (herbal) medicines and remedies that are known to keep the opening of the uterus firm and prevent the buildup of excessive moisture, which is conducive to slipperiness and infection. The expectant mother should regularly eat fresh young capons, deer, lamb, veal, partridges, or hazel hens, avoiding, however, gluttony, "a temptation to which many succumb today." She should seek a physician's counsel for persistent coughing, vomiting, diarrhea, tenasmon, and nose or vaginal bleeding (these latter conditions indicate that she has become too ripe with blood and should be bled to remove the excess). She should also avoid heavy exercise and work, running and jumping, excessive standing and walking, and situations that frighten or terrify her.[24]

Rösslin provided two regimens for the expectant mother, one for the month before birth, the second for the hour of birth itself. Here, as throughout his work, advice that is sound and sensible, occasionally touchingly so, alternates with somewhat bizarre, perhaps even harmful, suggestions. Such contradictions reflect not only the ambivalent state of the art in the sixteenth century, but also the earnestness with which people at this time attacked the terrifying problems of childbirth. Taken as a whole, however, Rösslin's work is a profound understanding and recommendation of the best features of what we today call natural childbirth.

In the last weeks of pregnancy the expectant mother is advised to avoid all foods and activities known to hinder birth and to treat any complicating ailments. Among the specific do's and don't's are the following. Medicate anal, vaginal, and urethral ulcers or boils that might inhibit expansion of the birth canal during delivery. Eat nonconstipating foods that moisten but do not fatten, like fried apples with sugar wine, sweet apple juice, and figs, and avoid baked and fried foods, rice, hard-boiled eggs, and millet, which dry, stop up, and constrict. If constipated, take a mild enema of chicken or beef broth or a mild laxative, or make a suppository of soap, bacon, or egg yolk. Prepare for birth by including in one's diet and daily activities things that are known to slacken the birth canal and render one open, wide, flexible, and pliant (*alle dingen die offnen/weyt lind und weich machen*). This advice is especially important for a woman with a small, narrow vagina or an older woman whose uterus and vagina may have become less flexible with age. The ex-

Anothomia oder abconterfectung eines

Weybs leyb/wie er innwendig gestaltet ist.

Das Hirn ist kelter vnd feüchter dañ alle andern gelider.

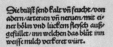

Die brüst send kalt vñ feücht/von adern/arterien vñ neruen/mit einer höln vnd luckem fleysch außgefüllet/inn welchen das blůt inn weysse milch verkeret würt.

Dyafragma ist einn fellin/welchs do abteylet die ernerende gelider/von dene so dz leben vfenthalten.

Der Mag ist ein hafen/darin alle speys võ d leben gekocht würt/vnd auß jm das haupt/hertz/vnd alle glider gespeyset vnnd erneret/Auch alles geplüt auß dem Magen von der lebern geborn.

Die Leber ist eyn bunn aller natürlichen geyst vñ krefften/eyn zůsamen gerunnen blůt/welche von der speys des Magens das edelst an sich zichet/vnd darauß eyn ran lauter geplüt macht/den schaum daruon abgesündert/welches ist die feüchte Colera in das heütlin der gallen/Die heef aber/welche die melancoly ist/schabt sye in das miltz/Die menstrua oder weybs fluß hat iren vrsprung von der lebern/vn aber die sich herab zeycht in den vohoff der müter/wie hie verzaichet ist.

Die Nieren send warm vñ truckem/durch welche/alle feüchtein von dem Magen in die blasen gefüret werden.

Die müter ist ein fürgeordnet faß von Gott dem Herrn/darin die Fündlin empfangen erneret vnnd zů einem menschen Körper formiert werden/An der müter hangen eyn bloß lin oder fläßlin/daruon leyt des weybs blům von der leber herab versamlet vnd durch das casser ro der müter daruon auch die blůß versläist/sich zů i ger außschüttet/Auch ist die müter mit zweyen Körlin/Hödlin zů böden seiten angehenckt/aneckder zwey/seynd hangen viel spermatica genant.

Zwo adern gond innwendig von den brüsten inn die müter herab/daruon das Fündlin erneret vnnd aufsgehalten würt.

Die Lung ist ein deckel vñ beheltnüs des hertzens/von welcher etwan kompt Fäche/vrsach der verstopfung der lungen röt/Etwan võ grosser kelte vñ feüchtin/auch von vbriger truckne/ire geschwär send Periplomonia/hitzig von der flegma/Pleurese von der Colera/Ptisis von disen beden.

Das hertz ist das hitzigst glid des gantzen leybs/eyn sitz vñ wonung der seelen vnd des lebens.

Das Miltz ist kalt vnd trucken ein hefel alles geplüts/auß welche die Melancoley im hindern theyl des haupts geborn würt.

Die blos ist formiert wie eyn wasser/glas/welche an die müter angehenckt/vñ sich nit durch die müter/sonder zů allerforderst in dem ror der scham außlasset/wie auch der weyber blům/dann die müter ligt noch ferrer inwendig vnd hart verschlossen/welche sich zů der zeit des Ehelichs wercks öffnet/nachmals widerumb vff das hertest zů schleüst ꝛc.

In dem hindern darm/den man den mastdarm nennet/seyd fünff adern/die man Emorroidas oder Varraure/das ist die gulden ader nennet/durch welche/etwan vill bös geplüt außgefürt würt/gleich als durch der weyber kranckheyt/darinnen würt auch gemählde aber Venaflux welche zů hindern lybt im darm nach grad hat/gehet biß an die müter/darnach sich theylen in zwen äst oder adern/eyn in den lincken/die ander in den rechten schenckel.

Mit Kayserlicher Mapestat freyheit.
Getruckt zů Augspurg durch Jobst de Negker Fürmsinder.
Im M. D. xxxviij. Jar.

Anatomy of a Pregnant Woman

The internal organs related to sex, conception, and fetal nurture are described as follows:

The breasts are cold and moist and filled with vessels, arteries, and nerves. Within each breast are cavities in which blood is transformed into white milk. The breasts are connected to the womb [uterus] by two vessels through which the fetus is nourished and maintained.

The womb lies deep within [the lower abdominal cavity] and is tightly sealed. During sexual intercourse it opens, and afterward it closes as tightly as possible.

The mentrual flow originates in the liver and discharges through a vessel in the front of the womb.

The womb is a receptacle preordained by God the Lord, wherein a child is conceived, nourished, and assumes human form. Little receptacles or vessels hang on the womb. They gather the menstrual flow from the liver and discharge it when the time is right through the outer veins of the womb . . . The womb also has two fleshly stems hanging on its sides. From these are suspended two little containers called vessels of seed [ovaries, *vasa spermatis.*]

---

pectant mother should regularly drink broth made from fat young hens or capons and should lubricate their privates with chicken, duck, or goose grease, or with herbal oils.

If ulcers, boils, or constipation persist to within two weeks of delivery, Rösslin recommended warm baths up to the navel in water saturated with softening agents (mallow, myrrh root, chamomile flowers, sycamore seeds, fenugreek seeds, marshmallow, bentwort, and *bingelkrut*); external soaks; the insertion into the vagina and/or anus of sponges or woolballs saturated with softening agents; or internal flushing by enema. He also favored treating infected privates by penetration with "good odors"; the expectant mother is advised to straddle hot coals over which musk, amber or *gallia muscata* has been poured. Under no circumstances, however, should she take steambaths or visit public baths (Rösslin was concerned with both possible infection and propriety).[25]

Rösslin gave the expectant mother a twofold regimen for the hour of birth, one part designed to speed the baby through the birth canal, the other to lessen the mother's pain. To hasten birth, he recommended that the mother alternately stand and sit during dilation. Breathing instructions were provided to assist in controlling the bowels. He also allowed medicines that induce birth. Once the actual birth begins, however, the pain of childbirth is better handled if the mother assumes a reclining position, halfway between lying down and standing (Rösslin included a sketch of a special birthing chair said to be popular in Germany and Italy).[26] If the mother is obese, it is recommended that she not sit but rather lie on the floor with her knees tucked under her and her forehead on the ground so that downward pressure is exerted on the womb.

At this point the midwife assumes control, instructing and maneuvering the mother, telling her when to breathe, giving her refreshment as needed, pressing her stomach, "and with positive, soft words encouraging her to work" (*mit guten senfften worten die frawen zu arbeitten ermanen*). Rösslin advised the midwife to console the expectant mother "by telling her that the birth is going to be a happy one, that she is going to have a boy." The mother should also be well lubricated with lily oil and, if necessary, the midwife may manually widen the vagina. If the water sac has not broken, she should puncture it with her fingernail; this failing, a knife or scissors should be used, taking care not to wound the baby.[27] If the child is breech, the midwife should try to reposition it. This can be done by pushing the feet into the front of the womb and bringing the head to the back, down, and around to the opening of the uterus. If the arms are above the head, the midwife should try to bring them down to the sides of the body. If these efforts fail and the child cannot be turned around, then the midwife must bind the feet with a soft cord and gently draw it out. "This is the most difficult birth" (*die aller sorgklichst geburt*).[28] Rösslin discussed and illustrated every conceivable position a child might take in the womb — one foot down, sideways, bowlegged, knees first, one hand first, two hands down, bottom first, back first, hands and feet first, belly first — as well as the possible positions of twins. In each instance he provided detailed instruction on the safest delivery from such a position.

Imaginative and unusual methods were suggested to facilitate birth, for example: make the mother sneeze with hellebore or pepper; lubricate the vagina and uterus with duck fat, lily oil, barleycorns saturated with saffron, musk oil, or various gum resins, or engulf them in medicinal vapors (among those recommended is dove dung); apply wool nets soaked in an acrid oil made from the evergreen leaves of rue, also known as "herb of grace"; give the mother medicinal brews and broths or special pills (among them an opiate and, said to be especially potent, a combination of *aristolochia longa* (birthwort), pepper, and myrrh, with wine as a binder, to be taken with water containing lupine or horsebean); finally, ply the mother with various plasters, the most highly recommended being coloquintida (a bitter herb and powerful cathartic)

A Woman in Labor

A midwife checks a woman in labor to see how far dilated she is. The expectant mother sits in a special birthing chair.

boiled in water and mixed with rue sap, myrrh, and wheatmeal and spread from the navel to the vagina.[29]

Rösslin mercilessly condemned midwives whose negligence caused a child to die at birth unbaptized and thereby consigned to hell for eternity. His condemnation was as much the expression of his desire to discipline midwifery as it was a revelation of traditional religious belief. But he did not recommend *non*medical aids for a woman and child in difficult labor. His total silence about traditional prayers and appeals to saints for women in labor anticipated a soon-to-surface Protestant point of view opposing superstitious aids in all spheres of life. Nine years after the publication of the *Rosengarten*, Luther discouraged the practice of consoling women in labor with the legends of St. Margaret, the patron saint of pregnant women, and "other silly old wives' tales." Anna Platter revealed the impact of such teaching on Protestant laity at the birth of her first child. When, in the name of St. Margaret, the midwives placed a wooden paternoster around her bed and urged that she have a mass said to assist her labor, Anna declined, saying, "Oh, I trust in the true God; he will help me through this." The newborn daughter was named Margaret.[30]

Rösslin listed a variety of tasks that a midwife might have to do after a birth: expel an afterbirth that was not delivered with the child (remedies range from having the mother hold her breath and push to warming her privates with the "sweet vapors of burned donkey hoofs");[31] manually reposition a prolapsed uterus or a displaced rectum; stop excessive uterine and vaginal bleeding (among the remedies: bind the arms, threaten to bleed the woman — a psychological cure — vinegar soaks, medicinal suppositories, herbal plasters, salves, pills, and baths); mend a lacerated womb; replace a popped-out navel; or stitch a torn vagina or anus.[32]

The most harrowing section of the *Rosengarten* is eight pages of instruction on the removal of a dead child from the womb. This circumstance posed the gravest threat to the mother's life because of the primitive surgical skills of the age. Rösslin cited twelve signs of infant death in the womb: the mother's breasts become flat and wither; movement within the womb ceases, after having previously existed; the child can be felt "rolling like a stone" from one side of the womb to the other when the mother turns around; the mother's womb turns cold; the mother has a foul-smelling vaginal discharge and develops a feverish illness; her eyes sink into the back of her head, the whites of her eyes turn brown, her ears and nose go numb, and her nose turns dark blue; pain in the womb makes the mother's face distorted and discolored; she craves food and drink that are contrary to a normal diet; she has persistent insomnia; a burning sensation accompanies urination and there is need to defecate but with little success; stinking breath (said to appear on the second or third day after fetal death); and a hand warmed in hot water and pressed against the womb elicits no response from the fetus.[33]

Before proceeding to remove a dead fetus from the womb, the midwife is instructed first to ascertain whether it can be done without killing the mother. Rösslin proposed that the midwife "let God settle the matter" if the mother becomes powerless, loses her memory, fails to respond to simple questions, makes croaking sounds, cannot eat, has a fast but weak pulse, or if trembling is seen in her veins and arteries. If, however, the mother remains reasonably strong, then the midwife may proceed with various medical remedies. Among these are the vapors of burned donkey hoofs or excrement, or vapors from a special concoction of myrrh, beaver oil, dove dung, and hawk dung, packed into a snakeskin and burned under the mother; a drink containing asafetida ("devil's dung," a stinking gum resin), dried rue, and myrrh mixed in white wine; and various equally potent suppositories. Still other suggested remedies are seasoned baths and, equally harmless yet revealing primitive magical belief, having the stricken mother drink the milk of another mother whose infant has recently died.[34]

If these remedies fail, the midwife is instructed to take hold of the baby with "hooks, force, and other instruments." The mother must now be held down by her arms so that she does not thrust forward when the dead child is pulled. The midwife inserts her left hand, well-greased, into the womb to determine the child's position "so that she knows where to set the hooks." "If the head of the dead child is first, she will place the hook in an eye of the child, or gums of the mouth, or under the chin in the neck, or in a shoulder blade, or other [accessible] member in which the hook can be [securely] set." (Rösslin provided similar instruction for dead infants in breech or other unnatural positions.) Two hooks must be set, the second placed directly over against and parallel with the first, so that the child is pulled on both sides with equal force. As obstructing arms and legs appear they should be cut off, and the hooks should be reset higher on the body as it protrudes. If the head is swollen with fluid and too large to pass through the birth canal, the midwife should rip it open with a knife so that it drains and reduces in size; if it is too large by nature, then it must be broken apart and extracted piece by piece.[35]

Rösslin also devoted a section to the reverse situation — when the mother has died, yet hope still exists for saving the child. He instructed the midwife to keep the dead mother's mouth, vagina, and uterus open so that the child continues to receive air. The midwife should cut into the mother's left side with shears (the left side is the less encumbered, because the liver fills the right) and remove the child "in accordance with a procedure used long ago to deliver the Roman Emperor Julius Caesar."[36]

Rösslin's instructions to midwives may usefully be compared with the advice on pregnancy and childbirth offered to fathers a century later in the popular vernacular housefather books.[37] These guides to estate management and household maintenance, intended primarily for landowners, provided solutions to problems the man of the house could reasonably expect to confront, not the least of which were the pregnancy of his wife and the birth of his children. Written expressly for laymen facing the situation for the first time rather than for midwives, the housefather books convey information about pregnancy and childbirth that is simpler, more practical, often less "scientific," but perhaps also more revealing of contemporary social attitudes than the work of Rösslin.

The *Haussbuch* of Coler, the acclaimed originator of the genre, was the most popular such work of the seventeenth century. The son of a Lutheran pastor and professor, Coler studied medicine and law as a youth but later turned to theology and became a preacher in the small towns of Doberan and Parchim in northern Germany. He wrote his *Haussbuch* professedly from his own observation and experience, rejecting "slavish dependence" on received (classical) wisdom. First published in six parts between 1591 and 1605 (actually in only four separate printings), the *Haussbuch* grew through subsequent editions (1609, 1627, 1638, 1645, 1656, 1665, 1668) into the mammoth encyclopedia of 1680, which persisted into the nineteenth century.[38]

Far more so than Rösslin's manual, Coler's *Haussbuch* includes the fanciful superstitions and astrological speculations of medieval folk medicine, beliefs Coler encountered in his village ministry and seems to have shared. As with Rösslin, we are still in the world of Galenic medicine, although Coler also addresses questions that did not occupy, if they ever crossed, Rösslin's mind. The most practical personal matters concern Coler. How does a woman who suspects she is pregnant know for sure? Despite his professed independence from ancient authority, Coler was not above learning from Hippocrates: give her mead before bedtime, and if pain afflicts her body throughout the night, she is pregnant (actually a simple test of her degree of nausea).[39] How does the expectant mother tell is she will have a boy or a girl? If her color is good, it will be a boy; if bad, a girl (again Hippocrates). Or place a few drops of the secretions from her breasts in a glass of water and if they sink to the bottom, expect a boy, if they float on top, a girl. Again, if the mother's nipples turn dark or black, that is a sign of a boy, if yellow, a girl.[40] Can the expectant mother do anything to make her child beautiful? Declaring that "nature is a marvelous imitator of all things," Coler suggests a measure taken by an ugly king to fulfill his wish for beautiful children: surround the bed of the pregnant wife with beautiful paintings so that she constantly contemplates them.[41] In an age of primitive medical skills, it was no doubt consoling to believe that nature might imitate art. Coler hastened to add that pregnant women could safely look upon rabbits and other animals, although he also believed that a woman who craved rabbit during her pregnancy or was frightened by one would likely bear a hare-lipped child.[42] Authors of housefather books were generally convinced that a pregnant woman's virtues and prayers would influence the moral character of her offspring, as would also her vices, so expectant mothers were universally urged to practice the strictest piety and morality.[43]

Like Rösslin, Coler had a list of do's and don't's for expectant mothers. He urged those with toddlers to cut back on nursing them at the midpoint in their pregnancy, ostensibly to preserve their own strength and that of the unborn baby, but surely also because of the change in the quality of milk that we know occurs with advanced pregnancy. During the last weeks of pregnancy the expectant mother is advised to eat only one meal a day, this in order to keep the child small and make delivery easier (*damit die kinder fein klein bleiben ad exitum paratiores*). She is warned not to scratch, much less to bend or crumple, her breasts, since this will make nursing painful. In the days before birth she should eat crushed aniseed (licorice), which is said to be beneficial both to the health of the child and to milk production. Terrifying situations should be avoided at all costs, since fright can damage the child and even bring on a miscarriage. Coler also understood the susceptibility of the fetus to the mother's diseases and the importance of personal hygiene; the expectant mother is instructed to stay away from her children if they become ill and to bathe often during the weeks before birth, taking special care to wash the privates with mallow and chamomile.[44]

Like Rösslin, Coler also discussed foods and medicines, again with advice both sensible and strange. He counseled against eating

strong purgatives, like saffron, cabbage, and celery. He thought
highly of balsam (which contains benzoic acid and is used today as a
base for cough syrups and many other medicines) and recommended
a spoonful each week during pregnancy, increasing to three spoonfuls before birth. He warned husbands that in the third month of
pregnancy their wives might develop a craving for unusual foods:
coal, peelings, chalk, glue, axle grease, human flesh(!), live fish, and
generally things that produce cold phlegmatic acid (*acida pituita*) in
the stomach. Coler associated such cravings with a female fetus,
who was apparently believed to trigger them when her hair begins
to grow and touch the womb.[45]

Coler strongly recommended, as an aid to swollen feet and for
safe and easy labor, purchasing a charm known as an "eagle stone,"
a hollow, round, clay-colored stone containing a smaller stone that
rattles when shaken. Fastened to a gold or silver chain and worn
across the womb, it was said to attract and hold the attention of the
unborn child within, to exercise and strengthen it. When tied to the
mother's right knee at the time of delivery, the stone was said to
guide the child to a safe and speedy birth. After birth the stone could
be hung on the child to protect it from deadly illness. While Coler
expressed skepticism that such charms actually fell from eagles, he
was emphatic about their effectiveness. He claimed that they were
sold at city hall itself in any well-provisioned city, the larger stones
in Frankfurt costing ten thaler, although Coler had seen some that
cost between two and four thaler.[46]

Coler instructed the father, as the hour of birth approached, to
summon "good, experienced, trustworthy, and licensed (*vereidete*,
sworn) midwives who know how to turn a child in the womb and
deliver it correctly, for much is here at stake." He was utterly
credulous of old wives' tales about the influence of the heavens on
the character and fate of the newborn. Children born during earth-
quakes were said to be always fearful; those born when thunder is
rolling, weak and timid; and those who arrive when a comet
streaks, mad. Children born under a full moon seldom live long,
and when they do they suffer terrible diseases (the full moon "rules
their degree of wetness," which determines proneness to disease). If
a comet appears at the child's rising sign when he is born he will die
immediately or very young, or will survive in ill health. Should a
comet shoot when the newborn's sign is in the tenth house, then he
is destined to suffer innocently many personal indignities and end
his life in disgrace. An eclipse at the hour of birth occasionally
means the death of both mother and child. Those born under a new
moon will be weak, die young, or grow up to be incurable melan-

cholics. Coler compiled a special list of misfortunes that befall Cancers, Leos, and Virgos (all summer babies), probably singling out this group because children born during the summer months are known to be the most vulnerable to winter colds and may have had mortality rates unusually high even for the sixteenth century.[47]

Coler commented briefly on the problem of a dead fetus in the womb, suggesting such odd solutions as draping a pressed snakeskin around the mother (obviously an act of imitative magic) and having her drink mugwort water or the urine of her husband (the latter is said to be ineffective if another man is the father of the child). He also revealed an apparently pervasive prejudice against children born prematurely, especially among common people, who are said to shriek at an early birth. Because of a premature child's need for special care and its often prolonged sickliness, parents greeted it as a burden, even as a divine punishment for some wrong they had done. Coler condemned such prejudice, insisting that a child who comes to term as early as seven months is normal, and reminding the reader how frequently children arrive four weeks early. Young wives, he pointed out, especially with their first pregnancy, often miscalculate and do not know for sure when they have become pregnant. He urged clergy not to punish women who deliver prematurely; apparently a new wife who gave birth early was often required to do penance, ostensibly because the birth indicated sexual activity before marriage. Nor did he approve of artisans demanding immediate payment of outstanding bills when a child arrived prematurely, as if it were a certain sign that a catastrophe would soon consume the parents. Opposing both Hippocrates and Roman law, Coler also defended the propriety of *late* births, having in mind widows who deliver as late as the eleventh month after their husbands have died.[48]

During labor and delivery Coler expected the father to be present or at least nearby so he could assist if needed. "If a woman faints in labor and after repeated coolings with a wet towel cannot be revived, then her husband should go to her, take her hand in his, and give her friendly encouragement. This is a great help to a wife in labor and the best way to revive her, for she soon hears her husband's voice and, encouraged by him, opens her eyes and looks around."[49] The village of Wallis required husbands to be present at the birth of their children "so they would be more patient with the midwives" (in the event of injury or death to the mother and/or child). Thomas Platter described how, at the birth of his daughter, the midwives attempted to obstruct his view, "but I knew exactly what was going on because my shirt was soaking wet."[50] Ralph Josselin recorded the day and often the hour of birth of all ten children that his wife gave birth to, and his account suggests not only that he was present but that he also assisted at the births.[51]

The Care of the Newborn

Much has been written about the perceived callousness of parents and their distance from their children in Reformation Europe, which scholars have attributed to the high mortality rates of infants and children. Because they frequently experienced the death of newborn and young children, parents, it has been suggested, felt "obliged to limit the degree of their psychological involvement," resulting in an alleged "low gradient affect"[52] between parents and children. The frequency of death, according to this theory, made children too ephemeral to acknowledge and love. In light of this argument, it is striking to find Rösslin and Coler writing at length, sympathetically and with imagination, on child care, setting forth remedies for every conceivable affliction of infancy and childhood, quite obviously in the belief that parents would spare no effort to secure the health and well-being of their children. The very detail in which they discussed these matters is itself a positive commentary on parental love in Reformation Europe.

Rösslin instructed the midwife to bathe the newborn baby in warm water, carefully clean out its nose, place a little olive oil in its eyes, open and massage its anus (to ease and stimulate movements), and keep the child warm and away from cold drafts. He also recommended smearing the newborn with nut oil to harden its skin so that it is not easily cut or bruised. When after three or four days the umbilical cord falls off, the mother is instructed to treat the navel with a mixture of ashes and mussels (the latter abundant in local ponds), ashes from burned calf's hoofs. or lead-ash well ground and mixed with wine. Coler urged mothers to save the cord, ostensibly as a kind of magical charm, for times when the child became sick, especially with stomachaches.[53]

Rösslin recommended bathing the child briefly two or three times a day after naps, but "only until its body becomes reddish and warm," taking care not to get water in its ears. Afterward its limbs should be stretched and the wrinkles smoothed, each member swaddled (*inbinden*) separately and thickly, with a light binding around the bladder (lower stomach) to assist urination. One or two drops of olive oil may be placed in the nose. When sleeping, the child should wear a tight-fitting cap, its head raised higher than its body, turned

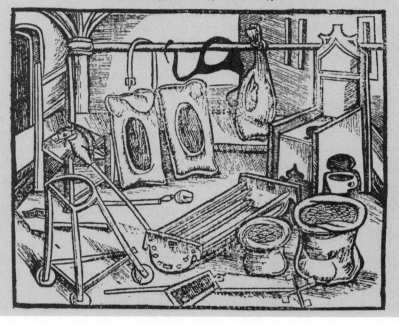

The Nursery

A "House Advice" book, a popular gift for newlyweds setting up housekeeping, lists the following items as "musts" for the nursery. Many can be discerned in the illustration.

Walking bench
Harnass to hold the child up when
　practicing on the bench
Bags of straw
Swaddling
Silk or linen sheets
Silk baptismal shirt
Two "red shoes" (apparently leather
　cradles for transporting the infant)

Wooden tub
Walker
Protective hat
Metal can
Drying table
Pan for pap
Potty chair
Stick horses

always toward the warmest part of the house and carefully shaded
from the sun if placed by a window.[54] Coler also instructed parents
to bathe the child daily, "taking great care to keep the oven warm."
The child should often be permitted to kick about freely on a pillow
so that it is not always swaddled. When the mother returns the child
to its bed, she should turn its legs so that its feet lie neatly beside one
another (this is conducive to a long, beautiful body).[55]

Swaddling, which could continue as long as eight or nine
months,[56] is not recommended in modern child care and has been
criticized for confining the child and being unsanitary. It did,
however, serve several positive functions for both mother and child.
By immobilizing the child it protected him from the danger and dirt
of the floor and freed the mother for her housework (in this sense it
was a forerunner of the playpen and babysitter).[57] Rösslin and Coler
saw two chief advantages: it helped the child's limbs grow straight
and kept him warm.

No part of infant care was more important to our authorities
than a mother's nursing her own child — this in opposition to the
practice, especially popular among the urban upper classes and the
nobility,[58] of putting infants out to hired wetnurses for up to eighteen months. Modern studies indicate that wetnursing at least
doubled infant mortality in cities; death rates as high as 75 percent
have been found among infants put out to nurse in some French pro-
vinces in the eighteenth century.[59] Not only were wetnurses usually
poorer than the families that hired them, they also regularly nursed
their own child or other children at the same time. An infant put out
to wetnurse could receive both an indigestible and an insufficient
milk supply. In terms of immunological and nutritional benefit, a
child was incontestably better off with its own mother.[60]

A welcomed convenience for the mother, wetnursing especially
served the father's sexual needs and his patrimonial ambitions.
Puritan authors commented directly on husbands' resistance to their
wives' nursing.[61] Many people apparently believed that sex spoiled a
mother's milk and that nursing mothers, for the health of their
children, should remain sexually abstemious. The church required
sexual abstinence during lactation under pain of penance.[62] Only
the most inexperienced nursing mother was unaware that a new
pregnancy shortened her milk supply. According to the medical
authorities, a mother's milk was transformed menstrual blood, and
when the menstrual blood was diverted to the nourishment of a new
fetus, milk production gradually ended.[63] Nursing mothers had
reason to fear for the health and well-being of their children if they
became pregnant again too quickly; hence, their sexual reluctance

with their husbands. Equally annoying to a husband was the fact
that nursing had a contraceptive effect, virtually preventing a new
pregnancy for at least six months after a birth; even after six months
a nursing mother was less likely to conceive (modern studies indicate
that only one in four women conceive while lactating). Ralph
Josselin's wife successfully spaced her pregnancies by prolonged
nursing of her children.[64] For many well-to-do and noble families,
however, the provision of male heirs was too important to be
postponed because of nursing.[65]

The church remained ambivalent about the practice of wetnursing. On the one hand, it supported it for the sake of the husband's
sexual needs; both Catholic and Protestant theologians argued that a
man could not be continent for more than a few days and was likely
to commit adultery if not pleasured regularly by his wife.[66] To
Martin Luther has been attributed the rhyme: "Twice in every
week, one hundred and four times a year, does harm to neither husband nor wife dear."[67] When moralists considered the welfare of infants, they were moved to agree with the medical authorities that
mothers should nurse their own children; but when conflicts arose
between maternal duty and conjugal duty, confessors instructed
nursing mothers to give the needs of their husbands priority and set
aside fears of losing their milk supply.[68]

For Rösslin, it was a simple matter of doing what was in-
contestedly best for the child. Mother's milk best suited a child; it
was consistent with the nourishment he had received in the womb,
he took it more readily, and he was manifestly healthier and happier
with it.[69] The housefather books scolded mothers who turned their
newborn babies over to nurses, thereby placing their own vanity
and convenience above the health of their children because they
"fancy their breasts to be decorative ornaments rather than the
means provided by God and nature to maintain children"; "God and
nature have created no wetnurses, only mothers."[70] Coler could be
eloquent on this issue, which he believed to be a vital one for both
mother and child. "God has provided each mother with two breasts
so that she can give her child milk and nourishment. He has further
placed these breasts near the heart so that the child may also gain
from its mother true childlike love, fear of God, wisdom and
understanding, discipline, and a sense of honor."[71]

Obviously occasions arose when illness or bad ("sharp," indigestible) milk forced a mother to hire a nurse. For those in search
of a truly qualified nurse, Rösslin provided a six-point test. She must
be a woman with good color, a strong neck, breasts firm and broad
but neither too large nor too hard. She should have given birth

neither too recently (at least one-and-a-half to two months earlier) nor too long ago, and she should be the mother of a boy. She should be healthy, neither too thin nor too fat, and her body should be firm and "fleshy." She should have demonstrably good morals and conduct and not be easily angered, depressed, or frightened (such traits physically endanger a child and also sour the milk). Hire neither a melancholy (neigerin) nor a stupid woman (dummfrawen), for a nurse's temperament and character are passed on to a child. Her milk should be white and sweet, not brown, green, yellow, or red, nor bitter, salty, or sour; it should not be too thin or too thick. Rösslin suggested that the parents spray some of the candidate's milk on a thumbnail and test its viscosity; the best milk beads up on the nail until it is turned downward, and then it runs off freely.[72] Finally, the wetnurse should not regularly have sex, since sexual activity reduces the milk supply and makes it distasteful to the child, who, according to Rösslin, will seldom take the milk on the morning after.[73]

Even more than Rösslin, Coler believed that a child imbibed the physical nature and moral values of its nursing mother. Viewing wetnurses generally as "loose people," often too impoverished to nourish their own children properly, much less those of others as well, Coler believed that only extreme ill health excused a mother from nursing her own child. When such circumstances forced her to acquire a wetnurse, it was imperative that she choose an honorable, god-fearing, loving, conscientious, and well-nourished woman who was not given to drink.[74]

Rösslin instructed nursing mothers to feed their infants only small amounts two or three times during the day. Too frequent nursing and overfeeding are said to invite pain and illness, signaled by a child's urine turning white, an indication of the undigested surplus of milk in his body.[75] Mothers are warned against nursing when their milk is hot, a sign of illness. In addition to sexual intercourse, Rösslin identified illness, clogged nipples, cold breasts, insufficient nursing, and poor diet as causes of an inadequate milk supply. He provided many remedies to increase the supply of milk and improve its quality — healthful herbal recipes; practical measures, such as improved diet, massaging the breasts, and soaking them in warm water; and cures that are perhaps best described as unexpected: eating a sheep's udder that has been cooked with its milk inside; drinking barley water containing dried, ground earthworms; and placing a bleeding glass under the breasts without actually cutting them (ostensibly a psychological cure for breasts that are simply being obstinate).[76] Coler too discussed breast care at length, alerting new mothers to such common problems as raw nipples and engorgement.[77] Rösslin offered a final, touching piece of advice to new mothers: after a child has been nursed, rock it to sleep slowly; otherwise the milk will be shaken up and turn bad.[78]

Finally, our authorities indicate that parents in the sixteenth and seventeenth centuries may have been weaning their children at an earlier age than tradition advised. Rösslin described "today's custom" as being "against Avicenna,"[79] who had instructed that children be nursed for two years. One gets the impression that children began to make the transition to mashed whole food as soon as they were physically able to do so, probably by the end of the first year. A critic of abrupt weaning (*stumpflingen entwenen*), Rösslin recommended bread and sugar balls as a transition food[80] that could be consumed well before the child had a mouth full of teeth. Coler suggested that whole foods could be substituted for mother's milk as early as birth when circumstances left no alternative. He provided a formula for newborn infants whose mothers, "as often happens," died in childbirth — a pap made of white flour, butter, and beer, to be alternated with whole milk — and he reported a peasant woman who claimed to have raised her son successfully from birth on beer alone.[81] Mrs. Josselin weaned each of her ten children sometime between the ages of twelve and nineteen months, nursing some of them for up to a year after their first teeth appeared, not because it was absolutely necessary to do so, but apparently to take advantage of the contraceptive effect.[82]

From reading Rösslin and Coler one has the impression that sending children to a wetnurse was the practice of a minority of women, largely confined to the upper classes; that it was undertaken to save the lives of infants as well as to serve the convenience, vanity, and patrimonial ambitions of parents; that infants were nursed (and wetnursed) for a shorter period than the two years modern scholars usually assume; that parents tried to place infants with healthy, responsible nurses; and that infants given over to nurses were not necessarily unloved or forgotten by their parents.[83]

The Trials of Infancy

Rösslin and Coler allocated large sections of their works to the afflictions and illnesses of infants and the best-known remedies from antiquity to the present. Rösslin composed a list of the thirty-five most common, ranging from canker sores to crossed eyes, drawn both from the medical literature and his own observation. The following brief summary of the main remedies conveys both the good sense of much traditional medical practice, derived from centuries of simple trial and error, and the deep concern that early modern parents had for their children.

Canker sores on the gums or jaws. Gently rub in chicken fat, chamomile oil with honey, or turpentine and honey.

Dysentery or diarrhea. Apply a plaster of rose seeds, caraway seeds, and aniseed to the stomach. Administer "goat tonic," that is, young goat's milk in cold water, in place of mother's milk for one day, or soft-boiled egg yolks, white boiled bread, and boiled, thin wheatmeal lumps. For yellow stools, Rösslin recommended a suppository made of elderberry sap, white powdered lead, opium, and sugar shaped into the thickness of a writing pen one to one and a half fingers long.[84]

Constipation. Use suppositories made of honey and oils, selected herbs, and, for severe cases, crushed mace and fat from the kidney of a he-goat. Feed the child honey in pea-sized drops and give him oil rubs. Or have the mother or a wetnurse take a laxative and feed the child for a day. Rösslin also recommended stomach plasters and a nutshell full of butter tied over the navel.[85]

Convulsions. These are said to be caused by teeth coming in, poor digestion, and/or poor circulation. Various oil rubs are recommended, together with baths in water containing mullein.[86]

Deep coughing and mucus. Bathe the child's head in very warm water every half hour and coat his tongue with honey. Depress the back of the tongue regularly so that mucus is broken up. In the morning and at night administer a mixture of gum resins and syrups in milk (recipes are provided), crushed sweet almonds boiled in water with oil of fennel, or simply fennel water and milk. If the mouth and throat become raw from coughing, mix two spoonfuls of strained quince slime with sugar *penidien* and sweet almond oil, thin with water, and administer often. The mother or nurse should avoid vinegar, salty foods, sharp foods, and nuts—foods said to be conducive to coughing—and she should lubricate her breasts with butter or *dyaltea* before nursing.[87]

Short, asthmatic breathing. Administer maple seeds mashed with honey, or cottonseeds crushed in a cooked egg yolk. Apply olive oil around the ears, especially behind them, and to the tongue. Should vomiting occur, rinse the mouth with warm water.

Boils or blisters on the tongue and mouth. These are said to be caused by the acidity of the mother's milk. Blisters may be black, red, yellow, or white, the yellow and white ones being the least harmful, the black ones capable of killing. The basic remedy for all types is crushed violets (*viol*) or a mixture of crushed violets, roses, and Saint-John's-bread (the fruit of *ceratonia siliqua*) liberally applied to the mouth. If, however, the sores are black and inflamed, aniseed is recommended.[88]

Chapped lips. These are said to be caused by the hardening of the mother's nipples. Make a warm salve of plantain, raw butter, and fresh chicken fat and apply with cotton.[89]

Ear infection (runny ears). This is traced to excessive fluid in the body, especially in the brain. Make an ear plug by soaking a rag in a mixture of honey, red wine, and powdered alum (or a little saffron), replacing the plug with a fresh one as it fills with fluid. If the ear runs pus, use boiled honey and water, or gallnut mixed with vinegar.[90]

An abscess on the brain (ein hitzig apostem des hirns). This is indicated by pain in the head and eyes and white or yellow discoloration of the face. Cool and moisten the brain by placing over the head a cloth soaked in pumpkin or gourd sap, nightshade, and purslane mixed with attar of roses.

Swelling of the eyes. Dampen a soft towel in *licium* (a sap), temper with milk, and place over the eyes, or wash the eyes with boiled water containing chamomile blossoms and basil.[91]

Discoloration of the eyes. This is usually caused by excessive crying; a solution of nightshade sap is recommended.

Fever ("unnatural bad heat"). The nursing mother or wetnurse should eat only foods that cool and moisten. Give the child pomegranate sap and pumpkin or gourd water with sugar and a little camphor. Also recommended are plasters and baths. Coler's remedies reflect folk practice and are less "scientific" than Rösslin's; among his cures for fever is tying a sack filled with three worms and selected herbs around the child's neck for three consecutive days.[92]

Stomachache. Tie around the stomach a cloth soaked in warm water and oil with a little wax.[93]

Swelling of the body. Wrap the swollen areas with a cloth soaked in a solution of elder tree shoots and elderberries that have been boiled in white wine.[94]

Chronic sneezing. Cool the child's head and have him inhale crushed basil.

Boils on the body. If they are black and pussy, boils can be deadly, and the more numerous the deadlier. Soak a cloth in a mixture of boiled roses, bilberry, and tamarisk leaves, and place on the boils. If the boils rupture, apply ointment of white lead (*ungentum de cerusa*), or wash them with honey water and nitrum (a salt).[95] In addition to warm herbal baths, Coler recommended applications of honey and fresh bread to draw out the blackheads.[96]

*Swelling or breaks in skin around the genitals and swelling of
the navel.* Treat with basic salves and plasters.[97]

Sleeplessness. If caused by excessive crying, apply to the
forehead and temples a paste made from a mixture of poppy stems or
flowers, poppy seeds, poppy oil, and the sap of wild lettuce (*Lac-
tuca*). If caused by bad milk, place violet oil and a little vinegar in
the child's nostrils, rub the head and stomach with a mixture of attar
of roses and wild lettuce sap, and administer a syrup of white poppy
seeds. A mixture of violet oil, saffron, and poppy paste may also be
rubbed on the forehead and temples. With all such ailments, if the
milk supply is suspect, the mother or nurse should immediately
change her diet.[98] Coler believed that mawworms and overeating
also caused sleeplessness in children. Although opposed to giving
children special sleeping potions, he also recommended poppy paste
for both child and nursing mother.[99]

Hiccups, belching, or sneezing. Crush an Indian nut, mix with
sugar, and give to the child. If caused by overfeeding or a cold
stomach, warm the stomach by rubbing it with laurel or bay oil or
by applying a plaster.[100]

Nausea and vomiting. Overfeeding, or thin or impure mother's
milk brings these on. Administer ground cloves equal in weight to
four barleycorns, or combine the following ingredients to make a
plaster for the stomach and the mouth: roasted wheat flour in
vinegar, hard egg yolks, mastic, frankincense, and Arabian gum
mixed with mint juice. For the accompanying stomachache, various
syrups and plasters are recommended.

Bad dreams. These also are said to result from overfeeding. Give
the child a little honey as a laxative. Also recommended are various
prepared medicines (*dynamuscum, dynapliris,* theriac [via Rhazes])
in milk.[101]

Incipient epilepsy. Overfeeding is said to predispose children to
epilepsy (hence the Latin name for epilepsy: *mater puerorum*). The
symptoms are frequent crying, screaming in sleep, poor sleeping,
feverishness, and bad breath. The best cure is to stop overfeeding
and make sure the milk supply is good. Also recommended are
dynapliris, dynamuscum, and theriac, which can be administered in
milk.[102]

Heavy, asthmatic, short, excited breathing while sleeping. Give
crushed maple seeds or caraway seeds in honey.

Hemorrhoids. Bathe the child in water in which the following
ingredients have been boiled: pomegranate bark and flowers, myrtle, acorn shells, alum, goat hoofs, and gallnut.

Tenasmon. The urgent desire, but inability, to defecate is said to be caused generally by coldness. In addition to warming the child, administer pulverized cress and caraway seeds mixed in old butter and cold water. Also recommended are turpentine vapors to the rectum.[103]

Worms in the lower intestine. These are either small ("the size of cheese maggots or smaller") or long. Administer couch grass water (*queckenwasser*, from *gramen*, a medicinal plant or grass) in milk. Use suppositories made of white currants, shaved ivory, baked harts horn, violet root, white sugar, and couch grass water. Also recommended are plasters of pulverized caraway seeds and ox gall. Olive oil is said to "kill all worms." After the worms have been killed, the child's rectum should be washed with wormwood or other medicinal oils and bathed in water containing boiled pear leaves and wormwood, or gallnuts and wormwood. A salve, containing among other ingredients wormwood and lupine, may also be applied.[104]

Diaper rash. Apply pulverized myrtle or, either separately or mixed together, *yrcos*, roses, wild mandrake, and tragacanth. Also recommended is a salve made from rose oil, frankincense, and camphor in attar of roses. Special ointments of white lead and roses may be obtained from an apothecary.[105] Coler recommended dusting the child with *Meel*, the wood powder produced by deathwatch beetles that inhabit wooden walls, which was used as a kind of primitive baby powder. He also thought highly of daily baths and rubs with Venetian or olive oil ("this produces frisky, healthy, fat children")[106]

Epilepsy. Epilepsy is said to be either congenital (caused by coldness and bad fluids in the brain) or accidental. If the former, both the child and its nurse should take only warm, dry foods. If it develops after birth, it can be regulated by closely monitoring the milk supply. The nurse should be purged with medicines, avoid all cold, moist foods, and not overfeed the child. Castor oil and other nosedrops may be used, as well as having the child inhale stinking asafetida as a jolting stimulant. Still another recommended remedy is a mixture of honey water and a rennet obtained from rabbits (*hasen renne/coagulum leprois*). Finally, revealing the desperation and credulity of the premodern physician, Rösslin suggests hanging mistletoe picked in March in waning moonlight around the child's neck. According to his authorities, if the affliction persisted in boys after age fifteen and in girls past their first menstrual period, the child would never be free of it.[107]

Chronically underweight, skinny children. Prepare a bath in which the head and feet of a ram have been boiled until the flesh peels off the bones. Bathe the child often in this. Afterward rub him with a mixture of raw butter, violet oil, pig fat, and white wax.[108]

Lameness. This is indicated by rubbery limbs and a child's inability to crawl or walk when it is time for him to do so. If at this time he is still nursing, give the nurse medicines known to induce warmth and dryness, along with baked and fried foods, but not milk, fish, or hearty meat. (Rösslin here implies that weaning begins at the time a child begins to crawl and/or walk.) Also recommended is massaging the child with castor oil, after baths. If the child is lame in all his members, a plaster of wax, *euphorbia*, and olive oil should be applied to his back.

Body tremors. This is said to be a sign of approaching lameness or epilepsy and should be treated with oil rubs along the spine.[109]

Stone in the bladder. The signs of this affliction are urethral burning; frequent, and at times painful and difficult, urination; pure and clear urine, and an erect penis. Bathe the child in warm water in which mallow, marshmallow, maple seeds, and Saint Peter's wort (*paritaria*) have been boiled. Give him mild diuretics and put bromide water (*bromber*) in his milk. Rub olive oil on his penis. Another suggested remedy is a rub consisting of ram's blood, cooked scorpion powder, and either scorpion or white lily oil.[110]

Crossed eyes. If one eye crosses in, arrange the cradle so that the child looks directly at daylight, not above himself or to his side. If one eye crosses out, turn the cradle so that daylight strikes the side of the uncrossed eye; also keep a candle burning day and night on the side of the uncrossed eye. (The light will pull the crossed eye toward it.) During the day hang a brightly colored towel (gold and green are said to be especially effective) before the child "so that his face is [exercised], turned and drawn away from the crossed eye, and inclined to the other side."[111]

If such detailed treatment of the afflictions of children reflects an age beseiged by infant and child mortality, it also suggests an age that was far from overwhelmed by it. Rösslin and Coler addressed parents who, they assumed, loved their children and were eager to pursue every possible measure to preserve them in good health.

A Child's Sense of Mortality

In adult life Hermann von Weinsberg wrote in great detail about his own infancy and childhood, drawing on his lively memory and the vivid recollections of his parents. His chronicle records both the physical torments and the peculiar delights of growing up in a sixteenth-century German city. As a child he had been made very conscious of his birth on January 3, 1518, by his mother's frequent recounting of a pilgrimage she had attempted to make shortly before that date, apparently to ensure the safe delivery of her first child. She had longed to go to a great shrine in Trier, but her pregnancy made the journey too much for her, and she had to settle instead for a nearby, lesser shrine in Aachen. "I was in Trier that year [in my thoughts]," she later told Hermann, "but I did not see it; and you were in Aachen [in fact], but did not see it."[112] Forty-one years later, in 1559, while visiting Aachen, Hermann recalled how he "had once before been to Aachen but had not seen it."[113]

Hermann was weaned prematurely, within five months of his birth, after a spring plague rendered his mother too ill to nurse him. The family acquired a wetnurse, a woman who later boarded with them, but she proved inadequate (it is unclear whether her milk supply was insufficient or her milk simply disagreed with Hermann.) So after five months Hermann was raised on pap and liquids (*Brei und Getrank*).[114] Measles struck him at age one and rendered him so sick and restless that his father had to comfort him through many nights, entertaining him by whistling through a glass.[115] In the same year (1519) his mother's maid tripped while carrying him across a street and he suffered a cut on his head so deep that he required a physician's care.[116]

From infancy through adulthood Hermann recalled infestations of lice, which the family adjusted to with grim humor. Once when he was three years old (1521), his body was so covered with lice that his parents and servants debated whether they should "scratch or bathe them off." Hermann suggested at the time that they "catch them in a net," a comment that greatly amused his parents and became a standing family joke, repeated thereafter whenever lice appeared.[117] Hermann recalled returning home with a friend from school in Emmerich when he was sixteen (1534), both of them covered with lice, "pants, jacket, shirt, and coat all full." In adulthood he and his second wife, Drutgin Bars, twice abandoned their residence under the Rathaus because of lice in their bedroom.[118]

When he was four (1522), Hermann had three brushes with death. He first fell into a large barrel of water and almost drowned. Then, far worse in his recollection, he became ill with worms to the point of delirium and fainting, passing worms from both his mouth and anus, too sick even to take worm wort and other medicinal poisons.[119] Finally, in the summer he was stricken by plague (*kinderpocken*), which claimed the lives of two of his sisters. The death and dying around him left him totally inconsolable; on one occasion his parents attempted to reassure him by telling him that God "sometimes tempted his friends whom he really loved" by letting them suffer, to which assurance the five-year-old Hermann replied: "There is no love in this for me; this is pure torment." Recording these events in his thirties, Hermann reflected fatalistically on his having survived the plague while his sisters had not: "Had I died with my sisters, it would not have mattered much and it might not have been unfortunate for me [an apparent reference to his eternal fate]: however, I am satisfied with God's decision to have spared me."[120] He remembered the great plague of 1541, which struck when he was in his early twenties, killing hundreds in one day, thousands before it relented; he walked the streets "in great terror" because he knew so many of those who were sick and dying. He sought prophylaxis in bleeding, burning incense, and consuming much garlic and vinegar, many "plague pills," and theriac. Among the dead were eight of his relatives, including a sister.[121] In other times of plague his family fled the city and went to the neighboring village of Dormagen, where they enjoyed the "natural beauty" and his father even managed to receive the daily newspaper from Cologne.[122]

When he was seven (1525) Hermann developed a nosebleed so severe that he "began to turn white." Among the unsuccessful remedies tried were being "hung somewhat by the neck," having his nostrils stuffed, and being immersed in cold water while he held red iron stones in each hand (the stones were believed to have the power to stop the flow of blood). The following year a man hunting crows accidentally creased Hermann's cheek and skull with a bullet. In 1527, at age nine, a lesion developed in his mouth and infected his gums to the point that tissue and several teeth had to be surgically removed. Recalling the pain of the procedure, he cried out in his chronicle against life's suffering: "O how much suffering must be borne by old and young alike; it is no surprise that so many die daily, for humankind is stalked by so many afflictions." He skipped school one day in 1529 on the feast of St. Appollonia, who was believed to have power over teeth, to pray for relief from the pain connected with the earlier lesion.[123] Also in 1527 Hermann suffered a severe hernia that plagued him lifelong, limiting his activity and rendering him shy and withdrawn. His mother blamed the injury on some cold fatty soup he had eaten, while his father suspected a cut received while he was screaming or running and jumping at school. Whatever the source, the ailment left Hermann something of a recluse, at least by temperament.[124] Finally, as a youth Hermann also had bouts with dysentery, which his mother treated with a pap made from goat's milk, and with boils, which on one occasion in his early twenties became so numerous on his legs that his flesh rotted to the shinbone.[125]

In addition to bearing extreme physical pain, Hermann witnessed many scenes of violence and cruelty, both official and gratuitous, in the course of his childhood. In 1529 he was present at the burning of two heretics, and he saw a fight in which a man's nose was hacked off. At fifteen (1532) he stood with his classmates at the execution of a criminal who refused to cooperate with the executioner by stretching out his neck for the ax; ordered to "hack away one hundred times if necessary," the executioner took a stout drink, wound up, and struck such a mighty blow that the man's head fell to the ground with one of his shoulders attached. Hermann recalled a stranger's mysterious strangling of a much-loved house dog, the loss of which caused his family to grieve as if a human member had been lost. In 1540 the city of Cologne was benumbed by a "great frightening eclipse" of the sun and by a summer drought so prolonged that people drank so much wine that they were left "lying about the street like pigs."[126]

But there were also happy memories, especially of time spent with siblings. Hermann recalled the birth of his first brother, Christian, in 1529 when he was eleven. After awaking to find his mother in labor, he stayed home from school that day. His aunt, who assisted with the delivery, bounded down the stairs and announced that Hermann would no longer be "the only son and *bobgin*" in the family. After the birth Hermann went late to school, where he excitedly reported that he had a brother. The schoolmaster and his classmates laughed at him because he was so emotionally caught up in the event, "as if," the schoolmaster teased, "you were the one having the baby."[127] Hermann also remembered the day in 1532 when his second brother Gotschalk was born, with a small "helmet" on his head (apparently a thick patch of skin) and "bowed, rider's legs," which Hermann's mother attributed to her (quite distant) infatuation with one Don Galzera de Cardona, a man with markedly bowed legs, who had accompanied the emperor to Cologne during her pregnancy.[128]

Hermann was fond of relating endearing stories about his siblings. One day in church, when his sister Trisgin was nine, Hermann noticed during confession that she placed her offering for the priest (*beichtspfennig*) on her head as she knelt before the father confessor (Hermann noticed because the penny had fallen off). Afterward he asked why she had done this. She replied earnestly that she had observed that the priest always put his hand on the head of each penitent and she assumed that he did so to collect the *beichtspfennig* for his services. Hermann set her straight and they had a good laugh. Once his eleven-year-old sister Marie (called Merg) caught a spark on her neck as she sat watching a fire. After a few moments' hesitation she ran to the beer barrel and took a hearty drink. Finding this curious, Hermann asked what she was doing and was amused when she told him she was putting out the spark before it could "settle within her body."[129] Hermann also delighted in telling about the time Merg was asked to fetch a "dash of wine" from the cellar and she started up the stairs with a full glass instead; realizing her error halfway up, she sat down and drank all but a dash, finally arriving at the top none too clear of head.[130] Then there was the time Hermann's seven-year-old sister Agnes was watching her grandmother eat the white part of her bread, but not the crust; as grandmother explained, she was too old to bite through the crust. Upon hearing this, Agnes removed the white part of her bread and put it into her dress pocket and proceeded to eat only the crust. When Hermann inquired about this, Agnes explained that she was going to "save the white part of her bread until she was old enough to eat it."[131]

Hermann related what he considered a "funny" episode about his then nine-year-old brother Christian. While on a journey with his mother and Christian to attend the ordination of a nephew, Hermann was ordered to kill two doves he had brought along (whether as pets or for food is unclear). Hermann took his brother aside to watch as he wrung their necks. Christian, saddened by their death, asked expectantly: "If you wring their necks in the reverse direction, will they come back to life?" Hermann commented that "Christian was still a child and mourned the death of doves."[132]

Hermann recalled a time in 1536 when his mother's false belief that she had been bewitched brought a new fear into the family. She attributed a sudden pain in and around her heart and breasts to retaliation by a neighbor who was reputed to be a witch, with whom she had had a conflict a full eight years earlier (1528). According to Hermann, he and his father were greatly disturbed by her interpretation of the pain's origin and "wanted to rid her mind of such fantasy," lest formal accusations of witchcraft ensnare the family in harmful conflict (one never knew exactly where a witchcraft trial, once begun, might lead). Despite their efforts, his mother clung to the belief that she had been bewitched; she had special masses said for her in church and took a special medicine prepared in a jug that had been buried underground. Finally, after much insistence, Hermann and his father, convinced that her ailment was the result of overwork, persuaded her to cut back on her household chores. Much to the relief of all, the pains subsided. "One did not thereafter speak again of bewitchment; but where the pain came from only God knows. My father did not, however, want her to have dealings with the Devil's followers."[133]

Reminded on every side of their mortality, the children of Reformation Europe amused themselves with simple pleasures.[134] The Weinsberg children took delight in activities that modern children would find peculiar at best. For example, they looked forward to the days on which the family was bled by its physician; whereas the adults bled themselves soberly as a health measure, the young did it "for fun" (aus lust), finding an excuse to be joyful, as they stayed home from school and got to drink wine as an aid to building new blood.[135] Johannes Coler described children as "the soul of the house" (anima Domus),[136] the force that brings it to life. Observing his children arguing and fighting one minute and reconciled and playing together gleefully the next, Martin Luther commented: "How pleased God must be with the life and play of children; all their sins [against one another] are forgiven sins."[137] In the minds of children, fun and fear, anger and forgiveness, life and death were still compatible.

·4·

The Rearing of Children

"Is there anything on earth more precious, friendly, and lovable," asked the Nuremberg reformer Veit Dietrich, "than a pious, disciplined, obedient, and teachable child?"[1] For Dietrich and his contemporaries this question was highly rhetorical. Never has the art of parenting been more highly praised and parental authority more wholeheartedly supported than in Reformation Europe. "There is no power on earth that is nobler or greater than that of parents," declared Luther, the father of six children, in an oft-repeated statement.[2] "The diligent rearing of children is the greatest service to the world, both in spiritual and temporal affairs, both for the present life and for posterity," agreed Justus Menius.[3] "Just as one turns young calves into strong cows and oxen, rears young colts to be brave stallions, and nurtures small tender shoots into great fruit-bearing trees, so must we bring up our children to be knowing and courageous adults, who serve both land and people and help both to prosper."[4] Therein Menius summarized the parental mandate of an age.

Parenting was not only or even primarily woman's work; it was too high a responsibility to be left to one parent. Mother and father shared it to an unusually high degree, the maternal role being greater in the infant and early childhood years, the father's role increasing in importance after age six or seven, when the maturing child could respond to a regular discipline. The bond between father and child was understood to be as intimate and as enduring as that between mother and child.[5]

Like the selection of a spouse, the rearing of a child was a rational art, not an emotional venture. Even monkeys, the author of a housefather book pointed out, exercise "instinctual" parental love, protecting their offspring and fulfilling their basic material needs.[6] Human parents must do more than this; they have a duty to prepare their children for both temporal and spiritual well-being; in addition to caring for their physical and material needs, they must methodically inculcate virtues and values. "If God's commandments are not impressed upon a child in his youth," warned Menius, "they will be lost on him when he is grown; for 'old dogs do not learn new tricks' and 'a tree rooted after it is grown will not yield fruit.' "[7]

The Measure of a Child

The cardinal sin of child rearing in Reformation Europe, a common one, according to the moralists, was willful indulgence of children. Critics perceived this to be especially true within wealthier families, which had the means to be indulgent, although permissiveness is said to have afflicted peasant households as well. Far from treating their children cruelly or with aloofness, as modern scholars have alleged,[8] early modern parents were inclined to spoil their children rotten, according to contemporary German observers and critics. Conrad Sam wrote of the children of Ulm's lords and Junkers:

> As soon as the child can move about, one throws a ragged frock on him and treats everything he does in the same [un-judgmental] way. Soon there are outbursts and tantrums, but these only delight the old, since they come from a dear little son who can do no wrong. Where one sows thorns and thistles in this way, how can anything other than weeds be expected to grow?[9]

In Sam's view such permissive child rearing accounted for the presence in society of so many "mercenaries, murderers, and criminals." The English "pediatricians" Thomas Phaire and John Jones also traced crime and laziness to the coddling and spoiling of children; such "strangling" of children, more than any other cause, was said to fill the jails and burden parish charities.[10] Sam offered parents the following advice:

> Whether you are a king, prince, count, knight, or servant, whether a townsman or a peasant, if you want to know joy in your children, take care that you teach them virtue. Do not do as is now done in the world, where children are taught to rule, but not to serve; to curse and insult, but not to pray; to ride, but not to speak properly. Children today are badly raised; not only do parents permit them their every selfish wish, but they even show them the way to it. God will hold parents strictly accountable for their

children, who [now] reward them [appropriately by their
bad behavior].[11]

Writers complained that too many parents thought childhood
"only a time for fun, joy, and amusement" (*nur lust/freud und
kurtzweil*) and viewed their main responsibility as that of giving
their children as much money as possible. Such parents were said to
treat their children as just another temporal possession (*jr eigen-
thumb*) rather than as God's temple (*Gottes heyligthumb*); "This is
why parents give no thought to God's discipline and indulge their
children's every petulant demand."[12] To the extent that a parent
subjected his child to standards that were pleasing to God, to that
extent he treated his child with dignity, as a creature made in God's
image.

In midcentury the Nuremberg pastor Veit Dietrich found
negligent, permissive parents "all too common."

Today you find few parents who once mention study or
work to their children. They let them creep about idly,
eating and drinking whenever they please, casually dressed
in ragged pants and jackets. Through bad example and lax
discipline, children learn to curse and swear, lie and steal.
Parents aid and abet such ill breeding by laughing at small
children when they curse or repeat bawdy rhymes. Later
[when their children are older] they rage at such indiscipline and self-indulgence [which has then ceased to be
so funny]. When children stay out dancing till midnight or
carouse around the public houses, father and mother do not
say them nay; but neither do they wake them up on Sunday
morning, take them to church, and ask them what they
have learned from the sermon, as if in this too nothing were
at stake.[13]

No age subscribed more completely to the notion that the hand
that rocked the cradle ruled the world. Today's children were
tomorrow's subjects and rulers, and they would shape society as they
had themselves been shaped at home. Indulgent parents who
"loosened the reins too much" in rearing their children sowed the
wind both for themselves and for society. "Your children will
become wanton and scorn you," warned Menius, "and when they
are grown they will be wild and malicious, harmful people, who
also scorn government."[14] The Hessian churchman Corvinus,
criticizing the nobility, from whose ranks he assumed future

political rulers would ascend, accused parents of corrupting their children with materialism and, by slighting their intellectual and spiritual growth, of betraying both present and future generations.

> You think that if you leave your children many houses, much money, and property, it is not necessary to concern yourself also with their acquisition of the skills, wisdom, and cunning (kunst/weisheyt/und kluckheyt) by which a land and people must be ruled . . . It was precisely for this reason [namely, to make them fit to rule] that the ancients schooled the nobility in the liberal arts.[15]

For Corvinus, the fatal flaw of the upper classes was that parents let their children discover too soon just how fortunate they were. When aristocratic youth learn that they are rich and powerful and exalted above all other social groups, they thereafter "resist all rational rearing (sie sich . . . nicht leiderlich ziehen lesset) and develop a taste for horses, dogs, hunting, debauchery, feasting, and drunkenness, all the things that keep youth from study and learning."[16] When society's leaders are thus raised without proper self-discipline and training in the Arts and religion, they can only come to rule as crude tyrants who burden their subjects to the point of revolt. Society's political hope must rather be placed in children reared at the hand of "pious and learned disciplinarians" (Zuchtmeister); only as such children come to rule over a land, Corvinus concluded, can its subjects take heart that their fatherland is secure and will prosper.[17]

Modern scholars at least since Max Weber have closely associated this concern for morals and discipline with the Protestant Reformation, and the commentators cited above were indeed Protestants. Protestants may well have been more sensitive than others on this issue; they were understandably preoccupied with developing the internal and external controls necessary to preserve and enlarge their newly won religious freedoms. But preoccupation with morals and discipline was a pervasive feature of the sixteenth and seventeenth centuries; in the minds of most thoughtful people an ordered life was the only free and secure life, and the consequences of anarchy always seemed more dreadful than those of tyranny. The same detailed instruction that physicians and "household experts" devoted to pregnancy and infant care, the moralists and educators of the age gave to the orderly rearing of children. Just as an unskilled midwife endangered the physical life of a child, so an uninformed and negligent parent or teacher was a deadly menace to the child's

rational, moral, and Christian development. Erasmus summarized
a universal sentiment with his famous insistence that "human beings
are not born, but formed" (*homines non nascuntur, sed finguntur*).[18]

Consider two tracts on the discipline and education of children
that circulated widely in Latin and vernacular versions during the
1520s and 1530s, written by two of the century's most influential
and, to many modern scholars, also most "liberal" pedagogues: the
Strasbourg humanist and physician Otto Brunfels's *On Disciplining
and Instructing Children* (Latin, 1519, 1530; German, 1525),[19] and
Erasmus's *Behavior Befitting Well-Bred Youth* (Latin, 1530; German, 1531).

Brunfels's work was a synthesis of classical, patristic, and contemporary humanist teaching, incorporating sizable excerpts from
St. Jerome, Rudolf Agricola (the reputed father of German
humanism), and Erasmus. According to the translator, Fridolinus
Meyger, the purpose of the German version was to place at the
fingertips of ordinary fathers the best counsel of both antiquity and
modernity.

> For what more Christian thing could happen than that
> children be raised well and taught self-discipline, usable
> skills, and a sense of honor (*sye zu zucht/kunst und erberkeit
> weisen*)? What richer and better inheritance could any
> father give his children than to help them advance in these
> three things and become useful and reliable to themselves
> and to others? I can summarize [the message of this book] in
> no better way than by citing words I once read by a man of
> God: "If one wants to reform the world and make it Chris-
> tian, one must begin with children."[20]

Similar sentiments inspired Erasmus's work. Why should
children be disciplined and educated? According to Erasmus, for
four interconnected reasons: so that youthful hearts and minds
might gain a firm foundation in the things that bring respect and
honor; that they might come to know and love the liberal arts; that
the meaning of duty and office might be instilled; and that "graceful
virtues" (*zierliche sitten*) in body, dress, and play might become to
them a second nature. These virtues, the subject of Erasmus's work,
are said to spring from "upright hearts and minds" only as they are
properly disciplined by a pious, understanding, and diligent
taskmaster.[21]

The modern reader is unprepared for the degree to which these
two humanists regulated childhood behavior. Both considered a

child's external actions, manners, and expressions as profound commentaries on his innermost character, and for this reason necessitating the most diligent monitoring. If the degree of conformity in behavior seems to us excessive, their intended goal could not be more noble: to make a child able to control his own moral and intellectual destiny. Erasmus, who had raised himself above the liabilities of an illegitimate birth by his scholarly achievements, put it memorably in a statement that is surely also autobiographical: "While none is permitted to choose his own parents or fatherland, each may fashion for himself his own moral virtue and [gain his own level of] understanding."[22]

According to Erasmus, conformity between external behavior and internal character is *required* by nature and reason; both in bodily comportment and in inner disposition, youth, like young saplings, reflect the "graftings" and "bending" they have received. In the belief that appearance speaks volumes about a person, Erasmus elaborated rules for mannered behavior extending from the head to the feet. He paid special attention to facial gestures, in which the true qualities of a person were said to be reflected. For example, eyes with a "kind, modest, and honest glance" reveal a "well-bred, honorable, and pleasant person," while a furrowed brow and a dirty nose are unfailing marks of poor breeding, as is wiping one's nose on one's clothes, hands, or arms, or whistling through the nose, as crows and elephants do. A child's cheeks should maintain their natural color and placement; puffed out, they indicate pride; sagging, they show melancholy and despair. Gestures of the mouth especially betray character. Tightly pressed lips do not recommend one, and a mouth agape suggests a fool. Biting one's lower lip is a threatening act, while licking one's lips, even when preparing, in good German custom, for a greeting kiss, suggests animal behavior, as does poking out one's tongue at another. Yawning is never funny in a child. Laughing at shameless jokes or pranks is boorish behavior, while laughter without cause is the mark of either a fool or a madman. At no age is it proper to laugh so uproariously that one's entire body shakes, for this reveals an absence of inner control. Nor should happiness and joy ever overcome one to the point that one loses facial composure; if laughter overwhelms one, disguise such defeat with a hand or a handkerchief. Can anyone doubt the implications of whinnying like a horse or baring one's teeth like a dog when laughing?[23]

Another type of damnable behavior involving the mouth is spitting. If this must be done, turn one's back toward others and take care to rub out the sputum with one's foot or catch it in a napkin.

Children should know that coughing while speaking to another is a
trick liars use to gain time to fabricate their stories. A child should
always speak softly, with proper deference, and not too fast; never
should a child swear, especially girls, "for what is more shameful today than the fact that young girls in several lands swear openly over
bread and wine?" The disciplined mouth is clean as well as circumspect. Rinse every morning with fresh water and avoid overuse
of salt and alum as cleansers, for while they brighten the teeth, they
also harm the gums. If at table a particle of food should become
lodged between two teeth, do not remove it with a table knife or,
still worse, with one's fingernails "like a dog or a cat," but take a
small quill or the splinter from a chicken leg.[24]

Hairstyles, too, are said to reveal the inner person. Children
should have neatly combed hair that does not cover their forehead or
reach the back of their shoulders or swish to and fro like the mane of
a wild horse. Scratching the head, crooking the neck (a sure sign of
laziness), expanding the chest (a prideful display), and standing
with uneven shoulders are habits to be avoided. Children should
also learn to be ashamed of displaying those members of their bodies
that "nature" has covered; unless one is forced by necessity, urination properly occurs in private.[25]

Erasmus also discerned a person's true spirit in the clothes he
wore. Although he recognized that clothing was relative to time and
place, he believed that people everywhere and at all times had
associated neatness in dress with good character, and disorderly, excessive, lewd, and pompous attire with bad character. Games too
were seen to expose a child's character; incipient liars, hotheads,
bullies, and the vaingloriously ambitious show their true colors in
fierce competition. By contrast, "a well-natured child, whether at
table or at play, always maintains a singular temperament" (*allweg
gleich gesinnet*).[26]

"Singularity of temperament"—that is what differentiated
human from animal character. Although each child was thought to
have an inner disposition to rationality and moral virtue, Erasmus
and his contemporaries also believed that the bestial could triumph
over rationality in a child. On this issue Erasmus and Luther agreed,
and it was not by chance that each characterized unacceptable
behavior as animal-like. The modern reader will not begin to
fathom sixteenth-century childrearing and family dynamics until he
appreciates the depth of this fear. A child was not believed to be
truly human simply by birthright; he was a creature in search of
humanity—unpredictable, capable of animal indolence, selfishness,
and savagery—traits that would dominate his adult life if they were

not controlled in childhood. The rational and moral self-control that raised humans above animals did not come as an inalienable endowment of nature; it was a state of maturity into which each child had to grow by hard, persistent exercise under vigilant parental and tutorial discipline.[27]

Otto Brunfels traced a typical day in the life of a *properly* reared child, defining acceptable behavior from the moment he awakened until he retired from the dinner table in the evening. These are some of the habits Brunfels expected a god-fearing child to internalize.

> Sleep neither too little nor too much [seven hours is the recommended amount]. Begin each day by blessing it in God's name and saying the Lord's Prayer. Thank God for keeping you through the night and ask his help for the new day. Greet your parents. Comb your hair and wash your face and hands. Before departing for school, ask Christ to send his Spirit, without whom there is no true understanding, remembering also, however, that the Spirit only helps those who help themselves. Do *not* greet the saints or ask them for enlightenment.[28]

> At school be happily obedient (*gern gehorsam*); do everything wholeheartedly. When called on, answer quickly and modestly (*züchtiglich*). Expect disgusting behavior not only to be rebuked with sarcasm, but punished firmly. Above all, do not let the teacher strike you with cause. Harm neither your teachers nor your peers in either word or deed. Try to learn from those who criticize you rather than simply turn them aside.
> Read incessantly; make your heart a "library of Christ." Read something specific from Scripture every day; do not go to sleep until you have memorized a few new verses. Punish yourself when you have neglected your readings. Tackle special personal faults and persist against them until they are overcome. Let no day pass when you do not do something that makes you a better person. To acquire rhetorical skills and master the arts only to gain knowledge and not also to become a *better* person is devilish. Good discourse is useful only when virtue is one's master; the morals of a speaker move those around him more than his speech.[29]

After school go directly home; do not tarry in the streets. If your parents need help when you arrive, obey their requests without question. If you have time remaining after your chores, use it to review and reflect on what you have read at school, remembering that nothing in this life is more precious than time, for once time is lost, it is lost forever.[30]

Brunfels gave table manners more attention than any other topic, and Erasmus also treated them fully, although not so disproportionately. The table provided the most regular occasion and the most structured setting for teaching a child his place in the family and in society. Here, in ways both subtle and overt, parents sought to instill habits of deference and self-sacrifice, virtues neither family nor society could long function without. Also, at a crowded table in the presence of guests, a child's breeding became most visible and consequential for the family — a potential source of praise and pride or of embarrassment and shame. These are some of the things Brunfels expected a child to bear in mind when he came to table.

Make sure your nails are cut and your hands washed. Sit up straight, comply with the requests of those around you, do not drink too much wine, and be mindful of what is fitting for one your age. Serve yourself only after others have been served.[31] If seconds are placed on the table, politely refuse; if you are not permitted to say no, take a modest portion, expressing thanks, and return the plate or pass it to the one nearest you. Take care *not* to pass to a woman when her husband is present, nor to royalty, or to a great lord. You may pass to your parents, friends, and relatives. If a delicacy is offered, say eel liver or carp tongue, take very sparingly from it and pass the remainder. If someone in good German custom offers you a drink, wait cheerfully, but take from him only a little and wish him good health; should you not be thirsty, empty your glass anyway.

Listen attentively to all who speak, but say nothing yourself unless you are addressed.[32] If someone says something improper or shameful at table, do not laugh, but look puzzled, as if you do not understand what has been said. Let no insults, slanders, or idle gossip cross your lips. Do not belittle others or brag on yourself. Be friendly to those who have had bad luck and praise the success of others without envy.[33]

Do not cut your bread on your chest or in your hands.

Eat directly in front of yourself. If you want something from
a serving plate, take it with your knife. Do not fall upon
your plate like a pig upon a trough. Do not mix your food
together. Do not eat with your fingers. When eating a soft-
boiled egg, first cut a piece of bread for a sop. Take care not
to drip the egg on the table or on your chest. Eat it quickly,
laying the shell, uncrushed, on your plate.[34]

Do not put candles out with your fingers (it leaves a foul
odor). Do not poke your fingers into salt dishes and other
table bowls. Take modest bites. Do not spit chewed food out
of your mouth onto your plate. Do not scratch your head
while eating. Expect punishment for incessant giggling at
table and ridicule if you dunk bread in your wine. After
drinking, wipe your lips with two fingers. Permit no morsels
of fat to swim about in your glass. Do not eat and speak at
the same time, or recline on your elbows, or lean back in
your chair. Do not throw bones under the table.

If the meal goes on too long and you become tired, ask
permission to leave and politely excuse yourself.[35]

The outstanding trait of a properly reared child Brunfels called
"moderation" (*Messigkeit*) and Erasmus described as "a singular
temperament." These terms, favored by sixteenth-century parental
advisers and educational theorists, summarized a Judeo-Christian
and classical ideal of measured action and willed self-control. The
common goal of parents and tutors, to which all lesser exercises in
self-control were aimed, was the fashioning of a person who could
freely subject emotion to reason, and selfish motive to altruistic purpose, placing the public good of family and fatherland above the
private pleasures of the individual. While such self-control was
believed to be within the power of a properly disciplined child
(otherwise parents and teachers could only despair), it was
understood that so benevolent a temperament was in competition
with a natural disposition to the contrary; hence, control had to be
inculcated diligently from infancy. At meals children should be fed
in moderation and taught patience and deference; their dress should
be always clean, orderly, and understated, not designed to call attention or to flatter; and at play children should be forbidden to indulge in the "games [of private greed that] rascals play" (chess, dic-
ing, cards, and, ever popular, swimming — condemned because of
its purely individual and frivolous nature). Instead they should turn
to exercises that are said to build character and a spirit of teamwork:
ballgames, calisthenics, round dancing, running, singing, and,

Ein Tischzucht.

Hör mensch so du zů tisch wil gon
Dein hend soltu gewaschen han
Lang negel zymmen auch nit wol
Die man heymlich abschneyden soll
Am Tisch setz dich nit oben an
Der haußuatter wölle dann selber han
Der Benedeyung nit vergiß
Jnn Gottes namen heb an vnnd iß
Den eltesten anfahen laß
Darnach iß züchtiglicher maß
Nit schnaude oder sey wisch schmatz
Nit vngestüm nach dem brot platz
Das du kein gschir vmbstoffen thůst
Das brot schneyd nit an deiner prust
Das geschnitten brot oder weck
Nit deinen benden nit verdeck
Vnnd brock nit mit den zennen ein
Vnnd greyff auch für dein orth allein
Thů nit inn der schüffel vmb stüren
Darüber haken will nit gepüren
Den löffel nim auch nit zů vol
Wenn du tryffeft es stet nit wol
Greyff auch nach keiner speyse mer
Biß dir deinmunde sey worden ler
Red nit mit vollem mundt sey meffig

Sey inn der schüffel nit gefreffig
Der aller letst drin ob dem Tisch
Zerschneyd das fleysch vnd půch die visch
Vnnd kewe mit verschloffen mundt
Schlag nit die zung auß gleich ein hundt
Zů ecken thů nit geynig schlincken
Vnnd wisch den munde ehe du wilt trincken
Das du nit schmaltzig machst den wein
Trinck sitlich vnnd nit hüst darein
Thů auch nit groltzen oder kreyßen
Schür dich auch nit vnnd sey am weyßen
Setz hupslich vngeschüret nider
Bring kein andern zůtrincken wide
Füll kein glas mit dem andern nicht
Würff auch auff niemandt dein gesicht
Als ob du merckeft auff sein effen
Wer neben dir am Tisch ist gefeffen
Den jere mit mit dein Elpogen
Sitz auff gerichtet sein geschmogen
Ruck nit hin vnnd her auff der penck
Das du nit machest ein geftenck
Dein füß laß vnterm Tisch nit gampern
Darzů hüt dich vor allen schampern
Worten nachreden gespöt vnnd lachen
Sey erbarlich mit allen fachen

Zů pulerey laß dich nit mercken
Thů auch niemandt auff hader stercken
Gezenck am Tisch gar vbel ftat
Sag nichts darob man grawen hat
Vnnd thů dich auch am Tisch nit schneützen
Das andere nit vor dir thů scheutzen
Gee nit vmb zausen vnn der nasen
Jm kopff soltu dich auch nit krawen
Der gleych sollen Junckfraw vnd frawen
Nach keynem floch hinunder fischen
Ans Tischtůch soll sich niemandt wischen
Auch leg dein kopff nit vnn dein hendt
Len dich nit hinden an die wendt
Biß das das mal hat sein außganck
Denn sag Gott heimlich lob vnd danck
Der dir dein speyse hat bescherdt
Auß Vetterlicher hande ernerdt
Darnach soltu vom Tisch auff stehn
Dein hend waschen vnd wider gen
An dein gewerb vnnd arbeyt schwer
So spruchet Hans Sachs Schůhmacher.

Wolffgang Resch formschneyder.
zů Nürmberg.

Table Manners

Listen you children who are going to
table.
Wash your hands and cut your nails.
Do not sit at the head of the table;
This is reserved for the father of the
house.
Do not commence eating until a
blessing is said.
Dine in God's name
And permit the eldest to begin first.
Proceed in a disciplined manner.
Do not snort or smack like a pig.
Do not reach violently for bread,
Lest you may knock over a glass.
Do not cut bread on your chest,
Or conceal pieces of bread or pastry
under your hands.
Do not tear pieces for your plate with
your teeth.
Do not stir food around in your plate
Or linger over it.
Do not fill your spoon too full.
Rushing through your meal is bad
manners.
Do not reach for more food
While your mouth is still full,
Nor talk with your mouth full.
Be moderate; do not fall upon your
plate like an animal.
Be the last to cut your meat and break
your fish.
Chew your food with your mouth
closed.
Do not lick the corners of your mouth
like a dog.
Do not hover greedily over your food.
Wipe your mouth before you drink,
So that you do not grease up your wine.
Drink politely and avoid coughing into
your cup.
Do not belch or cry out.
With drink be most prudent.
Sit smartly, undisturbed, humble.

Do not toast a person a second time.
Fill no glass with another.
Do not stare at a person
As if you were watching him eat.
Do not elbow the person sitting next to
you.
Sit up straight; be a model of
gracefulness.
Do not rock back and forth on the
bench,
Lest you let loose a stink.
Do not kick your feet under the table.
Guard yourself against all shameful
Words, gossip, ridicule, and laughter
And be honorable in all matters.
If sexual play occurs at table,
Pretend you do not see it.
Never start a quarrel,
Quarreling at table is most despicable.
Say nothing that might offend another.
Do not blow your nose
Or do other shocking things.
Do not pick your nose.
If you must pick your teeth, be discreet
about it.
Never scratch your head
(This goes for girls and women too),
Or fish out lice.
Let no one wipe his mouth on the table
cloth,
Or lay his head in his hands.
Do not lean back against the wall
Until the meal is finished.
Silently praise and thank God
For the food he has graciously provided
And you have received from his fatherly
hand.
Now you rise from the table,
Wash your hands,
And return diligently to your business
or work.
Thus sayeth Hans Sachs, shoemaker.

when done in the presence of a schoolmaster and without envy and hatred on the part of the participants, fencing.[36]

Discipline, Duty, and Love

Medieval theologians held children accountable for their acts when they reached six or seven years of age, at which time they were considered capable of mortal sin and subject to a special child's confession and penance.[37] Classical educators had also considered six or seven a good age to apply regular discipline, although Quintilian, perhaps the most influential classical pedagogue in Reformation Europe, spoke more generally of "the time when the child reaches understanding." The Lutheran Corvinus, who patterned his advice after classical theories of child rearing, believed that a sensitive father "naturally knows" when it is time to introduce his child to "proper godliness."[38] Obviously discipline could not succeed until a child was amenable to argument and persuasion, and since the precise age varied from child to child, parents were generally advised to adjust discipline to circumstances.

Johannes Coler, who wrote almost a century after Corvinus, urged special treatment for children under seven, whom he considered both physically and emotionally incapable of an adult regimen. He warned parents that hard physical labor during these tender years will stunt their children's growth and leave them "small as dwarfs." Between the third and the seventh year he advised parents not to deal severely with their children (*nit zu gar ernst und scharff halten*), lest they emotionally stunt them; "for children can be completely intimidated, even paralyzed, by fear." After age six or seven, children should be sent off to school, to be raised "gently and rationally" (*sanfft und vernünfftig*).[39]

Although sixteenth-century parents disciplined children in earnest from at least age seven, they felt that childhood extended to the ages of twelve for girls and fourteen for boys, the canonical ages when children theoretically could legally marry. At those ages Catholic law subjected them to the adult requirements of annual penance, normally during the Easter season. By those ages most Protestant educators expected moral character to be shaped forevermore.[40]

Authorities insisted that discipline at any age be carefully "measured" and related to the purpose of maturing the child. Appealing to Quintilian, the humanist von Eyb warned parents that harsh, arbitrary discipline would not create a docile and trusting

The Ages of Man

This depiction of the ages of man portrays no fewer than six activities of infancy and childhood, which are distinguished from adulthood and old age. Reading clockwise from the bottom, center: in the cradle; sitting up; learning to walk; first play and playmates; jousting on stick horses; and spinning tops.

child, but one who was "resentful and rebellious," despised all instruction, and despaired of his ability ever to do anything good.
Erasmus believed this to be as true in school as at home; just as a
father cannot instill self-discipline in a child by coercion alone, no
more can the teacher or tutor, who stands very consciously *in loco
parentis*, drum knowledge into a pupil by authority alone. As the
goal of parental discipline was internal self-control, not bare, external conformity, so the goal of education must be true understanding, not rote learning. In the hands of a good teacher, pupils should
both fathom a subject and learn to relate what they have learned to
their life experience.[41] Menius, the archetypal Lutheran, spoke for
his generation when he advised fathers in all their dealings, whether
with wives, servants, or children, to seek a middle course between
harsh, arbitrary discipline and unjudgmental permissiveness (*ymer-
dar nach dem mittel sehen*). Menius took special offense at men who
treated their servants, maids, and day laborers "like axes or hatchets
that required no special care or maintenance," and he suspected that
such men were also lacking as husbands and fathers.[42] Von Eyb
liked the advice of the Roman comedian Terence, who recommended that parents control their children not by the terror of
physical punishment but by instilling in them a conscience, that is, a
sense of shame, giving them freedom to test it and then dealing
kindly with them when the inevitable guilt struck (*mit schame mit
freyheit und mit gutigkeit*).[43] "Measured threats" also aided the for-
mation of good character; the authors of the housefather books
recommended both warnings of divine punishment and promises of
divine reward as useful ways to encourage moral behavior in
children.[44]

Menius especially favored putting children to work as the best
way to teach them self-control and develop good character. A child
who has regular chores learns not to take things for granted,
becomes vigilant, and develops a sense of responsibility and duty. In
addition, work protects youth from the many pitfalls of idleness;
does not a working child know less about lying, deceit, drunkenness,
gambling, cheating, fornication, and stealing than one who is
idle?[45]

The disavowal of harsh discipline did not gainsay corporal
punishment. While a mean between severity and indulgence was the
professed ideal in child rearing, many moralists were convinced that
too little discipline was more harmful than too much.[46] Purely
"praise-based" discipline also was viewed with suspicion and even
ridicule; nothing seemed to make a child more prideful and
rebellious against authority than undeserved or excessive praise.[47]

Sparing the rod not only spoiled the child; it also shirked parental duty when the going got tough, a sure mark of a parent who did *not* properly love his child. Menno Simons mocked the "too lenient" parent who is always quick to take the child's side as one motivated more by fear of the child than by love, "frightened whenever he hears a cry."[48]

Although condemnable, the harsh parent was thought to err less than one who was too lenient, for an indulgent and permissive parent who neglected the discipline of his children spurned the most basic responsibility of parenthood: to instill in a child the inner virtues and qualities that will enable him to serve and survive in the world and before God. The overly zealous disciplinarian, on the other hand, at least appeared to care deeply for his children and to take seriously — all too seriously — his responsibility for shaping their lives. Precisely for this reason, the authors of the housefather books, fearing that mothers would always be too soft, too filled with blind, indulgent love for their children to administer a regular discipline, insisted that the father should take the dominant role in child rearing after age six or seven. Men, they believed, could better be depended on to administer corporal punishment, whereas a woman's more pliant nature made her less of a match for the charm and fury of a child.[49]

In those periods of a child's life when self-control eluded his grasp and animal behavior gained the upper hand, a parent had to deal with him on a level befitting his character and conduct: he deserved to be spanked. The purpose of corporal punishment was frankly to achieve by fear the obedience a child would not give freely out of love or a sense of duty. This did not mean that children who had not yet attained the "age of reason" should be frequently spanked. To the contrary, Luther and his followers believed that the "sleep" of a child's reason during the first five years of his life actually aided the task of Christian moral instruction; with the full awakening of reason came new ways to plot against God, as Luther found all too evident in adults.[50] Although this was a pessimistic commentary on how human nature matured, it was also a more positive view of childhood than the popular idea reflected in much contemporary literature and proverbs, which frequently characterized children under seven as totally witless and untrustworthy.[51] The plasticity of the preadolescent gave parents, educators, and evangelists alike their best opportunity to shape his character in accordance with God's commandments; the older and more worldly wise the child, the more difficult this task became. From this perspective, parental discipline and vigilance were both more necessary and more futile as the child grew older. This did not encourage Lutherans to spank younger children less or older children more; it did perhaps incline them to marvel more than others in the presence of well-disciplined youth.

When the unpleasant task of spanking was necessary, always as a *last* resort, the housefather books, summarizing generations of advice on corporal punishment, instructed fathers never to punish a child to the point that he became terrorized, embittered, or moved to anger against a parent; fathers, after all, are not "hangmen." A proper spanking should be timely, coming on the heels of the infraction; "coolly" administered; calmly explained and justified in advance (a spanking was a *rational* exercise); and accompanied by profuse assurance of parental love (it *should* hurt the parent as much as the child).[52] Spanking a child also required a degree of humility on the part of the parent because its very occurrence attested the incompleteness, if not also the imperfection, of his child rearing.

How frequently and severely were children spanked? There are horror stories. The humanist Johannes Butzbach (1477–1526) reported in his chronicle of 1506 that as punishment for neglecting his studies he was tied to a post and beaten bloody by a schoolmaster in Erfurt before finally being rescued by his mother. However, the schoolmaster was removed from his post for this action, a clear indication that contemporaries deemed such punishment extreme and reprehensible. Butzbach also related that during the first days of school, teachers used sweets and flattery to build enthusiasm among new students for their studies.[53] Brutality toward children is also suggested in the famous episodes reported by Luther of being beaten by his mother until the blood ran for stealing a nut and of feeling alienated from his father after receiving a painful thrashing. Although Luther as a child did occasionally receive rough treatment and later could administer is as a father, harsh, arbitrary discipline was not characteristic either of his childhood or of his children's.[54] He made a revealing comment in a tabletalk of 1537 when he explained that his entrance into the monastery had been a cowardly act resulting from his parents' strict discipline. He did not believe that the discipline itself had been wrong, but that his parents had not sufficiently taken into account its effect on him. He described them as failing to adjust their punishment to his peculiar temperament as a child so that their discipline would strengthen rather than weaken him.[55] A proper discipline required parents to tailor the punishment to each child's disposition.

Hermann von Weinsberg's experience with parental discipline may have been typical of the age. Hermann recalled two especially memorable spankings when he was seven years old. The first came at the hand of his mother, who one day "with good cause" struck him hard, "as she often did." Hermann fled for comfort to his father, who teasingly asked him what he thought they should do with his mother for spanking him: drive her away from the house or let her live downstairs (while he and Hermann lived together upstairs). When Hermann chose the latter, it pleased his father, who commented that it "showed maturity not to want to drive his mother away because of a little spanking" (*ein wenich sclains*). Hermann's second spanking was administered by a schoolmaster in his first year at school. According to Hermann, this teacher struck students "very hard" (*seir strack*) and had often struck him without just cause ("not because I had been mischievous"). Hermann quickly added: "But I dearly loved this teacher because after he punished me, he consoled me and was friendly."[56]

Hermann conveys the impression that spankings at school occurred frequently in the early years, but gradually ended as a student got older and presumably conformed more readily to pedagogical expectations. He insisted that he was never spanked in school at Emmerich, where he enrolled at age twelve (1531), nor in the students' hostel where he resided, although he claims to have deserved a thrashing on at least one occasion. In the strictly run hostel where he lodged during his first year at school, he was once spanked by the monks — justifiably, he believed — for running off to a neighboring town without permission.[57]

Later, in his midthirties, Hermann struck one of his wife's grandchildren hard ("he fell like an ox"), ostensibly because the child was throwing a tantrum (for his "disobedience and anger"). The episode greatly upset Hermann, who hastened to assure the reader of his chronicle that it was very unusual for him either to curse or to strike a child.[58]

Moderate corporal punishment was a regular and encouraged part of discipline both at home and at school in Reformation Europe, especially during the formative years between six and twelve. Both children and adults, however, viewed harsh and arbitrary discipline as exceptional and condemned it, while outright brutality brought firings and fines and even deep personal remorse.

Among the kinds of youthful behavior requiring special parental vigilance, some moralists worried most about fornication (*hurerey*), the vice to which, they observed, the young were most inclined. Parents were urged to regulate so far as possible the circumstances conductive to illicit sex, namely, idleness, bad company, loose language, drunkenness, and lewd behavior.[59] Catholic and Protestant writers alike expected adolescent boys and girls to remain chaste, by sheer force of will, until they married. The self-discipline required to do so was described as part of the "vocation" (*stand*) of youth,[60] that is, as something particularly incumbent upon a teenager. As it was the special duty of fathers to toil in the world and of mothers to labor in childbirth, so it was a special responsibility of the young to maintain sexual purity until marriage. Other authorities, Martin Luther prominent among them, perhaps more sympathetic to the sexual passion of youth and certainly more realistic about its force, urged the remedy of an early marriage. "If parents find that their children lack the ability to remain chaste" (*ungeschickt zur keüshait*), counseled one family specialist, "let them marry when the time is right, for this natural mischief can be managed in no other way."[61] Such advice contradicted the more deeply held belief that marriage should be based on mutual respect and companionable qualities, not entered lightly, on the wings of emotion, by those who were immature and unemployed. Obviously, however, when children became sexually active and pregnancies occurred, parents developed their own special appreciation of St. Paul's counsel that it was better to marry than to burn with uncontrollable sexual desire.

Although their hopes, like their responsibilities, were exceedingly high, parents in the sixteenth century had few illusions about child rearing, and no group was more realistic than the Lutherans. The best parental efforts could fail; good parents also had bad children. Some children, admitted the Nuremberg pastor Dietrich, remain impossible lifelong; despite the best parental examples, sparing neither warnings, encouragement, nor the rod, some children still grow up to be scoundrels who spurn the church and its teachings, as the Devil spurned the cross of Jesus. This is a painful thing for parents, who love their children and want them to become honorable and successful adults. But there is absolutely nothing they can do, Dietrich concluded, save to persist in what they know to be right, setting their children the best example they can; otherwise their children, who may still turn out badly, will have no chance at all.[62]

There was widespread sensitivity not only to parents' mistreatment of children but also to children's neglect and abuse of their parents. The responsibilities of children to their parents were repeatedly enumerated. In a special instruction for the youth of Augsburg written in 1550, Johann Moeckard summarized the three basic duties that catechists everywhere urged upon children. First, children owe their parents honor and respect as God's representatives and servants in their lives (*gotes stathalter und diener*). They should defer to their parents by maintaining a neat appearance, standing in their presence, removing their hat, and addressing them humbly and politely with titles of respect. Cited as an authority was Tobias 4: "Honor your mother all the days of her life and never forget the pain she suffered in her body on your behalf." This reminder of parental self-sacrifice also extended to fathers, who were seen to suffer no less for their children in laboring to support them.[63] Strong criticism fell on successful children who, having risen to positions of power and importance in the world, came to despise their lowly origins (*dass sie nit von ansechlicheren/verstendigeren und reichern eltern geborn seind*) and to look on their doddering and cantankerous old parents as a burden and an embarrassment. "O, you children!" Moeckard scolded; "it should make no difference to you whether your parents are wise, learned, rich, and powerful, or simple, unimportant, poor, and despised; think first what a great thing it is that you have parents through whom God has given you life."[64]

A child's second duty logically followed from the first: obedience. The commands of honorable parents could be expected to be moral and godly and in a child's best interest.[65] But if they were manifestly not so, a child was no more obliged to obey them than he would be to follow the immoral and godless command of a magistrate, for he, like his parents, must obey God rather than man. But if his parents were righteous, the child's obedience should be immediate and unquestioning. The moral ordinance of Augsburg declared that children not only owed their parents "every reasonable obedience in submission to their will," but they also had an obligation to spare their parents worry and embarrassment by maintaining self-discipline, taking good care of themselves, avoiding bad company, and obeying the law.[66] Coler's housefather book itemized the child's obedience, stressing the importance of his loyalty to family unity and prosperity:

> Be submissive to parents; be alert to problems within the household and the faults of servants, reporting them promptly to parents; avoid collusion with servants; do not fight, argue, or in any way set one member of the household against another; do not steal from parents and hide the stolen items in the servants' quarters; do not become too friendly with servants or succumb to their loose morals; avoid such obvious vices as laziness, gluttony, drunkenness, gaming, and cheating; be sober, thrifty, righteous, and

honest, so that all members of the household will respect
and obey you in your parents' absence; avoid gossip in front
of servants, who circulate what they hear thoughout the
household and onto the city streets; take care to learn
everything that pertains to *Haushalten*.[67]

The final duty of children to their parents was to return their
love and care when age, poverty, or illness made the parents dependent on others.[68] Moeckard pointed to the biblical example of King
David, who kept his parents with him and cared for them in their
old age, and he criticized what he reported to be a common practice, of dumping aged and infirm parents into hospices and
monasteries or letting them eke out a meager existence on public
alms and donations from common chests. He reported a popular saying: "One father gives more love and care to ten children than ten
children to one father."[69] The housefather books, doubtless reflecting the neglect of aged parents, warned parents against giving all
their possessions to their children during their lifetime, thus becoming totally dependent on them.[70] Corvinus found the same social
problem in a somewhat different form among Hessian noblemen,
who were said to abandon their widowed mothers after taking
young wives. "When your young men have taken a wife," he
charged, "soon what is old in the house must be thrown out like gar-
bage. Can any justify this practice? It is right that you love your
wife, but you must also honor your mother."[71]

Peter Laslett has explained the rarity of extended families in
early modern England by giving the example of a son who evicted
his mother and sister, abandoning them to public charity when he
received his inheritance and married.[72] In 1580 Hermann von
Weinsberg singled out England as having the worst examples of the
evils of primogeniture in the whole of Europe. By contrast, in
sixteenth-century Germany partible inheritance was becoming the
rule. Although as the eldest son Hermann received the father's house
(*Stamhaus*) after both parents died, he freely shared it with his siblings, partly because he had no need of it and partly because he
believed it to be the right thing to do. The remainder of the inheritance was divided among the siblings, with each receiving a fair
share.[73] The practice of partible inheritance won the strong endorse-
ment of Protestants because of its fairness and apparently also
because they feared that strict adherence to primogeniture would
drive deprived younger sons back into Catholicism, where they
could find a monastic vocation if deprived of a livable inheritance.[74]

But partible inheritance did not remove the threat to a widowed or dependent parent posed by greedy children. The last will and testament of Hermann's parents, written in 1538, stressed that the children should not challenge the surviving parent and force a premature division of the estate, but that each child should be satisfied with what the surviving parent gives him, waiting until both parents are dead before "amicably" dividing the estate.[75] A few days before his death in 1549, Hermann's father gathered his wife and children together and ordered the children to honor and obey their mother and to remain at peace with one another. Hermann, as the eldest son, received the special mandate "to hold his hands over his mother's head," that is, to be watchful and protective of her. The fulfillment of this mandate, which Hermann earnestly undertook, later involved him in an altercation with his brother Christian, who one day tried to run him through with a sword, in part because Hermann had repeatedly censured him for failing to heed his mother's will.[76] In a well-known statement, Martin Luther declared his hostility to the practice of placing a deceased male's estate in the hands of a male trustee ("Den Vormunden bin ich feindt") and directly constituted his wife Katherine "heir to everything" (*haeredem omnium*), also expecting his children to abide by her will so long as she lived.[77]

Lutheran theology subjected parents and children to a divine plan in both their domestic and their religious life. This plan enjoined on each clear moral duties, the fulfillment of which would create a higher bond between parent and child than that of their natural relationship; faith was thicker than blood. This was one reason why in Lutheran lands public schools so readily took over the education of children. In urging magistrates to provide compulsory education in religion and the arts for all boys and girls, Luther reminded parents: "Your children are not so completely yours that you have no obligations to God on their behalf; God has his rights in the lives of your children; they are more his than yours (*sie sind auch mehr sein denn dein*)."[78] Hence, they also belonged to those public officials who guided them in the realization of God's plan for their lives. The only authority parents, teachers, or magistrates had over children was that which derived from the responsibility to rear them in accordance with God's law and discipline.[79] The elevation of God's plan over all other authority may also have enhanced maternal responsibility in child rearing. It certainly encouraged elementary education for girls, as Lutherans, continuing a fifteenth-century German movement, insisted on at least one hour of formal schooling per day; and emphasizing a divine plan in the rearing of children may also have helped Lutherans justify their recruitment of women teachers in the schools, something humanists like Erasmus had opposed.[80]

In setting forth the duties of children to parents, Johann Moeckard placed "love" third in his series, after honor and obedience. By love he meant willing self-sacrifice, not emotional desire or attachment. Although in third rank, such love was not the least of a child's duties; to the contrary, Moeckard considered it the child's noblest achievement. To love one's aged and ill parents meant to accept onerous responsibilities, giving freely of oneself, one's time, and one's possessions. Both between spouses and between parents and children such love was seen to develop only slowly over time, requiring maturity and self-control to the point of self-sacrifice.

In a unique "quantitative" investigation of how love was ranked in popular French catechisms, Jean-Louis Flandrin found that love of parents was the first duty of children in only one-half of the sampled pre-1688 catechisms; it rose to first rank in all the sampled post-1688 catechisms, which also enjoined parents to reciprocate. From such evidence Flandrin concluded that parents and children in France first learned to share "natural emotional love," that is, to love one another in the healthy modern way, in the late seventeenth century, having previously distrusted such love as "animalistic" and even harmful because of its permissive and self-indulgent nature.[81] Given the fact that Flandrin's sources were confessional manuals written by unmarried clerics, it may be that the love they raised to first rank was actually closer to the self-sacrificial love about which our sixteenth-century authors were writing than to modern romantic love. Be that as it may, it would certainly have struck moralists like Moeckard odd to find purely emotional love praised as a peculiar human achievement or goal; indeed, they would have found it demeaning of humankind to attach such importance to something so common and so resistant to the love born of duty and discipline.

The Weinsberg Men as Fathers

Hermann von Weinsberg had vivid memories of his childhood and youth, especially of his relationship with his father. While very firm when the circumstances required it, the elder Weinsberg approached child rearing with a degree of subtlety and a certain vulnerability. Hermann recalled making a journey on foot with him from Cologne to neighboring Dormagen when he was five. Along the way he grew tired and wanted to stop, but his father was determined to go on. To this end he involved his son in a game; taking a stone from a wall, he threw it ahead and commanded Hermann to fetch it and do likewise. Before Hermann realized it, they had arrived at their destination. Hermann's grandmother believed he was raised too permissively. One day when he was six, she criticized his parents for letting him play unsupervised in the streets and accused them of "raising him to be soft" (*man verzarte mich*). Thereafter he was kept in the house more often, although he still managed to cavort with his friends by extending his absences when sent out on errands. During one such excursion when he was eight, he hung his coat on a tree while he played in the street, only to find it stolen when he returned for it. For such negligence his father spanked him "soundly" (*wol und bess*). On the other hand, Hermann could proudly brag that his father bought him a new suit of clothes, not a used one, when he was ten, "because I was then still his only son" (as he would remain for two more years).[82]

He remembered spending many days winding yarn for his mother on a machine his father had devised. Visiting neighbors commented to his mother that in comparison with other children, Hermann was an "angel" to stay in and help in this way. When they were alone, his mother, aware of his displeasure at being housebound, twitted him: "You may be an angel to be off the streets, but in the house you are a young devil." In retrospect Hermann agreed: "If I was an angel at that time, I was a raw one" (*rau engel*), and he documented this judgment be recalling such mischief as quarrels with his sisters, accidentally shooting a maid in the eye with a crossbow after she had offered him her rear as a target, and joining his classmates at night to throw stones at abandoned houses.[83]

When he was thirteen (1531), Hermann went off to school in Emmerich, his first difficult steps into manhood. During his first semester he lived in a strictly regulated hostel run by monks and was extremely homesick. At spring break (March 1532), he petitioned his father to let him take lodging where he would have more autonomy. His father granted him permission "to do what he thought best" (*was mich duchte gut sin*), thus extending adult responsibility to his then fourteen-year-old son.[84] So Hermann moved into the home of John Passan with ten or twelve other students for the spring semester. His new freedom, however, proved too much for him; unable to turn down his friends' requests for money and the many temptations in food and drink offered by the city, he was dead broke within three months. For the first time in his life he experienced poverty, often going an entire week on only fruit and milk. Finally, he borrowed money from an Emmerich wine merchant, a business associate of his

father. The merchant, however, proved no confidant and sent
Hermann's "IOU" on to his father, who learned of his son's disorderly life with great disappointment.

Impoverished and unprepared to take his exams, Hermann
returned home unexpectedly in August 1532. Already wounded by
his son's prodigality, the father found further insult in Hermann's
coming home unannounced and without his permission. Hermann
recalled being greeted by a "stern countenance" and not receiving
the "hand of friendship." In October Hermann returned to Emmerich in a deep depression, having argued with his father the night
before his departure. He described his departure as "the most painful experience of my life," not only because of the unprecedented
estrangement from his parents, but also because he knew he would
not be able to return again to his beloved Haus Weinsberg until he
had proven himself. On the jouney he was unable either to eat or to
drink.[85]

In Emmerich his father had arranged new lodging with "very
good people" and had sent advance instructions that Hermann's
household chores should be limited and his studies encouraged. During the winter term Hermann fell seriously ill with recurrent chills
and high fever. He kept his illness from his parents until the spring
when, during a relapse, he wrote that he wanted to return home but
was physically unable to do so. This news occasioned a long letter of
reconciliation from his father, who wrote of his deep pride in Hermann's "talent for learning," a gift he personally envied, and his
own hope that his son "would achieve great things" (*dat du zu
groissen dingen komen machs*). While he reminded Hermann of his
lack of diligence and indecision, he stressed that his son's life was his
own to make or break, and that while his son's success would bring
him happiness, the gain, like the achievement, belonged solely to
Hermann. In an emotional postscript, he urged Hermann to keep
the letter so that in future years when he was more mature, and
especially after his father had died, he would know from it how his
father had felt about him.[86] Needless to say, Hermann was over-
joyed by the letter.

Despite predictions by friends that "he would never see Cologne
again," by summer Hermann had fully recovered from his illness.
He answered his father's letter with one in Latin, an exhibition of his
new scholarly resolve. In August his father wrote again, deeply
moved by the "special friendship and honor" Hermann had shown
by writing to him in Latin—although he had learned from the
translator of the letter that much of it had come from a known

source and not out of Hermann's own head! (Hermann acknowledged receiving some "help" in its composition, but he also defended his own contribution.) His father now blessed his son and expressed contentment that his money had not been wasted by sending him to school. "I now find in you a special joy."[87]

Throughout his life Hermann felt obliged to please his father, yet he never expressed a sense of injustice or any resentment when accommodation to his father's wishes clearly ran counter to his own. He continued his studies "in accordance with my father's will," declaring that he would have been just as diligent and satisfied if his father had placed him in a trade or apprenticed him to a merchant. In 1535 he took holy orders to fulfill his father's wish that he be eligible for a benefice to support his education. Two years later he turned to a career in civil law because he and his father found it "more congenial." The only time he expressed real disappointment over his father's influence in his life came in 1537, when his father thwarted his desire to play a musical instrument. Hermann had considered taking up the lute, spinet, clavichord, or organ in the belief that playing a musical instrument would "drive away depression." His father objected, saying his talents lay elsewhere and he should strive to be "among those for whom others play music."[88]

Over his father's protests, his mother taught him to play chess, arguing that it was a game he would learn sooner or later despite his parents' wishes and that he should learn it from one who would not take advantage of him. His father taught him cards with a similar motive, teasing him mercilessly when he lost, in the hope that this would instill a disinclination to gamble. Hermann acknowledged that losing did discourage him from both chess and cards in later years.[89]

When he took his first job at twenty-one in 1539, as rector of the Cronenbursa, a student hostel (a controversial appointment because he was so young), he received managerial assistance from his mother, whose advice he regularly sought. In 1542, when his father asked his advice before deciding to become *hausmeister* in the city council, a time-consuming and difficult post that Hermann also later held, it puzzled Hermann that his father, "who knew best what was advisable," should seek his counsel.[90]

In September 1549 Hermann's father fell ill with quartan fever (a fever that recurred violently every fourth day), from which he would die seven weeks later. He directly informed Hermann of the prospect of his death and asked him to stay by his side until the end. The discovery of his father's imminent death left Hermann "sickened in the heart." Shortly thereafter the illness also struck his mother, but she recovered. Hermann recorded his father's anxiety and fatalism as he approached death.

> It frightens me [my father would often say to me] that I must die; it makes me anxious and pains my heart. I am such a weak creature, such a poor worm. May God console, help, and be merciful to me. I will not come again alive to Weinsberg; I will not again see my friendly wife and my dear children. But then, nothing is lasting on this earth; everything comes to a quick end.[91]

When Hermann's mother approached his father's bed, he would look at her sadly and ask, "Is this to be our last day together?"[92] Hermann stood by his father, as he had promised, until the end; he was the last to speak with him before he died.

For some time thereafter, Hermann was inconsolable. He confided in his chronicle: "Never in my life have I been so near losing control over myself than at the time of my father's death and burial; for my father loved me and I loved him, so much so that my wife Weisgin often expressed her suprise when two days would pass and we had not been together."[93] Some months later Hermann beheld in a dream his father standing with his mother, the Virgin and child, and various friends and relatives "in a beautiful summer house" receiving a blessing in Latin from Mary and Jesus. Although he was not sure what to make of this vision, he found it very consoling.[94]

Hermann was also a father. In November 1546 Greitgin Olup, a maid in his mother's employ, with whom he had been intimate for over a year, gave birth to his only child, a daughter. Although Hermann had no direct contact with the child until she was seven years old, his covert care for her began at birth; the exercise of paternal duty at a distance was the burden of bastardy in Reformation Europe. Covertness gradually gave way over the years to direct dealings, warm expressions of paternal affection, and considerable paternal pride. Hermann's family took the child from her mother on the day of her birth, baptized and named her Anna, and arranged with a woman in the neighboring village of Ichendorf to nurse and raise her. Hermann paid maternity expenses, "damages" to Greitgin, and support payments of sixteen gulden a year to the nurse in Ichendorf. In 1548 Greitgin married a wool weaver, and the couple lived only a short distance from Hermann and his new wife Weisgin, who, to Hermann's distress, had frequent business dealings with Greitgin's husband, since they were both in the wool business.

When rumors circulated about Weisgin's commerce with the husband of Hermann's old mistress, Weisgin, who was unperturbed by Hermann's past, assured him that they would defeat gossip "by living well and friendly together."[95]

Hermann claimed to have first seen Anna in January 1554, when Weisgin fetched her from Ichendorf to begin work and school in Cologne. He described her at the time as "completely deformed in body and dress . . . her stomach swollen like that of a young pig," obviously a casualty of surrogate mothering, about which the century's moralists so frequently warned. Anna spent several weeks with Hermann's neighbor and friend Theis Muller van Aich and his wife, who saw to her rehabilitation. Healthier and better clothed, she then went to live and work with Hermann's bastard sister Geirt and her husband Peter Muller van Aich, a tailor, and also to attend school. In July 1554 Hermann negotiated a share of Anna's deceased mother's inheritance for her after Greitgin's sole surviving son Johann died (Greitgin and her husband had earlier fallen victim to plague). In 1556 Anna left the van Aichs to work for a brewer's family, again with the stipulation that she be allowed to continue her schooling.[96]

In May 1557 Anna, now ten years old, came to live with her father. Hermann described her as a "visitor" (*als frembt*) within the house, with responsibilities to serve the other women. Observing her one day, he expressed the hope that "God will grant that she may turn out to be a good person" (*ein gut menschs*).[97]

In March 1559 Anna was sent to live with Hermann's mother, where she learned to sew and embroider. At that time he reported that she had learned "to read and write somewhat."[98] The following year Hermann's sister Sibilla and his brother Christian acted as sponsors at her confirmation, which occurred without Hermann's knowledge for reasons that are not explained (there may have been complications relating to her illegitimacy, or Hermann may have been in one of his occasional anticlerical tempers). When he wrote his will in 1564, Hermann arranged for his brothers to advise and assist Anna after his death, and he instructed them to give her the following statement: "that she should consider all the things I have given her and done for her and not complain about what I have failed to give and do, because what has been done and what has been left undone have their reasons, and in all matters on her behalf I have acted with forethought. She should be satisfied with this and act honorably and wisely and remember me in her prayers."[99]

When Anna was twenty (May 1566), she entered the convent of Maria of Bethlehem. She had desired to pursue a religious vocation in another cloister, but her father persuaded her to enter this nearby family cloister. The decision pleased Hermann, who made detailed arrangements for her support there during and after his lifetime.[100] Anna's formal "clothing" (*inkleidung*) occurred on April 27, 1567, a solemn ceremony of marriage to Christ in which she removed a fancy wedding dress and donned the gray attire of a Franciscan nun. Her father celebrated the occasion with a great feast for the sisters, relatives, and friends and also gave Anna expensive gifts, including a relic-laden statue of Jesus ("there was none more beautiful in the cloister"). The bill for the gala and the presents came to well over a hundred gulden.[101] Anna professed her vows the following year in another elaborate ceremony (June 1568), this time receiving from her father gifts and nun's accessories (among them a wooden bed frame) costing eighty-three gulden.[102]

As the years passed, Hermann and Anna visited each other regularly, and a constant stream of gifts flowed into the cloister, both special (for example, a golden canister given to Hermann by an old Carthusian monk) and routine (money and wine). On Anna's birthdays Hermann seems always to have sent a cake.[103]

In September 1580 Anna became mother superior, and Hermann watched with pride as she received the keys to the cloister. A sister who had also aspired to the office refused her obedience, creating something of a scene; Hermann described the new position as "nothing but great worry and burdens" for Anna. During and after the ceremony, however, he was by his own description "unusually joyful"; "Many commented that they had never seen me so happy in my life." He made a big hit with the sisters, joking that they were now his "grandchildren," since Anna was their "mother." He commented on what the day meant to him: "Although it was only a poor Franciscan cloister . . . it pleased me much that Sister Entgin (Anna) had been so recognized and raised above all the others to this honor and office." In subsequent years he occasionally referred to her in his chronicle by her title, "the mother of the convent Maria of Bethlehem."[104]

Although Hermann had no sons, he did take a special interest in rearing a nephew, his brother Christian's eldest son Hermann, after Christian died. Young Hermann had problems at school, and his uncle, perhaps recalling his own difficult days as an arts student, was tolerant and encouraging almost to a fault. At twenty years of age, young Hermann had not yet completed the arts course, prerequisite for the study of law to which the family hoped he was destined. Hermann was initially patient with his nephew's dawdling and "let him rove about somewhat," thinking that being with people and conversing informally might aid his maturation. But young-Hermann's refusal to heed advice and succeed at school progressively strained their relationship. On one occasion Hermann described him as still "almost timid and childish," despite the physical signs of manhood. After young Hermann spent the summer of 1580 wandering aimlessly, despite an agreement with his uncle that he would pursue his studies, Hermann complained about an "abuse of my goodness and favor" and lectured him on the many opportunities he had squandered, "far more than any of his siblings had." Observing young Hermann to be "too old to learn a trade and physically too weak to work as a laborer," Hermann arranged for him to receive private instruction at home so that he might finish his arts course. In 1582 he gave him money to travel about for ten weeks in the hope that he might find a position somewhere. When young Hermann returned still unemployed, he settled down for a long stay with his uncle in the latter's adopted home, the Haus Cronenberg, helping with household chores and business matters and doing some writing, reading, and studying. In 1586 he became a notary public in Cologne and later (1590) gained an official post in Arsberg. During these years of close association with his uncle, they became fast friends; Hermann wrote of frequent intimate bedside conversations and of sharing the "secrets" of his will with his nephew.[105]

Hermann took a special interest in his nephew's career in large part because young Hermann was the male leader of the new Weinsberg generation; after Hermann's brother Gotschalk, he was next in line for Hermann's inheritance and the executorship of the Weinsberg estate. But they seem also to have liked one another, as a father a son and a son a father.

Sin and Mortality

Recent studies, as we have seen, have credited the Reformation with a new appreciation of the affective side of marriage, even with indirectly encouraging the practice of contraception by increasing sensitivity to the extrareproductive purposes of marriage.[106] Protestants have also been praised for pedagogical experiments that pointed in the direction of primary education for all. Still, the Reformation's overall effect on child rearing is considered, even by those who make such concessions, negative and even harmful, at least by modern standards. If a husband's authority over a wife was beginning to moderate in the sixteenth century, the authority of parents over their children is said to have reached new heights. Protestants generally are accused of repressive child rearing and educational techniques, of attempting to socialize children by fear of damnation and corporal punishment. Convinced that children were creatures depraved from conception by original sin, Protestant parents and schoolmasters proceeded, we are told, to scare the hell and beat the Devil out of them.[107] Even when children became adults, parents continued to influence strongly their vocational and marital choices, dominating their children as long as possible.[108]

There can be no argument that child rearing in modern times has adopted a more positive view of a child's willfulness and desire for autonomy and that the goal of controlling the lives of children has been largely abandoned. But surely the hubris of an age reaches a certain peak when it accuses another age of being incapable of loving its children properly. Such a judgment on the family of the past, pervasive today in both scholarly and popular media, is invariably based on a highly selective reading of sources and influenced by present-day values. Direct evidence of widespread brutality or even harsh treatment of children by sixteenth-century Protestants has yet to be presented.[109] There is little basis in fact for believing that the parents of Reformation Europe loved their children any less or mistreated them any more than modern parents do.

Even when examples of alleged maltreatment are found, what one group considered inhumane and godless treatment was humane and godly child care for another. Lutherans, for example, cried out against what they considered to be the "cruel" child-rearing practices of the Moravian Hutterites, who removed children from their parents between the ages of two and three and raised them communally, permitting only minimal parental contact.[110] The practice was described by Stephan Gerlach, who visited his sister in a Moravian community in September 1578. "All [Hutterite] settlements have a school in which they place children above two years (up to this point they remain with their mothers) in order to learn to pray and read . . . The daughters commonly learn only prayer . . . the boys, however, learn to read and write until they are a little older, at which time they are allowed to learn a handicraft or some other work. The children go a few times every day into the field or the neighboring woods in order that they may not be constantly on top of one another and may get some fresh air. They are also provided with certain women who do nothing else but watch over them, wash them, wait on them, and keep their beds and clothes clean and neat. After they are older they sleep together by twos."[111]

In Hutterite communities today a child is still considered a "house child" and primarily under the care of his parents until he is

three years old, after which time communal child rearing in
kindergarten begins. But even with this highly regimented, communal approach to child rearing, today as in the past, the greatest
care is devoted to the health, education, and vocational training of
each child, indoctrinating and integrating him into the larger
religious community. Neither the sixteenth-century nor the modern
visitor to Hutterite communities has found any lack of expressed love
and affection for children.[112]

Even at their seeming pedagogical worst, Protestants could be
surprisingly kind and enlightened. Perhaps the best case in point is
their handling of the delicate issue of a child's original sin. Although
Protestants believed that children, as members of the human race,
were innately depraved, this theological abstraction did not sanction harsh treatment of children. The doctrine of original sin explained for them, as it had for generations of Christians, the selfish,
possessive, irrational, and unaltruistic behavior of both young and
old, something manifest, they believed, not only to the student of
Holy Scripture, but to any casual observer of human conduct. Protestant reformers, like classical educators, knew that such behavior
could not be the foundation of either society or salvation; obedience
to a higher standard of conduct had to be established if a child was
to emerge as an adult with a civil and religious will. To this latter
end, which was hardly ignoble, parents must take the responsibility
of breaking their children's selfish, antisocial behavior by regular
discipline, using verbal threats and corporal punishment when love
and reason failed to persuade. Much was here at stake; the child
who did not learn to honor, obey, and love his parents and teachers
would grow up without a sense of duty and self-sacrifice to society
and hence would not be of service either to his fellowman or to
God.[113] A society of such individuals could only be at war with
itself. Nothing seemed clearer to people in the sixteenth century. If
they perceived a loss of individual autonomy in this (I suspect they
did not), the gain in social cohesion and harmony was believed to far
outweigh it.

Childhood discipline, then, sought to create a confident, responsible adult who accepted his place in the larger scheme of things and
was prepared to demand that others accept their place as well. This
was hardly the passive, diffident individual, certain only of his sin
and weakness, that some modern scholars have alleged.[114]

This is made clear especially in sermons and catechisms designed
for study at home. These short vernacular guides on issues of
popular concern compose a genre of instructional literature that is
distinct from, although by no means contradictory to, the large, for-

mal, proscriptive catechisms used in Protestant schools and churches. The highly public and official nature of the formal catechisms necessarily forced upon them rhetorical and theological correctness, giving them an unbending and remote quality, characteristic of official documents in any age. Such catechisms were better adapted to being memorized and repeated in unison than as guides to daily life; they may only marginally reflect and be relevant to the actual religious concerns and practices of individuals in the sixteenth century. The short topical pamphlet sermons and catechisms, by contrast, were written for the present, not for eternity; they gave priority to the practical consequences of a doctrine, not to its correct statement. For this reason, as sources they may better reveal the Protestant reformers' basic instincts and true expectations beneath the theological abstractions they felt obliged to defend.[115]

Take, for example, two sermons from the mid-1520s that addressed the nature of original sin in infants and the effect of baptism on their inborn depravity, questions that deeply concerned both the merely credulous and the deeply pious parents at this time. Both sermons assumed the inherited sinfulness of children and embraced a traditional concept of it. Both attempted to console married couples who, according to one sermon, refuse to have sex because they have been made so fearful by the traditional belief that infants go to hell if they die at birth unbaptized.[116] The author went on to say that some have consoled these couples with the equally false doctrine that all children are by nature guiltless and hence automatically go to heaven when they die, whether or not they have been baptized. The author cited a current popular saying that summarized this false belief: "I wish that I had died in infancy so that I could be sure of my salvation."[117]

The second sermon described the infant's sinfulness by merciless analogy with the inborn instincts of animals. According to the author, just as a cat craves mice, a fox chickens, and a wolf cub sheep, so infant humans are inclined in their hearts to adultery, fornication, impure desires, lewdness, idol worship, belief in magic, hostility, quarreling, passion, anger, strife, dissension, factiousness, hatred, murder, drunkenness, gluttony, and more.[118]

The authors clearly had no intention of surrendering the traditional belief in original sin; they were in fact totally oblivious to this option. They did, however, want to relieve the anxiety of parents who had become convinced by traditional teaching that infants who died unbaptized "die in their sins" and hence must be presumed to go to hell. The authors reported that new mothers were known to rush about frantically to find a priest "when their infants are barely halfway out of the womb" (*wenn sie kaum halb geporn sind*).[119] While such fear and anxiety may strike a modern reader as preposterous, they were all too real in an age of fervent religious belief. The physician Eucharius Rösslin warned midwives of the terrible consequences both for themselves and for any infant who died unbaptized as a result of their negligence or incompetence. "If a child dies without baptism and the midwife is responsible, she will be denied God's face for eternity. Heaven closes itself to her so that she may never repent this child whose death she caused. Nor can she bring it about that this child, who perished through her incompetence, will see the face of God."[120]

To counteract the fear of having a child die unbaptized in infancy, our pamphleteers insisted that baptism alone saved no one, neither infant nor adult. Even if an infant was baptized — which the authors believed to be a good thing and urged all parents to do — still it could not be saved unless it had *faith* — this in spite of the seeming injustice of damning one who apparently knows neither right nor wrong and who has not transgressed the law of God or man in actual thought or deed.[121]

But how can an infant have faith? Where is there any hope for a parent in this? At this point our authors appear to have removed the consolation of traditional baptism completely, leaving the parents of children who die in infancy or early childhood no hope whatsoever of their children's salvation. This, however, proves not to be the case at all. So irrepressibly inclined were our authors to console and strengthen that they flew in the face of their theological logic to do so: infants not only can have faith, but infant faith is declared to be the most effective kind, and more easily come by than the faith of adults.

> You ask: "But how can faith be in an infant which has no reason?" Answer: A child has as perfect and as rational a soul, one formed in the image of God, as any fully grown adult; the child is only hindered by the immaturity of his body. And God can infuse the gift of faith into the soul of a child [as easily as into the soul of an adult], although a child is not conscious of it until he reaches the age of reason or dies [presumably coming to consciousness in heaven] — just as a sleeping adult remains unaware of his faith until he is awakened.[122]

Infants, then are baptized precisely because age and the ability to reason have nothing to do with faith and salvation. "A young child can have faith as well as a grown man; if God can give faith to a grown man, he can also give it to a young child . . . [Indeed], no one is more ready for faith and baptism than an infant, who lacks cunning, reasoning, and fleshly cleverness."[123]

No married couple, then, should hesitate to have children for fear of their damnation should they die at birth; spouses should rather be fruitful and multiply, as God has commanded them to do, and entrust the eternal fate of their children to the One who finally decides all such matters.[124] Belief in original sin, properly understood, should inspire in a pious parent trust in God, not doubts about parenthood. Upon examination, we find that the doctrine of original sin actually could inspire *sympathy* for children.

Modern scholars have also considered the high rates of infant and child mortality to be factors in the allegedly pervasive indifference of parents and harshness toward children in Reformation Europe. But would parents be likely to withhold affection because their children proved to be physically fragile any more than because they shared the human condition of original sin? Why should the experience of repeated infant and child deaths not make surviving children all the more beloved by their parents? Why should giving a newborn infant the name of a child who had recently died indicate "a lack of a sense that the child was a unique being"[125] and not simply fondness for a family name and determination to see it persist?

Self-consciously expressed attitudes toward the death of infants and young children do not abound in sixteenth-century sources, but instructive comments can be found. The Ulm pastor Conrad Sam, for example, in a sermon on the prophet David, commented on the effect on parents of the death of infants, and his words suggest that a richer and more complex response may underlie perceived parental insensitivity to infant and child mortality than modern historians have assumed. According to the biblical narrative, David's first child, born of his marrige to Bathsheba, was cursed by God and died in infancy after a seven-day illness. During these seven days David fasted and wept for his child; after the child's death, he abruptly ended his mourning and returned to his work, as if nothing had happened. When his servants accused him of being callous and indifferent, David explained his behavior by saying that after the child had died, the matter was completely out of his hands. The Ulm pastor, agreeing, elaborated on David's explanation:

It serves no useful purpose to sorrow for the dead, while to be concerned for the living is not in vain . . . Here David reminds us that we are not to hold death in such honor that we mourn and lament a dead friend as if there were no hope or consolation. We should, however, ponder deeply the fact that we too must go this way, for as with the dead so will it be with all people.[126]

Remarkably similar is the attitude expressed a century later by the Puritan pastor Ralph Josselin, who told his flock that "grieving as others which have no hope" did not befit Christians. In a 1652 sermon he alluded to the once painful death of his first child Mary at eight years of age:

> Christians should . . . think about the dead without too much sorrow . . . When others go to the Tombs and Graves to mourn, Christians go to rejoyce . . . If their [deaths] sting you the consideration of their state in death is Honey that cureth and asswageth your grief . . . If you can consider their present state . . . you will finde your tears not brinish, but pleasant, this Sir, I have found and do finde an experienced truth . . . I have thoughts of my sweetest Daughter now with comfort, [I] who have [had] thoughts of her like the bitternesse of death.[127]

Parental grief over the death of a child seems to have increased with the child's age and the degree of familiarity and association. Josselin did not grieve the loss of children in infancy or after they had grown up and left home as deeply as he did that of children in the intervening years, such as his eight-year-old daughter. He described her in his diary as "a precious child, a bundle of myrrhe, a bundle of sweetness . . . a child of ten thousand, full of wisedome, womanlike gravity, knowledge, sweet expressions of God, apt in her learning . . . [who] lived desired and dyed lamented, [and whose] memory is and will be sweete unto mee."[128]

A still more revealing personal example of paternal grieving over children, again daughters, is provided by Martin Luther. He had six children (Hans, Elizabeth, Magdelene, Martin, Paul, and Margarethe), two of whom died during his lifetime—Elizabeth at eight months and Magdelene at thirteen years. Luther, who referred to his newborns as "little heathens," could be a harsh father; once, for example, he punished Hans for an unspecified "moral lapse" by forbidding him to be in his presence for three days and requiring him to write a letter begging his father's forgiveness, to which letter Luther replied that he would sooner have his son dead than ill-bred.[129] But the death of his children completely devastated this housefather, much to his own surprise and seeming incomprehension. He wrote of the death of Elizabeth at eight months: "I so lamented her death that I was exquisitely sick, my heart rendered soft and weak (*ein wundersam krankes, fast weibisches Herz*); never had I thought that a father's heart could be so broken for his children's sake" (*so weich gegen die Kinder*).[130] The death of Magdelene at thirteen overwhelmed him to the point that his very faith in God faltered. He wrote of it to his friend Justus Jonas, pointing out that while he and his wife should be thanking God that Magdelene was now "free of the flesh, the world, the Turk, and the Devil," neither was able to do so.

> The force of our natural love is so great that we are unable to do this without crying and grieving in our hearts . . . [and] experiencing death ourselves . . . The features, the words, and the movement of our living and dying daughter, who was so very obedient and respectful, remain engraved in our hearts; even the death of Christ . . . is unable to take all this away as it should. You, therefore, please give thanks to God in our stead.[131]

Despite the lessons of his own heart, Luther, like pastors Sam and Josselin, continued to look upon deep grieving as an unchristian tribute to death and a temptation all Christians must resist. "Should any thought of . . . death frighten us," he wrote to his dying mother in 1531, "let us . . . say . . . , 'Dear death . . . how is it that you are alive and terrifying me? Do you not know that you have been overcome [by Christ]? Do you not know that you, death, are quite dead?' "[132] After Magdelene's death, her elder brother Hans, with whom she had been particularly close, fell into deep depression and grieving. Upon Han's return to Latin school in Torgau, Luther wrote his teacher urging that he help Hans, then sixteen, overcome this "womanish feeling" and "childlike weakness" of grieving. "This is the reason he has been sent away [to school], that he may learn something and become hardened."[133] When the wife and newborn daughter of the Nuremberg reformer Osiander died in childbirth, Luther wrote a letter of consolation urging him to accept God's will and not succumb to that "most intense and bitter of human emotions" (grief), before which Luther confessed he had fallen and had not yet fully recovered.[134] After the death of their infant daughter, Thomas Platter and his wife Anna "cried from pain, but also from joy, because she was freed from suffering." Anna, however, suc-

cumbed to deep grieving, "unable to sing and be happy as before."
On a physician's advice, Thomas took her away to Zurich.[135]

Hermann von Weinsberg recorded numerous reactions, both his
own and others', to the death of children, which attest how emotionally consuming the deaths were, despite the surface calm that
parents and relatives attempted to maintain. The death of his
nephew Conrad at age seven (August, 1569), after he had long endured pain no medicine could relieve, led Hermann, like Luther
before him, to ponder the justice of God: "This poor sheep [Conrad]
has not committed many sins, yet he must suffer such weakness and
pain; O God be specially merciful to us adults."[136] In August 1588,
when his greatnephew Benedictus died at two years of age,
Hermann was overcome by emotion at seeing Benedictus' twin
brother, Gotschalk, bend over the corpse and kiss his brother good-
by in "an act of such great natural love and sadness that Gotschalk,
because still so young, did not comprehend it."[137] In March 1591
Hermann recorded an unusual, even slightly macabre, example of
parental love for a deceased child. A shoemaker's daughter, aged
eight or nine, had died after having been lame and sick for three
years. An autopsy discovered an enlarged liver, which the surgeon
attributed to the child's drinking undiluted beer. The autopsy had
occurred at the insistence of the girl's mother, who stood by and
watched it to completion "even though she deeply loved her child."
"I would not have wanted to watch, had she been my child," writes
Hermann; "perhaps the mother desired to see the cause of her
daughter's illness because the girl had suffered so much from it. But
what good did it do to locate the disease? Some say it may help
another who suffers from the same malady, if we learn more about
it. That may be, only God knows; but this does not please me."[138]

In the sixteenth and seventeenth centuries, outward insensitivity
to death, whether that of a child or of an adult, was considered a
moral and religious obligation, behavior every Christian should
strive to achieve. A "hardened" response to death was both appropriate social etiquette and an indication of character for a person
who was confident about the meaning of his own life and that of the
deceased. But as the above examples make clear, successful
resistance to grieving did not indicate any absence of love and affection for the deceased, especially for a child; indeed, particularly in
the case of deceased children emotional love proved an overpowering temptation.

Neither belief in original sin nor the experience of high infant
mortality inhibited a positive and caring attitude toward the
children of Reformation Europe. Such negative associations appear

to reflect the logic of a modern mind far more than they do the experience of people in the sixteenth century.

Evidence of strong parental affection for children can also be gleaned from children's catechisms, especially those designed for use at home. A striking example of this genre is the *Ten Dialogues for Children Who Have Begun to Speak* (1550), written by the Lutheran pastor and poet Erasmus Alberus. The author dedicated this work to the children of Hamburg to commemorate a visit there. It is a booklet, only a couple of inches in length and width, made for tiny hands. In the dedication he praised children as "the first Christians to die for Christ," a reference to the slaughter of the innocents by King Herod.[139] Alberus first composed catechetical dialogues for his own children as aids to their religious and secular education "as soon as they began to speak and understand a little." Subsequently he prepared them also for the children of his friends, among them the Reder family of Hamburg, with whom he lodged during his visit; two of the ten dialogues were between Reder's daughters, Christina and Dorothea, and Alberus.

In the preface Alberus shared a bittersweet confirmation of the benefit of such exercises for both parents and children, reporting how they consoled his "beautiful little daughter Cecilia" in her final moments of life. Asked on her deathbed, "How did Christ die for us?" she answered by stretching out her arms like Christ on the cross as she died.[140] Such physical gestures were generally taught small children as a means of consolation and comfort. Brunfels, for example, instructed children at bedtime, after they had said their prayers and been tucked in, to "lie neither on your face nor on your back, but first on your right side, your arms in the figure of a cross protecting your heart, stretching your right hand to your left shoulder and your left hand to your right."[141]

Alberus believed his dialogues would help children become informed, pious, and courageous Christians. "The reason so few people today are God-fearing," he wrote, "is that they were not raised to reverence God during childhood." Parents who failed to prepare their children for life by providing them with religious training he accused of "spiritually abusing," even "murdering" them.[142] Alberus thought this was especially true of the Anabaptists, the chief among the "Kindermörderer" in his opinion, because they denied infants entrance into God's kingdom through baptism.

Here are two dialogues, the fiirst complete, the second excerpted, which Alberus composed for himself and his three-and-a-half-year-old daughter Gertrude.[143] They reveal how one very influential Protestant father went about instilling the "fear of God" in his children.

ALBERUS: Do you love Jesus?
GERTRUDE: Yes, father.
A: Who is the Lord Jesus?
G: God and Mary's son.
A: How is his dear Mother called?
G: Mary.
A: Why do you love Jesus? What has he done to make you love him?
G: He has shed his blood for me.
A: He has shed his blood for you?
G: Yes, father.
A: Could you be saved if he had not shed his blood for you?
G: Oh no!
A: What would then have happened?
G: We would all be damned.
A: We would all be damned?
G: Yes, father.
A: O Lord God, it would have been bad for us poor people, if the Lord had not shed his blood for us.
G: Had the child Jesus not been born, we would be lost altogether.
A: Do you thank the Lord Christ that he has shed his blood for you?
G: Yes, father.
A: How? Tell me, child.
G: I thank you, Lord Jesus Christ, that you have become my brother and saved me from all want through your holy death. I praise you eternally for your great goodness.

The second dialogue:

A: Is Christ your brother?
G: Yes, father.
A: God's only begotten son, the son of the living God, is your brother?
G: Yes, father, really.
A: So you are for sure a great and powerful queen in heaven, because Christ in

heaven is your brother?

G: That I am, praise God.

A: So you are his dear little sister?

G: Yes, and I am also his dear daughter and dear bride.

A: You are also his dear daughter and dear bride?

G: Yes, praise God.

A: How blessed are you! The Lord has done a great thing for me.

G: Yes he has. For he saves a poor damned child from the Devil's kingdom and gives me eternal life.[144]

Not all children's catechisms, to be sure, were as short and light as Alberus's, but read in their entirety their intention invariably seems to have been supportive and reassuring. Eberlin von Günzburg captured their spirit in a catechism prepared for adult laity, in which he instructed parents to teach their children to think of Christ as "their best, truest, and friendliest friend (*den besten, getrewesten, frintlichsten fründ*), more friendly, loving, and trustworthy to them than all the angels and saints."[145]

The Faith of Our Fathers

Instead of being the tools by which church authority undermined the confidence of generations of children, Protestant catechisms may have had the reverse effect: to cast doubt on traditional religious belief and institutions by making children all too confident and sure where truth lay in ultimate matters. The catechisms for children that were popular in the first half of the sixteenth century repeatedly scorned the errors and superstitions of traditional religion and in the process transformed the anticlerical rhetoric of the later Middle Ages into a child's language. What must have been the long-term effect on children when criticism and ridicule of traditional authority were constantly drummed into their heads, while at the same time they were assured of the infallibility and certitude of the new faith? Such sustained catechetical mocking of the external rites of religion and exaltation of the internal faith of the individual created a two-edged sword, capable of challenging new Protestant "papacies" as well as that of the old church.[146] The Protestant catechism, so often deplored by modern scholars as an assault on the freedom and autonomy of children, may instead have been the chief means of their liberation from the internal bonds of authoritarian religion. Consider the following examples.

The popular *Catechism of the Brethren* (1523) posed the question: "Where do people place false hope?" and provided children the following answer.

In the grace of God without betterment of life; in dead faith without love; in a future penance and reception of the sacrament at the hour of death; in church services and frequent communion; in fasting, prayer, and almsgiving; in the canonical hours and verbal confessions of faith; in obedience to the pope and the Roman church; in clever intellectual hearing and reading of the word of God; in saints, intercessory prayer, and pilgrimages; in saying the rosary, the Ave Maria, and other contrived prayers; in the "third hell" of Purgatory; in gifts to the church and its servants; in the Mass; in special works of mercy; in the external performance of God's commandments; and in good works.[147]

The longest article in Johann Agricola's *One Hundred and Fifty-Six Common Questions for Young Children in the German School for Girls in Eisleben* (1528) — a catechism condensed and translated for private use from the author's work for the Latin schools — elaborated the practical consequences of St. Paul's question in Romans 8:32: "If God has given us his son, has he not also given us all things with him?" Instructs Agricola:

It follows that going on pilgrimages makes pilgrims, but not Christians; reading the canonical hours makes people who can pray seven times a day, but not Christians; holding Mass and reading vigils makes celebrants of the Mass and readers of vigils, but not Christians; endowing churches and monastic cells makes patrons of churches, but not Christians; fasting makes people who fast, but not Christians; [wearing] cowls and tonsures makes people who wear cowls and tonsures, but not Christians; [entering] holy orders and cloisters makes Carthusian, Franciscan, Dominican, and Benedictine monks, nuns, and regulars, but not Christians. In sum, Christ teaches that only spiritual things make one a Christian, and for this reason we take up nothing but Christ through faith. No external thing can make one a Christian. He who does many works is a worker, but not a Christian. [And the litany begins anew.][148]

The Strasbourg catechism for children and youth (1534) appended a special dialogue for father and child, the repeated use of which could only have given children who understood it the greatest confidence about their relationship with their Creator and Savior, who are presented as allies more powerful and sure than their own parents.

> FATHER: What does it mean to have God for one's father?
>
> CHILD: Two things . . . As I have been created by God and recreated to eternal life, I love God totally . . . [and] I shall never forget that he is my father and that out of his fatherly love he will give and do more for me than any earthly parent ever could.
>
> F: What does it mean to know that all things are in God's hand?
>
> C: That I hold God above all things and desire his grace . . . and trust in his protection and fatherly favor in all adversity.
>
> F: What does it mean to you that Christ sits at the right hand of God in heaven?
>
> C: That I can trust completely in my lord Jesus to whom the Father has given all power in heaven and earth and have no doubt that he will in the end save me from all sin and misfortune and let me dwell with him in heaven in eternal blessedness.[149]

Although the Reformation did come to extol the patriarchal family, its initial success lay in persuading a generation to abandon the faith of its fathers. Ezekiel 21:18 became a banner for Protestant reformers: "Do not walk in the statutes of your fathers, nor observe their ordinances, nor defile yourselves with their idols." One pamphleteer revealed how difficult such an action was in an age that prized parental authority:

> Here [Ezekiel 21:18] God commands us not to live in the faith and laws of parents (*in der eltern glauben noch rechten*). Yet, blind heads cry out day and night: "I must stand by my parents; I will not turn to the new doctrine, for it is not possible that God has permitted our parents to err so long. . ." But our elders are as human as we and err as easily as we. For this reason, we must take God's word as our model, not the lives of our parents.[150]

The Nuremberg city secretary Lazarus Spengler ridiculed childlike fidelity to "parental" religion, which he found to be a major obstacle to the new faith:

> How can one with a Christian mind and true heart say that, for salvation's sake, he wants to follow his parents and believe as they have done? Surely there are few today who are unaware that their parents, with good intentions and following the instruction of the clergy, relied on their own works, believing that they became pious and righteous and were saved by them. They placed their faith in indulgences, pilgrimages, and many external church services, attaching God's honor to lighting candles, the repetition of special prayers, building churches, decorating altars, and the like. They sought to absolve their sins by buying indulgences, calling on dead saints to aid and intercede for them, and endowing many masses — all because they knew no better. Now, shall we, who have been shown the folly of these things by God's grace and the light of his true holy word, cling to our parents' errors, to which they were misled by others, and die in them, following after our parents in what we know, recognize, and cannot deny to have been manifestly wrong? What is this but to deny Christ and openly embrace idolatry? We would be ashamed to wear our parents' long, obscene, pointed shoes and imitate other of their human vanities, yet we cling to their all-too-human and uncertain beliefs, even though we know that even the saints can err . . . Christ after all commanded us to *honor* our father and mother, not to *trust* and *believe* in them. Only one who trusts in him [Christ], not in any other person, will be saved.[151]

The fidelity to higher divine law that Protestant catechists urged upon children occasionally reached such idealistic heights that some children must have had difficulty coping with the purported religious importance of their lives. Take, for example, the following description of the sacrifices expected of Christians, which appeared in Agricola's vernacular catechism.

CHILD: If I live by faith alone, will tyrants drive me from the land and take all that I have?

ANSWER: That is the risk you must take [as a Christian]; for as soon as you embrace the gospel and Christ, you must think to yourself:

> "Now I deprive myself of body and
> life . . . and all that I have."
>
> C: Why do I do that?
> A: So that when it actually happens to you,
> you can take it in stride and say: "This is
> nothing new; I have known all long that
> this would come about."
> C: Will it really cost me my life?
> A: You must obey God more than man . . .
> C: But life is dear.
> A: For that reason it is your most
> treacherous and harmful enemy; as
> Christ says, "The enemies of man are his
> own family."
> C: How am I to understand that?
> A: The closer a friend, the worse an enemy
> and the worse an enemy, the closer a
> friend; a spouse, a child, life itself are
> more harmful to you than death and all
> misfortune.[152]

These were not sentiments to make young people cower before their parents or any other authority; nor were they the beliefs of people who shirked responsibility and self-sacrifice. By their inculcation of individual religious certitude and their incessant ridicule of unscriptural, hypocritical, and merely external religious practices, Protestant catechisms, so carefully designed to teach the child to obey, were at the same time programming him to defy. Heroism as well as subservience filled these catechisms. In every type of literary source and official record we can find reformers, educators, and magistrates urging parents to imbue their children with a sense of religious worth and the self-confidence necessary to manage the world and please God. Like Luther's free yet bound Christian, the obedient and disciplined child was also to be a "lord over all."

Our authors believed that few parents were willing to rear their children on so noble a model and that few children could live up to it. They frequently portrayed parents as denying their children the self-discipline that could make them strong, useful citizens and subjects. They especially accused the nobility of raising self-indulgent children more disposed to tyrannize society than to be its proper masters. So long as such neglect of parental responsibility held sway across the social spectrum, the moralists of the Reformation believed the result would be predictable: an unstable populace, alternately timid and unruly, and magistrates inclined to govern unjustly and cruelly.

It has recently been argued that a "fundamental inversion of the principles of familial morality" has occurred since the seventeenth century, that in former times a father had more rights over his children than duties toward them, whereas today "procreation gives a father more duties toward his children than rights over them."[153] In sixteenth-century Germany the rights and duties of parents were always more intertwined than this statement claims. Although a parent properly exercised his own best judgment in such matters, no parent was supposed to override the mature wishes of his child in choosing either a vocation or a spouse; if a parent attempted to do so, the child courageous enough to pursue them had both informal and legal alternatives. It is a great, self-serving myth of the modern world that the children of former times were raised as near slaves by domineering, loveless fathers who owed them nothing, the home a training ground for the docile subjects of absolute rulers. To the contrary, from prenatal care to their indoctrination in the schools, there is every evidence that children were considered special and were loved by their parents and teachers, their nurture the highest of human vocations, their proper moral and vocational training humankind's best hope. Parenthood was a conditional trust, not an absolute right, and the home was a model of benevolent and just rule for the "state" to emulate.

The inversion of familial morality that has occurred in modern times may better be appreciated if the matter is addressed from the point of view of the child. In the sixteenth century children were raised and educated above all to be *social* beings; in this sense they had more duties toward their parents and society than they had rights independent of them. This did not mean that the family lacked an internal identity or that loving relationships failed to develop between spouses, between parents and children, and among siblings. Privacy and social extension were not perceived as contradictory. The great fear was not that children would be abused by adult authority but that children might grow up to place their own individual wants above society's common good. To the people of Reformation Europe no specter was more fearsome than a society in which the desires of individuals eclipsed their sense of social duty. The prevention of just that possibility became the common duty of every Christian parent, teacher, and magistrate.

Works Frequently Cited
Notes
Index

Abbreviations

Das Buch Weinsberg	*Das Buch Weinsberg. Kölner Denkwürdigkeiten aus dem 16. Jahrhundert*, vols. I, II, ed. Konstantin Höhlbaum (Leipzig, 1886, 1887); vol. V, ed. Josef Stein (Bonn, 1926)
Köhler, *Zürcher ehegericht*	Walther Köhler, *Zürcher ehegericht und Genfer konsistorium*, I: *Das Zürcher ehegericht und seine Auswirkung in der Deutschen Schweiz zur Zeit Zwinglis* (Leipzig, 1932)
LW	*Luther's Works*, ed. J. Pelikan and H. Lehman (St. Louis, 1957–)
Tü fiche	*Flugschriften des frühen 16. Jahrhunderts. Microfiche Serie 1978*, ed. Hans-Joachim Köhler (Zug, 1978–)
WA	*D. Martin Luthers Werke: Kritische Gesamtausgabe* (Weimar, 1883–)
WABr	*D. Martin Luthers Werke: Briefwechsel* (Weimar, 1930–1948)
B.M.	British Museum
Ox-Bod, T.L.	Oxford University, Bodleian Library, Tracts Lutheran

Works Frequently Cited

Brenz, Johannes, *Wie in Ehesachen/und inn den fellen/so sich derhalben/zu tragen/nach Götlichen billichen Rechten/Christenlich zu handeln sey* (Wittenberg, 1531).

Das Buch Weinsberg. Kölner Denkwürdigkeiten aus dem 16. Jahrhundert, vols. I, II, ed. Konstantin Höhlbaum (Leipzig, 1886, 1887); vol. V, ed. Josef Stein (Bonn, 1926).

Bugenhagen, Johannes, *Vom Ehebruch und Weglauffen* (Wittenberg, 1540).

Clemen, Otto, ed., *Luthers Werke in Auswahl*, 1–8, 5th ed. (Berlin, 1950–51).

Coler(us), Johannes, *Oeconomia ruralis et domestica. Darinn das gantz Ampt aller trewen/Hauss-Vätter und Hauss-Mütter/bestandiges und allgemeines Hauss-Buch etc.* (Frankfurt, 1680).

De Mause, Lloyd, ed., *The History of Childhood* (New York, 1974).

Dieterich, Hartweg, *Das protestantische Eherecht in Deutschland bis zur Mitte des 17. Jahrhundert* (Munich, 1970).

Eyb, Albrecht von, *Ob einem mannen sey zu nemmen ein eelichs weyb oder nicht*, in *Ehebüchlein. Faksimile der Originalausgabe von Anton Koberger Nürnberg 1472* (Wiesbaden, 1966).

Flandrin, Jean-Louis, *Families in Former Times: Kinship, Household and Sexuality* (Cambridge, 1979).

Hoffmann, Julius, *Die "Hausväterliteratur" und die "Predigten über den christlichen Hausstand." Lehre vom Hause und Bildung für das häusliche Leben im 16., 17. und 18. Jahrhundert* (Weinheim, 1959).

Irwin, Joyce, ed., *Womanhood in Radical Protestantism, 1525–1675* (New York, 1979).

Köhler, Walther, *Zürcher ehegericht und Genfer konsistorium*, I: *Das Zürcher ehegericht und seine Auswirkung in der Deutschen Schweiz zur Zeit Zwinglis* (Leipzig, 1932).

Menius, Justus, *An die hochgeborne Fürstin/fraw Sibilla Herzogin zu Sachsen/Oeconomia Christiana/das ist von Christlicher Hausshaltung* (Nuremberg, 1530).

Rösslin, Eucharius, *Rosengarten* (1513), in *Alte Meister der Medizin und Naturkunde in Facsimile-Ausgaben und Neudrucken nach Werken des 15.–18. Jahrhunderts*, ed. Josef Stein (Munich, 1910).

Staehelin, Adrian, *Die Einführung der Ehescheidung in Basel zur Zeit der Reformation* (Basel, 1957).

Wendel, François, *Le mariage à Strasbourg à l'epoque de la Reforme 1520–1692* (Strasbourg, 1928).

Notes

1. In Defense of Marriage

1. Jeffrey B. Russell, *A History of Witchcraft: Sorcerers, Heretics and Pagans* (London, 1980), pp. 114–15, discussing H. C. Erik Midelfort, *Witchhunting in Southwestern Germany, 1562–1684: The Social and Intellectual Foundations* (Stanford, 1972).

2. Robert Wheaton, "Recent Trends in the Historical Study of the French Family," in *Family and Sexuality in French History*, ed. Robert Wheaton et al. (Philadelphia, 1980), pp. 3–26. See below p. 216, n. 7.

3. Nachman Ben-Yehuda, "The European Witch Craze of the Fourteenth to Seventeenth Centuries: A Sociologist's Perspective," *American Journal of Sociology* 86 (1980): 6; Christina Larner, *Enemies of God: The Witchhunt in Scotland* (Baltimore, 1981), p. 92; Richard Kieckhefer, *European Witch Trials: Their Foundations in Popular and Learned Culture, 1300–1500* (Berkeley, 1976), P. 96; H. C. Erik Midelfort, "Witchcraft, Magic, and the Occult," in *Reformation Europe: A Guide to Research*, ed. Steven Ozment (St. Louis, 1982), p. 191.

4. Waldemar Kawerau long ago pointed out the peculiarity of Protestant *Ehespiegel*, in contrast to earlier ones, in their treatment of marriage and family in opposition to celibacy. *Die Reformation und die Ehe* (Halle, 1892), p. 67.

5. "Hat man in Alten und newen Testament das volck zum Ehelichen leben angehalten. Bey unns aber können sy nichts / dann Junckfrawschafft preisen / und den Ehelichen standt vernichten / besorgen sich der muhe / und arbait / angst und not / so darinnen ist / sölcher beschwärung understeet sich niemandt gern / darumb fleücht und meydet yderman den Ehelichen standt. In sonderhait wären sich fast unser gaistlichen / so man in saget / sy mögen Ehelich werden / besorgen sich / mann werd jnen jr buben leben nit weytter gestatten / sonder sy in die mühsam Ehe treiben . . . Es haben der selbigen etzliche der Junckfrawschafft wöllen rathsam sein unnd jr mit macht ain zaum ins maul legen / haben sich von beiwesen der lewt abgesondert / und in die clöster gesteckt / darinn sy weiber weder hören noch sehen möchten / seinds vertrawens / durchs abwesen jr junkfrawschafft dester leichter zuhalten." Thomas Stör, *Der Ehelich standt von got mit gebenedeyung auffgesetzt / soll umb schwärhait wegen der seltzsamen*

gaben der Junckfrawschafft yederman frey sein / und niemant verboten werden (1524) [Ox-Bod, T.L. 37.122], p. A 4 b.

6. See my essays: "The Pamphlet Literature of the German Reformation" in *Reformation Europe: A Guide to Research*, pp. 85–106; "The Social History of the Reformation: What Can We Learn From Pamphlets?" in *Flugschriften als Massenmedium der Reformationszeit*, ed. Hans-Joachim Köhler (Stuttgart, 1981), pp. 171–204.

7. Even the bare housekeeping or budget book listing daily expenses of a household can be a mine of information. The *Haushaltbuch* of the Nuremberg merchant and city treasurer (*losunger*) Anton Tucher, for example, provides details of daily expenditures for kitchen and cellar, taxes, clothes, gifts, purchases of appliances and furniture, and payments to servants and laborers — information that permits one to measure inflation, buying habits, fluctuations in wages, even religiosity (as indicated by expenditures for religious services). *Anton Tuchers Haushaltbuch (1507 bis 1517)*, ed. Wilhelm Loose (Tübingen, 1877).

8. See the pioneering effort of R. W. Scribner, *For the Sake of Simple Folk: Popular Propaganda for the German Reformation* (Cambridge, 1982).

9. There are two handy collections of evangelical catechisms designed primarily for use in both Latin and German schools and churches: *Die evangelischen Katechismusversuche vor Luthers Enchiridion*, I–IV, ed. Ferdinand Cohrs (Berlin, 1900–1902); *Quellen zur Geschichte des kirchlichen Unterrichts im evangelischen Deutschland zwischen 1530 und 1600*, I–XI, ed. Johann Michael Reu (Gütersloh, 1900–1902). Many of these catechisms are large, official, and "correct" and may give the impression of being boring, merciless forms of indoctrination. I have favored the excerpted or smaller vernacular catechisms in my arguments here, suspecting that they were more adaptable to home or private use and closer to actual religious belief and practice because of their greater directness and simplicity. Compare the recent survey by Robert Kolb, "The Layman's Bible: The Use of Luther's Catechisms in the German Late Reformation," in *Luther's Catechisms — 450 Years*, ed. D. P. Scaer and R. D. Preus (Fort Wayne, Ind., 1979), pp. 16–26. On the success of catechisms in winning the hearts and minds of laity, see the sharply joined debate between Gerald Strauss and James M. Kittelson, as focused in Kittelson, "Successes and Failures in the German Reformation: The Report from Strasbourg," *Archiv für Reformationsgeschichte* 73 (1982): 153–175.

10. The importance of self-conscious comments by individuals both as a source in social history and as a corrective to gross generalizations from uninterpreted statistical data has been nicely argued by Heide Stratenwert. "Selbstzeugnisse als Quellen zur Sozialgeschichte des 16. Jahrhundert," in *Festgabe für E. W. Zeeden zum 60. Geburtstag*, ed. H. Rabe et al. (Münster / Westfalen, 1976), pp. 21–35. See especially her treatment of the conflict between the modern scholars' statistical data and personal comments by contemporaries on the meaning of infant (and adult) mortality in this period. Ibid., pp. 29–30.

11. *On the Estate of Marriage*, *LW*, 45, p. 36; Eileen Power, *Medieval*

Women, ed. M. M. Postan (Cambridge, 1975), pp. 16, 30. Luther's rejection of the misogynist literature of the Middle Ages is discussed by Elisabeth Ahme, "Wertung und Bedeutung der Frau bei Martin Luther," *Luther* 35 (1964): 61–68. Ahme considers Luther's influence a very positive one for women as a whole. On this subject, see also Kawerau, *Die Reformation und die Ehe*, pp. 41–63, and Miriam Usher Chrisman, who documents misogynist literature in late medieval Strasbourg. *Lay Culture, Learned Culture, 1480–1599* (New Haven, 1982), pp. 104–105, 111–112.

12. Quoted in *Womanhood in Radical Protestantism, 1525–1675*, ed. and trans. Joyce L. Irwin (New York, 1979), p. 67.

13. "Dieweyl in der Welt der Ehelich stand so ubel zerrissen / verschmehet und verworffen wirdt / als ein elender verachter stand / welches auch die jungen leüt von der Ehe schreckt das sie sehen / wie es so wunderlich zu gehet / und sprechen: Es gehort vil jm ein hauss." "Es ist bey vilen jetzundt ein abergraw / und ein schwers in vile der kinder / unnd ir vil förchten sich darvor." Leonard Culman, *Jungen gesellen / Jungkfrauwen und Witwen / so Ehelich wöllen werden / zu nutz ein unterrichtung / wie sie in ehelichen stand richten sollen* (Augsburg, 1568; first pub. 1534) [B.M., 8416.22.34], pp. A 3 a, D 6 b.

14. "Gesehen das solche muhe / angst / smertzen / nodt / sorge / und arbeyt / sey im ehelichen standt / sie wollten yhn einem hünde nicht günnen / bringen also yhre eigne kinder den teuffell heym / schaffen yhne gutte tage am leybe / unnd die hellen an der selen." *Über das Evangelion Johannis / da Christus seine Mutter auch seine Junger / wären auff die Hochtzeyt geladen / Wass mit worten und wercken daselbst gehandelt. Eyn Sermon dem Ehlichen standt fast freudsam und nützlicht* (1534) [Ox-Bod, T.L. 39.178], p. B 1 a.

15. *Das Buch Weinsberg*, II, 147–148. See below, pp. 158–160.

16. Ibid., p. 192.

17. Ibid., p. 183.

18. Tabletalk no. 3566A (1537), in *Luthers Werke in Auswahl*, 8, ed. Otto Clemen (Berlin, 1950), p. 111.

19. "So wollen sich etzliche dieses seliges ehestandes ewssern / und lieber hurerey und ein Sodomytisch leben haben / auss der ursach / sprechen es wehr gut ehelich werden wie will ich mich aber erneren / ich habe nichts ja nym ein weib / yss uns tryngt dar von / Es hat vill plage / vill sorge / vill muhe und arbeyt / da klagets weib / ist kranck / da tzannen und plerren die kinder / das wyl trincken / das wil essen / jah wol wo nemen / Dyss ist freylich die grost hindernuss das auff das allermeyst die ehe hyndert." *Über das Evangelion Johannis*, pp. B 1 b–B 2 a. See also note 5 above.

20. "Also haben sie [the clergy] uns arme ehemänner und leyen / wie sie uns nennen / bei der nassen umbgefürt / sein so keusch und fürsichtig gewesen / das wir schier weder frawen noch junckfrawen / Döchter noch kint / vor jnen ongeschmecht behalten haben / und haben auff die letst mit jren leeren und leben / uns arme layen auch dahin bracht / das wir den ehebruch / junckfrawen schwechen / unnd weyber schenden / etc gering oder fur nichts geacht haben / dann wir haben sollichs von jnen in jren

leeren und leben gehört und gesehen / Es ist auch sollichs nit grosse sündt zu sein von jnen erfaren worden / dann so wir beychtet haben / ist es einem ehebrecher umb ein Groschen oder Batzen gewesen / so sein wir von dem ehebruch etc. frey ledig und absolviert worden / Ja meyn ich eben wie den hundt der flech / darauss dann wir abgenommen haben / dz es nit gross schwere sünd sey / sonderlich weil es so leücht in der beycht abgehe und dieweil auch Pfarrer und prediger / Münich und pfaffen / Pfarrhöffheuser und Clöster / sollicher beischlaff / huren und köchin vol stecken." *Concubinarii. Underricht auss Götlichen und Gaistlichen Rechten / ob ein Priester ein Eheweyb / oder Concubin / das ist / ein beyschläfferin haben mög* (1545) [B.M., 3908.ccc.65], p. C 4 a. This was a prominent argument of early Protestant pamphleteers; an anonymous pamphlet of 1523, for example, described as "great fools" those laity who tried to justify adultery by appealing to clerical example — "darumb dass die / die ain gaystlichs klaydt antragen / Eebruch offentlich treyben / und andere laster mer." *Ayn kurtzlich Antwort ainer Ordens schwester / jrem natürlichen bruder Cartheüser ordens zugeschickt / uber seine Christliche / und Evangelische lere und ermanung* [Tü fiche, 68–177], p. A 3 b.

21. An anticlerical pamphlet, probably from the early 1520s, alleges the financial stake of bishops in concubines and priests' children as the reason behind the church's toleration of concubinage. Hanns Kolb, *Ein Reformation notturfftig in der Christenheit mit den pfaffen und iren magten* (n.d., n.p.) [Tü fiche, 328–924]. See also Ozment, *Reformation in the Cities* (New Haven, 1980), pp. 60–61, 113–114.

22. *Syben frumm aber trostloss pfaffen klagen ihre not* (Basel, 1521), in *Johann Eberlin von Günzburg. Sämtliche Schriften*, 2, ed. Ludwig Enders (Halle, 1900), pp. 60–63.

23. *Ein new Apologia unnd verantwortung Martini Luthers wyder der Papisten Mortgeschrey* (Bamberg, 1523), in *Flugschriften aus den ersten Jahren der Reformation*, I, ed. Otto Clemen (Leipzig, 1907), 161.

24. Ibid., pp. 163–164.

25. François Wendel, *Le mariage à Strasbourg à l'epoque de la Reforme 1520–1692* (Strasbourg, 1928), pp. 20–24; John T. Noonan, Jr., *Contraception: A History of Its Treatment by the Catholic Theologians and Canonists* (New York, 1967), pp. 221–244.

26. "Es gilt gleich als vil bey Got / du seyest Junckfraw oder Ehelich / dann ayns als wol gottes gab ist / als das ander / und werden also bayde zugleich für Got gepreisst . . . . freyen gegen junckfrawschafft / ist ain böss ding / aber doch ist brennen erger / darumb ist besser die unlustige ehe dann die unlustige keüschait / besser ain sawre und schwere ehe / dann ain sawre und schwere keüchait. Ursach / es ist besser freyen dann brennen. . . Ain Priester ist je ain man / gottes Creatur und werck / sich zu meren und zubesamen / wie ander lewt geschaffen." Stör, *Der Ehelich stand*, pp. B 2 b, C 1 a–C 2 a.

27. *Der frummen pfaffen trost*, in Enders, 2, p. 81.

28. John K. Yost, "The Value of Married Life for the Social Order in

the early English Renaissance," *Societas* 6 (1976): 29–31; John B. Payne, *Erasmus: His Theology of the Sacraments* (Richmond, Va., 1970), pp. 107–108.

29. "So ist auch die Ee ein frölichs luspers und fuss ding. was mag frolicher und susser gesein dann der name des vaters der muter und der kinder so die hangen an den helsen der eltern und manchen sussen kuss von in empfahen und so beide eeleute solliche lieb willen und freundschafft zueinander haben was eines will das es auch wolle das ander und was eines redt mit imselbst geredt und in beiden gutes und ubel gemein ist das gute dester frolich und das widerwertig dester leichter. Solliche und ander mer ursachen . . . preyssen und loben die heilligen wirdigen Ee und anzaigen die antwort auff die . . . frage des einem manne sey zunemen ein weyb." Albrecht von Eyb, *Ob einem mannen sey zu nemmen ein eelichs weyb oder nicht*, in *Ehebüchlein. Faksimile der Originalausgabe von Anton Koberger Nürnberg 1472* (Wiesbaden, 1966), p. 81. An edition was published in Augsburg in 1517 [Ox-Bod, T.L. 85. 14].

30. Ibid., p. 55.

31. "Da bedarff es weyter nicht vil fragens noch bedenckens / ob man sol ehelich werden / oder nicht / hilfft auch nichts / Eben so wenig / als wenn du dich bedencken wöllest / ob du dich des lebendigen odems essen / trinckens und ander natürlicher notturfften brauchen wöllest / Denn da wirt nichts anders auss / welchen Got zum Man geschaffenn hat / der sol und muss sein weib haben / und widerumb ein yekliches weib jren man." *Erinnerung wass denen so sich inn Ehestant begeben / zu bedencken sey* (Wittenberg, 1528) [Ox-Bod, T.L. 51.13], p. B 1 a. Menius notes that the Bible recognizes some who are "anders geschaffen," blessed by God with the special gift of chastity, but he does not elaborate.

32. "Wer aber recht sihet / dem kehret Gott das Wort um / und spricht nicht / es gehort vil in ein hauss / sonder es gehet vil auss eim hauss." Culman, *Jungen gesellen*, p. A 4 b.

33. *On the Estate of Marriage*, *LW*, 45, p. 40.

34. "Die Ee ist ein nutzs heilsams ding durch die werden die landt stet und heüser gepawen gemeret und in fride behalten. manich streyt schwer krieg und veintschafft hindergelegt und gestillet. gut frenschafft und syppe undter frembden personen gemacht und das gantz menschlich geschlecht geewigt." *Ehebüchlein*, pp. 80–81.

35. *On the Estate of Marriage*, p. 44.

36. Johann Bugenhagen, *Wye man die / so zu der Ehe greyffen / Eynleitet zu Wittenberg* (Wittenberg, 1524) [Tü fiche, 432–1173].

37. *Einleitunge der Eheleut wie sie zu Nürmberg braucht und gehalten wirdt* (Nuremberg, 1526) [Ox-Bod, T.L. 47.49].

38. "Solche leute / so landen und leuten dienen sollen / von kindheyt mussen aufferzogen werden / oder nichts werd. . . Wil man landen und leuten wol rathen und helffen. . . so muss mans warlich am ersten in der Oeconomia mit der jugent anfahen / Sol die jugent aber wol erzogen und underrichtet werden / so muss man jhr auch warlich die Gottes forcht ein-

bilden." Justus Menius, *An die hochgeborne Furstin / fraw Sibilla Herzogin zu Sachsen / Oeconomia Christiana / das ist von Christlicher Hausshaltung* (Nuremberg, 1530 [first ed., 1529]), pp. c 2 b–c 3 a.

39. The most popular of this genre, Joannes Coler(us)'s *Oeconomia ruralis et domestica*, defines "Haushaltung" as "eine sonderliche Geschicklichkeit / mit allem deme / das ein Hausswirt in und ausserhalb seines Hauses zu Erb und eigen hat / also und auff diese Weise umzugehen und zu bewähren / dass er nicht allein sich / sein Weib / Kinder / Gesinde und Viehe zur Nothdurfft ausshalten: sondern auch das Jahr durch / etwas simliches erübrigen kan / damit er folgendes Kirchen und Schulen / seinem Vatterlande / Weib und Kindern / guten Freunden / und anderen Hauss- oder sonst armen Leuten / willfahren und dienen kan." *Oeconomia ruralis et domestica. Darinn das gantz Ampt aller trewen Hauss-Vätter und Hauss-Mütter / bestandiges und allgemeines Hauss-Buch etc.* (Frankfurt, 1680), pt. I, bk.1, ch. ii, p. 2. The first edition appeared between 1593–1603 with other surviving editions in 1604, 1606, and 1645. See Julius Hoffmann, *Die "Hausväterliteratur" und die "Predigten über den christlichen Hausstand." Lehre vom Hause und Bildung für das hausliche Leben im 16., 17. und 18. Jahrhundert* (Weinheim, 1959), pp. 65–75.

40. See Ian Maclean, *The Renaissance Notion of Woman: A Study in the Fortunes of Scholasticism and Medical Science in European Intellectual Life* (Cambridge, 1980); Vern Bullough, "Medieval Medical and Scientific Views of Women," *Viator* 4 (1973): 485–501.

41. Power, *Medieval Women*, pp. 9, 16, 30.

42. Written between 1395 and 1398, Jean Gerson, *Oeuvres complètes*, VII, ed. Palemon Glorieux (Paris, 1966), 416–421.

43. *The Spiritual Exercises of St. Ignatius*, trans. A. Mottola (Garden City, N.Y., 1964), pp. 139–141.

44. James Brundage, "Carnal Delight: Canonistic Theories of Sexuality," in *Proceedings of the Fifth International Congress of Medieval Canon Law, Salamanca 21–25 Sept. 1976*, ed. Stephan Kuttner et al. (1980), p. 364.

45. According to St. Augustine, before the fall sexual intercourse occurred without lust, the organs of reproduction being activated by calm rational volition, not by uncontrollable passion, as man's will and reason were then in perfect harmony with God. *The City of God*, trans. Marcus Dods, in *A Select Library of the Nicene and Post-Nicene Fathers of the Christian Church*, II, ed. Philip Schaff (Grand Rapids, Mich., 1956), bk. 14, chs. 15–16, pp. 274–276.

46. In Yost, "The Value of Married Life," p. 36.

47. So Hartweg Dieterich, *Das Protestantische Eherecht in Deutschland bis zur Mitte des 17. Jahrhunderts* (Munich, 1970), pp. 32–33. However, to the contrary, see Olavi Lähteemäki, *Sexus und Ehe bei Luther* (1955), p. 49; and Heiko A. Oberman, *Luther: Mensch zwischen Gott und Teufel* (Berlin, 1982), p. 287. Manfred Fleischer interprets Luther's declaration "in conjugio non potest esse unkeuscheit" as a denial that sex in marriage is in any sense sinful. "The Garden of Laurentius Scholz: A Cultural Land-

mark of Late-Sixteenth Century Lutheranism," *Journal of Medieval and Renaissance Studies* 9 (1979): 43–44. On Luther's criticism of the church fathers, see *Luthers Werke im Auswahl*, 8, no. 3983 (1538), p. 209. Luther characteristically stressed the sexual sin that occurs *outside* the estate of marriage rather than that which occurs within it: "One cannot be *unmarried* without sin." Ibid., no. 244 (1532), p. 32. According to the Hutterite Ulrich Stadler, writing in 1536, "God will wink at our marital work . . . on behalf of the children and will not reckon it upon those who act in fear and discipline." Cited by Robert Friedmann, "Hutterite Marriage Practices," in *Hutterite Studies*, ed. H. S. Bender (Goshen, Ind., 1961), p. 123. For both Luther and Stadler, sexual intercourse within the proper context (marriage) and for the proper ends (procreation, avoidance of fornication) was pleasing to God and not reckoned by him to be sinful, although from the point of view of the (fallen) human participants, sex still entailed sinful elements of egoistic pleasure-seeking.

48. Thomas N. Tentler, *Sin and Confession on the Eve of the Reformation* (Princeton, 1977), pp. 224–225; Brundage, "Carnal Delight," pp. 366–367.

49. Cited in Brundage, "Carnal Delight," p. 377; see also Maclean, *The Renaissance Notion of Woman*, pp. 28–46. The authors of the *Malleus Maleficarum* (1486), the magisterial fifteenth-century guide to the detection of witches, were influenced by such sources in explaining the sexually predatory nature of women and their sexual commerce with the Devil.

50. Eleanor McLaughlin, "Equality of Souls, Inequality of Sexes: Women in Medieval Theology," in Rosemary R. Ruether, *Religion and Sexism: Images of Women in the Jewish and Christian Traditions* (New York, 1974), p. 241.

51. "Wann eeliche werck beschehen wider rechte ordnung und ausserhalb der stet die die natur darzu geordnet hat. Oder auch in solicher mainung daz verhindert werd die empfahung der frucht / und das ist allweg tötlich. Zu den anderen wann sich ein tail an jm selbs beflecken ist durch greiffung oder berurung des anderen." *Ain püchlein von der erkanntnuss der Sünd und auch ettlicher tugent* (Augsburg, 1494) [B.M., IA 6635], p. C 4 b.

52. Ibid., pp. C 4 b–C 5 a.

53. Nikolas Paulus, "Mittelalterliche Stimmen über den Eheorden," *Historisch-politische Blätter für das katholische Deutschland* 141 (1908): 1008–1024. See also Yost's discussion of William Harrington's *Commendacion of Matrymony*, whose fourth rule required married couples to abstain from sex during Lent, Rogation days, holy days and nights, menstruation, and pregnancy. "The Value of Married Life," p. 28.

54. Brundage, "Carnal Delight," p. 383.

55. Hans-Friedrich Rosenfeld and Hellmut Rosenfeld, *Deutsche Kultur im Spätmittelalter* (Wiesbaden, 1978), pp. 130–131. On women in the printing industry of late medieval Strasbourg, see Chrisman, *Lay Culture, Learned Culture*, pp. 22–23.

56. *Das Buch Weinsberg*, V, 250–251.

57. Erich Maschke, *Die Familie in der deutschen Stadt des späten Mit-*

telalters (Heidelberg, 1980), pp. 35–41; Power, *Medieval Women*, pp. 53–62; Natalie Davis, "City Women and Religious Change in Sixteenth Century France," in *A Sampler of Women's Studies*, ed. Dorothy G. McGuigan (Ann Arbor, 1973), pp. 21–22.

58. Rosenfeld, *Deutsche Kultur im Spätmittelalter*, p. 130; Steven Ozment, *The Age of Reform 1250–1550* (New Haven, 1980), pp. 91–92.

59. Mary M. McLaughlin, "Survivors and Surrogates: Children and Parents from the Ninth to the Thirteenth Centuries," in *The History of Childhood*, ed. Lloyd De Mause (New York, 1974), 129–133.

60. Cited by James B. Ross, "The Middle-Class Child in Urban Italy, Fourteenth to Early Sixteenth Century," in De Mause, *History of Childhood*, p. 206.

61. Of the many articles on this subject, see especially the now classic studies of Lucien Febvre, "The Origins of the French Reformation: A Badly-Put Question?" in *A New Kind of History and Other Essays*, ed. Peter Burke (New York, 1973), pp. 44–107; and Bernd Moeller, "Piety in Germany around 1500," in *The Reformation in Medieval Perspective*, ed. Steven Ozment (Chicago, 1971), pp. 50–75.

62. The appeal to women of nontraditional religious movements is discussed by Patrick Collinson, "The Role of Women in the English Reformation, Illustrated by the Life and Friendships of Anne Locke," *Studies in Church History* 2 (1965): 258–272; Nancy L. Roelker, "The Appeal of Calvinism to French Noblewomen in the Sixteenth Century," *Journal of Interdisciplinary History* 2 (1972): 391–418; Miriam Chrisman, "Women and the Reformation in Strasbourg 1490–1530," *Archiv für Reformationsgeschichte* 63 (1972): 143–168; Davis, "City Women and Religious Change," pp. 28–38; Jane D. Douglass, "Women and the Continental Reformation," in Ruether, *Religion and Sexism*, pp. 292–318. See also note 70 below.

63. See, for example, David B. Miller, "The Dissolution of the Religious Houses of Hesse during the Reformation" (Ph.D. diss., Yale University, 1971).

64. Lawrence Stone, *The Family, Sex and Marriage in England 1500–1800*, abbrev. ed. (New York, 1977), p. 38. Suzanne Wemple has made an impressive argument for the cloister as an alternative way of life with a new dignity and degree of autonomy previously unknown by married women in early medieval Frankish Society. *Women in Frankish Society: Marriage and the Cloister 500–900* (Philadelphia, 1981), pp. 157, 163, 190–191. Wemple's argument is not, however, a general one, and what may have been true for central Europe in the sixth and seventh centuries was not true on the eve of the Reformation.

65. Power, *Medieval Women*, pp. 89–91, 99.

66. McLaughlin, "Equality of Souls," p. 260.

67. Davis, "City Women and Religious Change," p. 38.

68. *Das Buch Weinsberg*, I, 127–128.

69. McLaughlin, "Equality of Souls," 241–244.

70. Gottfried Koch, *Frauenfrage und Ketzertum in Mittelalter: Die*

Frauenbewegung im Rahmen des Katharismus und des Waldensertums und ihre sozialen Wurzeln (12.–14. Jahrhundert) (Berlin, 1962); Claire Cross, " 'Great Reasoners in Scripture': The Activities of Women Lollards 1380–1530," in *Medieval Women*, ed. Derek Baker (Oxford, 1978), pp. 359–380; Keith Thomas, "Women and the Civil War Sects," *Past and Present* 13 (1958): 42–62.

71 ."Das man frawen klöster lass schulen sein der zucht ains christlichen wäsens, auch das man do selbst die kinde auff haushalten und arbeit ziehe, allso ob sie ein mol eefrawen werden das sie wissen hauss zu halten." *Ein Vermanung aller Christen das sie sich erbarmen uber die Klosterfrawen* in *Johann Eberlin von Günzburg. Sämtliche Schriften*, 1, ed. Ludwig Enders (Halle, 1896), 30. It was a common theme of Protestant pamphleteers that neither the Bible nor human experience recommended vows of celibacy. Exposés of the impossible ideals of the cloistered life abounded in the first half of the sixteenth century. Two of the best examples of this lively and often entertaining genre from the 1520s, especially revealing of the depths of lay anticlericalism, are Hans Sachs, *Eyn gesprech von den Scheinwercken der Gaistlichen / und yhren gelubde* (Nuremberg, 1524) [Yale, Beineke Library]; and the anonymous *Ayn freüntlichs gesprech / zwischen eynem Parfusser münch . . . und einem Löffelmacher* (n.p., n.d.) [Ox-Bod, T.L. 84.20].

72. Georg Buchwald, *D.M. Luther. Ein Lebensbild für das deutsche Haus* (Leipzig, 1902), pp. 341–346; Roland Bainton, *Here I Stand* (New York, 1950), pp. 224–226.

73. "Den hohisten kampff, nemlich umb die iungfrawschafft zu streytten / da kaumet und gar selten auch die ihenigen bestehen die mit gottis wortt allenhalben gerust und mit hoher seltzamer wunderbarlichen gnad erhaben sind." *Ursach und anttwort das iungkfrawen kloster gottlich verlassen mugen* (Wittenberg, 1523) [Tü fiche, 14–60], p. A 3 b.

74. "Eyn weybs bild ist nicht geschaffen iungfraw tzu seyn / sonder kinder zu tragen." Ibid., p. A 4 b. Declaring that only one nun in a thousand performed her cloistered chores "happily, *mit lust*, and uncoerced," Luther concluded that if a girl must do something she dislikes and that gives her no joy, it is better that she do it in the estate of marriage, where she at least serves her fellow man, that is, her husband, children, servants, and neighbors. Ibid.

75. *Ain schöner Sendtbrieff des Wolgebornen und Edeln Herrn Johannsen Herrn zu Schwartzenberg / An Bischoff (Weyganden) zu Bamberg aussgangen / Darinn er treffenliche und Christenliche ursachen anzaygt / wie und warumb er seyn Tochter auss dem Closter daselbst (zum Hayligen Grab genannt) hinweg gefürt / und wider unter seyn vätterlichen schutz und ober handt zu sich genommen hat. Ain vorred darinn die Münch jres zukünfftigen undtergangs erinnert / und ernstlich gewarnet werden. Andreas Osiander* (Nuremberg, 1524) [Ox-Bod, T.L. 38.170]. On Schwartzenberg and Bishop Weigand, see Werner Zeissner, *Altkirchliche Kräfte in Bamberg unter Bischof Weigand von Redwitz (1522–1556)* (Bamberg, 1975), pp. 73–75.

76. *Ain schöner Sendtbrieff . . . Johannsen . . . zu Schwartzenberg,* p. B 2 b. Although Schwartzenberg insisted that he was still loyal to the bishop and expressed the hope that the bishop would not hold the assault on the cloister against him, Osiander published the letter as a general exposé of cloisters and a rallying cry for other fathers with daughters in cloisters.

77. "Underweyset . . . mit senfftmütigen gayst . . . darumb hatt es kain reümen mitt dem steuppen / mit dem schlagen / mit dem disciplinen / mit dem strōen krentzlen / mit dem grossen und klain bann / mit dem kerckern / stocken und blocken / Gott geb euch allen seyn gayst / der senffmütigkait / guttigkait / und barmhertzigkeit." Noricus Philadelphus, *Wie alle Clöster und sonderlich Junckfrawen Clöster in ain Christlichs wesen möchten durch gottes gnade gebracht werden* (1524) [Tü fiche, 291–844], p. B 1 b.

78. Ibid., p. B 2 b.

79. The secular magistrates are described as protectors not only of the laity, but of the religious as well: "Als die / Amptlewtten oder Fürstlichen oberkaiten / nach götlichem Rechten ordenliche richter unnd obern nit allain der layen / sonder auch der vermaynten gaystligkait seynd." Ibid., p. C 2 a.

80. Ibid., p. C 3 a.

81. Ibid., p. C 1 a.

82. "Als ich 14. jar alt / und mein gemüt und geschickligkayt begund zu fulen unnd erkennen / befand ich / das gaystlicher stand aller meiner geschickligkeit und nattur entgegen / und als / das meiner seelen saligkait mir were zu halten unmüglich." *Ain Geschichte wie Got ainer Erbarn closter Junckfrawen aussgeholffen hatt. Mit ainem Sendtbrief Doct. Mar. Luther / An die Graffen zu Manssfeldt* (Wittenberg, 1524) [Ox-Bod, T.L. 96.10], p. B 1 a.

83. "Ich were nun eingesegnet / und hette gott durch die opfferung des Ringes / ewige raynigkait verhayssen und geschworn . . . kündt mich auch kayn Bapst noch Bischoff darvon absolviern." Ibid., p. B 1 a.

84. "Wenn ich gleych vill gefraget / hette ich doch nicht anders / denn was sy gerne gehört / dürffen sagen." Ibid., p. B 2 b.

85. "Saget mir die domina . . . ich möchte mich nun under allen meyner mitschwestern füsse / wie ain gefangene / der man fort weder getrawen noch glauben wurde." Ibid., p. B 3 a.

86. "Wie schmählich / schämlich / lesterlich und hönisch ich da von jr (die domina) und andern aussgericht / ist nicht vor frümen lewtten zu reden oder zu schreyben." Ibid., p. B 3 a.

87. *Der Durchleuthtigen hochgebornen F. Ursulen / Hertzogin zu Monsterberg etc. Grefin zu Glotz etc. Christlichs ursach des verlassen Klosters zu Freyberg* (Wittenberg, 1528) [Tü fiche, 292–846], p. A 3 a.

88. Ibid., p. C 2 a.

89. Ibid., pp. F 2 a–b.

90. "Welches bekentnis auch Gott hat gewircket yn den aller schwechesten werckgezeugen / nemlich ynn den iungfrawen und weibern / die natürlicher art eines schwachen / weichen und unbestendigen

gemütes sind gewesen / wie wir / welchs uns Gott auch geben kan." Ibid., P. D 3 a.

91. *Ain Sendtbrieff von ainer erbern frawen im Eelichen stand / an ain Klosterfrawen / gethon über berümung ettlicher hayliger geschrifft in Sermon begriffen / So die Klosterfraw verbrent / und darauff ain lange ungesaltzne geschrifft zu ursach erzelt hat* (n.p, n.d.) [Tü fiche, 170–466], p. D 2 a.

92. Ibid., pp. D 1 a–b.

93. *Ain Sendtbrieff an ettlich closterfrawen zu sant Katherina und zu sant Niclas in Augspurg* (1523) [Tü fiche, 225–632], pp. A 3 a–b.

94. Ibid., p. A 4 a.

95. "Ir kündt nitt speculieren unnd ain rechts anschawlichs leben fieren, dann ir seyt nit gelert." Ibid., p A 4 a.

96. "Ain eefraw / die jrem kindlin altag seine windelen weschet / den brey einstreicht / jren hausswurt zu essen gibt / die kinder im schwayss irs angesichts ernört / die würt euch vor lauffen / sy vertrawt allain auff Christum / ist nit hochfertig vermaint durch jr arbayt nit frumm zu werden sonder durch glauben in Christum / unnd jre werck thut sy jrem nechsten zu gutt / bekennt jr sünd / vertrauwt der barmhertzigkeit gottes / und last got in allen dingen / sein err." Ibid., p. B 2 a.

97. "Du darffst dich gantz nichts kümmern umb unser leib und sel / du darfst für uns nit gen himel noch gen hell faren." *Antwurt zwayer Closter frawen im Katheriner Closter zu Augspurg / an Bernhart Remen / Und hernach seyn gegen Antwurt* (Augsburg, 1523) [Ox-Bod, T.L. 31.183], pp. A 2 a–A 3 a. A similar exchange, between a contented cloistered sister and her apparently Lutheran brother, who accuses her of believing that salvation is gained by cowls, holy orders, prayers, and fasting, is recorded in a vernacular pamphlet, *Anntwurt auf den sendbrieff / ainer vermainten gaistlichen klosterfrawen / der von Mariestain aussganngen / kloster leben und gelübdt / betreffennde* (1524) [Ox-Bod, T.L. 38.159]. Better known is the resistance of a convent of nuns of the Order of St. Claire in Geneva to Calvinist efforts to dissolve them, preserved in the chronicle of Jeanne de Jussié (1526–35). *Le levain du calvinisme, ou Commencement de l'hérésie de Genève* (Cambery, 1611; reprinted, Geneva, 1865). See also Jane D. Douglass, "Women and the Continental Reformation," in Ruether, *Religion and Sexism*, pp. 292–318.

98. "Nach dem du dich / auss deynem Closter / ynn Leyen kleydern / wie ein tantzmeydlein / ghen Wittenberg auff die hoheschule begeben / Dich alda nach eynem Ratzschen knecht umgesehen / mit dem Luther (wie man sagt) in schnöde und offenliche untzucht gelebt / yhn auch entlich zu eynem Manne genommen / hast / Dardurch du also an deynem breuttigam Christo / mit gelubdbruchiger unehe / trewlosz / und meynedig worden bist." *Ein Sendtbrieff Kethen von Bhore Luthers vormeynthem eheweybe sampt eynem geschenck freuntlicher meynung tzuvorfertigt.* (Leipzig, 1528) [Tü fiche, 64–165], p. A 3 b.

99. Ibid., p. A 4 a–b.

100. Ibid., pp. C 1 b–C 2 a.

101. "Die sünde und schalckheyt ist meyn / meyn / meyn ist sie / Dergleichen miszhandlung ist nicht under den Menschen / Dann dis ist ein erschreckliche und scheuszliche Gotlossheyth." *Ibid.*, p. D 3 b.

102. *Eyn schöne underrichtung was die recht Ewangelisch geystlicheit sy / und was man von den Clösteren halten soll* (Cologne, 1528) [Tü fiche, 291–843], p. E 4 a.

103. On the strong family ties between aristocrats and convents in Strasbourg, see Thomas A. Brady, Jr., *Ruling Class, Regime and Reformation at Strasbourg, 1520–1555* (Leiden, 1978), p. 223. Such a tie also existed between the Weinsberg family of Cologne, who were petty bourgeois, and the small Franciscan convent Maria of Bethelehem, discussed below.

104. See, for example, the Bern religious ordinance. *Gemayn Reformation: und verbesserung der bisshergebrachten verwendten Gotsdiensten / und Ceremonien* (1528) [B.M., 3906.bb.88], arts. 7, 12. Especially revealing of the thoughtful steps taken to suppress cloisters with the least possible disruption and injustice to all concerned was the ordinance of Philip of Hesse, *Was der Durchleuchtig hochgeporn Fürst und Herr / Herr Philips Landtgraffe zu Hessen . . . mit den Closterpersonen / Pfarrherrn / und abgöttischen bildnussen / in seyner gnaden Fürstenthümbe . . . furgenummen hat (1528)* [B.M. 1226.a.79].

105. "Nonnen odder Begynen sol man nicht mehr machen." Johannes Bugenhagen, *Was man von closter leben halten sol am allermeist fur die Nonnen und Begynen geschrieben aus der heiligen schrifft* (1529) [B.M.], pp. H 2 b–H 4 a.

106. Compare, however, the argument of H. C. Erik Midelfort, "Protestant Monastery? A Reformation Hospital in Hesse," in *Reformation Principle and Practice: Essays in Honour of A. G. Dickens*, ed. Peter N. Brooks (London, 1980), pp. 71–94.

107. See Köhler, *Zürcher ehegericht*, pp. 1–2; Wendel, *Le mariage à Strasbourg*, pp. 71–72.

108. The categories were: informal and overlong engagement; seduction by a man who admitted breach of promise; a woman's breaching of an informal engagement; a man's breaching of an informal engagement; seduction by a man who denied having promised marriage; termination of informal engagement at the request of both partners; recognition of presumptive marriages, that is, relationships involving engagement and sexual intercourse "out of sight of the church." Beatrice Gottlieb, "The Meaning of Clandestine Marriage," in *Family and Sexuality in French History*, ed. Robert Wheaton and Tamara K. Hareven, pp. 57–65.

109. Wendel, *Le mariage à Strasbourg*, pp. 71–72.

110. Payne, *Erasmus*, p. 118.

111. Wendel, *Le mariage à Strasbourg*, p. 107.

112. Lucid summaries can be found in Adrian Staehelin, *Die Einführung der Ehescheidung in Basel zur Zeit der Reformation* (Basel, 1957), pp. 4–11; and Wendel, *Le mariage à Strasbourg*, pp. 26–30.

113. As Gottlieb has pointed out, Gratian held both that secret marriages "are not denied to be marriages" and that such marriages are "prohibited." "Meaning of Clandestine Marriage," pp. 50–52.

114. James Brundage, "Concubinage and Marriage in Medieval Canon Law," *Journal of Medieval History* 1 (1975): 7.

115. Staehelin, *Die Einführung der Ehescheidung in Basel*, pp. 4–5.

116. Ibid., pp. 8–9. See also Christian Gellinek, "Marriage by Consent in the Literary Sources of Germany," *Studia Gratiana. Collectanea Stephan Kuttner II*, 12 (1967): 558–576.

117. Maschke, *Die Familie in der deutschen Stadt*, p. 42.

118. Wheaton, "Recent Trends," p. 9.

119. Staehelin, *Die Einführung der Ehescheidung in Basel*, p. 11.

120. "Es erzeight sich auch wol her nach wen die kuss / wuchen fur ist / und kranckheyt die Spiegel und Schaufal umbwendt / was verharlicher treuw ynn dem lust Elichs wesens gefunden wirt." *Eyn Sermon in dem deutlich angezeigt und gelert ist die Pfaffen Ee / yn Evangelischer leer nitt zu der freiheyt des fleischs / und zu bekrefftygen den allten Adam . . . gefundiert* (Erfurt, 1523) [Tü fiche, 290–838], p. B 3 a.

121. "Hieraus so zwo junge person / heimlich on wissen und willen der Eltern / jnn ungehorsam / in unverstandener jugend / inn einer trunckenen weis / durch ergen mutwillen / durch betrug / durch kupplerey / durch hinderlistig schmeichelwort / odder andere unbilliche mittel / sich zusamen Ehelich verbunden / wer wolt nicht sagen / das solch verbündnus mehr von dem Satan / dann von unserm Herrn Gott geschehen were?" *Wie in Ehesachen / und inn den fellen / so sich derhalben / zu tragen / nach Götlichen billichen Rechten / Christenlich zu handeln sey. Mit Vorrhede Mart. Luthers* (Wittenberg, 1531) [Ox-Bod, T.L. 57.33], p. B 4 a.

122. Ibid., pp. B 2 a–b, C 2 a, C 3 a–b.

123. *De regno Christi*, in *Melanchthon and Bucer*, ed. and trans. Wilhelm Pauck (Philadelphia, 1969), p. 320.

124. Ibid., p. 322.

125. *A Christian Directory* (London, 1673), in Irwin, *Womanhood in Radical Protestantism*, p. 118.

126. Wendel, *Le mariage à Strasbourg*, pp. 106–109.

127. Dieterich, *Das protestantische Eherecht*, pp. 150–152.

128. Wendel, *Le mariage à Strasbourg*, pp. 77–78; Karl Koch, *Studium Pietatis. Martin Bucer als Ethiker* (Neukirchen, 1962), pp. 135–137; Gottfried Seebass, *Das reformatorische Werk des Andreas Osiander* (Nuremberg, 1967), pp. 184–185; Judith W. Harvey, "The Influence of the Reformation on Nuremberg Marriage Laws, 1520–1535" (Ph.D. diss., Ohio State University, 1972), pp. 98–100.

129. See Karl Holl, "Luther und das landesherrliche Kirchenregiment," in *Gesammelte Aufsätze zur Kirchengeschichte*, I (Tubingen, 1923), 326–380.

130. Dieterich, *Das protestantische Eherecht*, pp. 86–90.

131. Wendel, *Le mariage à Strasbourg*, p. 87.

132. *Ein new Apologia unnd verantworrtung Martini Luthers wyder der Papisten Mortgeschrey* ([Bamberg], 1523), in *Flugschriften aus den ersten Jahren der Reformation*, II, ed. Otto Clemen (Nieuwkoop, 1967), p. 160.

133. Dieterich, *Das protestantische Eherecht*, pp. 54–55.

134. Koch, *Studium Pietatis*, pp. 135, 147, 151.
135. Wendel, *Le mariage à Strasbourg*, pp. 79, 114.
136. Köhler, *Zürcher ehegericht*, pp. 35–40.
137. Ibid., p. 66.
138. Ibid., pp. 43–48.
139. Ibid., pp. 49–52.
140. Ibid., pp. 144–145.
141. Ibid., p. 85; for Nuremberg, see Harvey "Influence of the Reformation on Nuremberg Marriage Laws," pp. 24, 84–89.
142. *Die Ordnungen und erkandnussen / wie hinfür zu Zürich in der Statt über Eelich sachen gerich sol werden* (Zurich, 1525) [Ox-Bod, 8.K.31.Art.BS], pp. A 5 a–b.
143. Köhler, *Zürcher ehegericht*, p. 62.
144. Ibid., p. 85.
145. Ibid., p. 89.
146. Harvey, "Influence on the Reformation on Nuremberg Marriage Laws," p. 198.
147. *That Parents Should Neither Compel Nor Hinder the Marriage of Their Children, and That Children Should Not Become Engaged Without the Consent of Their Parents, LW*, 45, p. 384.
148. Gottlieb, "Meaning of Clandestine Marriage," p. 72.
149. Ibid., p. 71.
150. *Das Buch Weinsberg*, I, 32.
151. Ibid., II, 149–150, 159–160.
152. See below, chapter 4.
153. *Das Buch Weinsberg*, I, 257–258.
154. Ibid., I, 277.
155. Köhler, *Zürcher ehegericht*, pp. 74–76. The Augsburg marriage ordinance required for all valid marriages the counsel and permission of parents or guardian, or if these did not exist, of at least two blood relatives, or, these not existing, of three "honorable, pious, and honest persons." *Ains Erbern Rats / der Stat Augspurg Zucht und Pollicey Ordnung*, pp. B 3 b–B 4 a. An imperial ordinance of 1540, issued to regulate the moral life of Brussels and Flanders, required that girls be twenty and boys twenty-five before marrying without parental permission. *Ordnung / Statuten und Edict / Keiser Carols des fünfften / publiciert in der namhafften Stat Brüssel / in beisein irer Mayestet Schwester und Königin / Gubernant und Regent seiner Niderland* (1540) [Ox-Bod, T.L. 67.12b]. The Zurich ordinance, however, permitted orphaned children without parents or guardians to betroth themselves if a girl was fourteen and a boy sixteen years of age.
156. Köhler, *Zürcher ehegericht*, pp. 138–139.
157. Ibid., pp. 90, 98–100, 102–103.
158. "So söllent diejenigen, weliche fürhin vor dem offentlichen Kilchgang sich mit einanderen fleischlich vermischend, jedes insonderheit zächen pfund gelts zu buss geben, wer die buss nit hete, dieselb mit gfangenschaft abbüssen." Ibid., p. 104. Comments Köhler: "So schob sich jetzt der Kirchgang zwischen Eheabschluss und Ehekonsummierung.

'Bestätigung' blieb er, aber seine Relevanz wird die höchste, die unter dieser Voraussetzung möglich war." Ibid., p. 105.

159. "Dhweil bey ainem Christenlichen Volck / die hailig Ee /ye nit anderst / dann mit aller Forcht des allmechtigen Gots unnd Andacht / gehanndelt und volzogen werden solle / so wil ain Erber Rat / Das menigklich / die sich Eelich zusamen versprochen haben / ee unnd Sy solche versprochne Ee würcklich volziehen / zuvor den Segen und Ermanung auss dem Wort Gottes / vor der Gemaind Christi / in irer Pfarrkirchen / mit aller Zucht und Gotsforcht (Bey vermeidung ains Erbern Rats ernnstliche Straff) suchen / und empfahen." *Ains Erbern Rats / der Stat Augspurg / Zucht und Pollicey Ordnung*, p. C 1 a. For Nuremberg, see Harvey, "Influence of the Reformation on Nuremberg Marriage Laws," pp. 56–61.

160. E. William Monter, "The Consistory of Geneva, 1559–1569," in *Renaissance, Reformation, Resurgence: Papers and Responses Presented at the Colloquium on Calvin & Calvin Studies . . . April 22 & 23, 1976*, ed. Peter De Klerk (Grand Rapids, Mich., 1976), p. 68. Reprinted in *Bibliotheque d'Humanisme et Renaissance*, 38 (1976): 476–484.

161. In Augsburg adultery and forcible rape/seduction were punished by a mandatory four weeks in prison, at least eight days of which had to be served "with the body," while the other weeks could be served by payment of three gulden per day. The penalty was doubled at a second offense, and a third offense brought either exile or "severe punishment" in property, body, and/or life, as the Rat deemed. *Ains Erbern Rats / der Stat Augspurg / Zucht und Pollicey Ordnung*, p. C 2 a.

162. Wendel, *Le mariage à Strasbourg* p. 114; David Hunt, *Parents and Children in History: The Psychology of Family Life in Early Modern France* (New York, 1970), pp. 61–62.

163. According to an ordinance of 1687. Köhler, *Zürcher ehegericht*, pp. 104, 107.

164. "Damit sy not wurde betrogen, wie vil ist geschehen." Ibid., p. 104.

165. Staehelin, *Die Einführung der Ehescheidung in Basel*, pp. 42–43.

166. Köhler, *Zürcher ehegericht*, pp. 76–77. When a mother and father were divided on approval of their children's marriage, the board respected the father's wishes.

167. Thomas Robisheaux, "Peasants and Pastors: Rural Youth Control and the Reformation in Hohenlohe, 1540–1680," *Social History* 6 (1981): 281–300.

168. J. Hajnal, "European Marriage Patterns in Perspective," in D. V. Glass and D. E. L. Eversley, *Population in History: Essays in Historical Demography* (1965), pp. 101–146; Jean-Louis Flandrin, *Families in Former Times: Kinship, Household and Sexuality* (Cambridge, 1979), p. 53. The figures were reflected in the marriages of the Weinsberg family in sixteenth-century Cologne. Hermann von Weinsberg's parents married in 1517 when his father was twenty-eight and his mother nineteen (*Das Buch Weinsberg*, I, 17). Hermann was considered "too young" at twenty-five, when he was still a

student and not yet self-supporting, although his father attempted to arrange a marriage for him with a forty-eight-year-old widow when he was twenty-six (ibid., I, 198, 209). Hermann married his first wife when he was thirty and she thirty-six; his sister Catherine married for the first time at twenty-three a man of forty (ibid., I, p. 286).

169. Dieterich, *Das protestantische Eherecht*, pp. 95–96. In Thomas More's *Utopia*, men married at twenty-two, women at eighteen. (Noonan, *Contraception*, p. 422). In fifteenth-century Florence and Tuscany women married between seventeen and eighteen, well below Hajnal's late-marriage pattern. David Herlihy, "Deaths, Marriages, Births and the Tuscan Economy (ca. 1300–1550)," in Herlihy, *Cities and Society in Medieval Italy* (London, 1981), pp. 135–164; and Christiane Klapisch and Michel Demonet, " 'A uno pane e uno vino': The Rural Tuscan Family at the Beginning of the 15th century," in *Selections from the Annales*, ed. Robert Forster and Orest Ranum (Baltimore, 1976), pp. 41–63. On the age of majority in the empire, see above, note 155. Lawrence Stone finds women marrying at twenty in late-sixteenth-century England. *Family, Sex, and Marriage in England*, pp. 40–44.

170. Harvey, "Influence of the Reformation on Nuremberg Marriage Laws," p. 219.

171. Wendel, *Le mariage à Strasbourg*, p. 104.

172. Staehelin, *Die Einführung der Ehescheidung in Basel*, p. 45.

173. *Die Ordnungen und erkandnussen / wie hinfür zu Zürich in der Statt über Eelich sachen gerich sol werden*, p. A 5 a; Köhler, *Zürcher ehegericht*, pp. 74, 77.

174. Harvey, "Influence of the Reformation on Nuremberg Marriage Laws," pp. 195–219.

175. Wendel, *Le mariage à Strasbourg*, p. 106.

176. Dieterich, *Das protestantische Eherecht*, p. 58; Staehelin, *Die Einführung der Ehescheidung in Basel*, p. 45.

177. "Doch zu kainem Hayrat / der jnen unangenem / oder unanmutig und zuwider were / müssigen / noch zwinngen / Sonder in dem allem / der iungen / frommen und wolfart / der Personen und Guts halben / auf das trewlichest ansehen unnd fürdern." *Ains Erbern Rats / der Stat Augspurg / Zucht un Pollicey Ordnung*, p. B 4 a.

178. Power, *Medieval Women*, pp. 40–41. Parental pressure was obviously very influential. Bartholomäus Sastrow, Lutheran burghermeister of Stralsund, recounted the reluctant capitulation of his brother Johannes, at the time twenty-nine years old, to their parents' opposition to his marriage to a Schwäbisch girl he had fallen in love with. When the parents later reconsidered and agreed to the marriage, the girl in question had already married another (suggesting that their original judgment might have been the correct one). Ursula Brosthaus, *Bürgerleben im 16. Jahrhundert. Die Autobiographie des Stralsunder Bürgermeisters Bartholomäus Sastrow als kulturgeschichtliche Quelle* (Cologne, 1972), p. 54.

179. Martin Bucer advised children who were of age and seeking to make honorable vows, but arbitrarily impeded from doing so by their

parents, to resist, first by warnings and prayers, then by the urging of relatives and friends, then by the presbyters of the church. If all these failed, they should appeal to the magistrates, "lest anyone by the wickedness of his parents be either kept from marriage longer than is fair or driven to a less acceptable marriage." *De regno Christi,* in Pauck, *Melanchthon and Bucer,* p. 323.

180. *That Parents Should Neither Compel Nor Hinder the Marriage of Their Children, LW,* 45, pp. 388–389.

181. Ibid., p. 392.

182. Ibid., p. 390–391.

183. See also Zwingli, *Uber die gevatterschaft das sy die Ee nit hyndren sol noch mag* (Zurich, 1525).

184. *That Parents Should Neither Compel Nor Hinder the Marriage of Their Children,* p. 392.

185. *Luthers Werke in Auswahl,* 8, no. 185 (1532), p. 28. In another tabletalk, Luther opposed parents coercing their children into unwanted marriages, remembering when "we once here [in Wittenberg] permitted two youth to marry against the will of [the boy's] parents. The bridegroom was an honorable and wealthy fellow, his bride poor and happy to marry him, but the [boy's] father refused. [When the boy said] 'I must have her in the house,' [the father] responded, 'There are many servants here; choose another.' And they married." Ibid., no. 5441 (1542), p. 302.

186. *Thomas Platter. Lebensbeschreibung,* ed. Alfred Hartmann (Basel, 1944), pp. 87–90. A variety of sixteenth-century diaries are exerpted in *Die Autobiographie des späten Mittelalters und der frühen Neuzeit,* I, II, ed. Horst Wenzel (Munich, 1980).

187. John T. Noonan, Jr. "Power to Choose," *Viator* 4 (1973): 419–434; Flandrin, *Families in Former Times,* pp. 130–131.

188. Charles Donahue, Jr., "The Policy of Alexander III's Consent Theory of Marriage," in *Proceedings of the Fourth International Congress of Medieval Canon Law, Toronto,* ed. Stephan Kuttner et al. (1978), pp. 259, 277.

189. Roger Mols, S.J., "Population in Europe 1500–1700," in *The Fontana Economic History of Europe: The Sixteenth and Seventeenth Centuries,* ed. Carlo M. Cipolla (Glasgow, 1974), p. 47. Bartholomäus Sastrow reports frequent sexual indiscipline among Stralsund's burghers, alleging only one sexual lapse of his own, a love affair with a concubine while on a business trip to Rome. Brosthaus, *Bürgerleben im 16. Jahrhundert,* p. 57.

190. Brundage, "Concubinage and Marriage," p. 8.

191. Robert M. Kingdon, "The Control of Morals by the Earliest Calvinists," in De Klerk, *Renaissance, Reformation, Resurgence,* p. 98.

192. Hunt, *Parents and Children in History,* pp. 60–62.

193. Robisheaux, "Peasants and Pastors," p. 282.

194. Köhler, *Zürcher ehegericht,* pp. 148–152.

195. Flandrin, *Families in Former Times,* p. 133.

196. *Von der Kinderzucht / Auss dem Evangelio Luce 2. Lehr und Vermanung Durch Vitum Dietrich* (Nuremberg, 1566 [= 1546]), in *Etliche*

Schrifften für den gemeinen man / von unterricht Christlicher lehr und leben / unnd zum trost der engstigen gewissen. Durch V. Dietrich . . . (Nürnberg M.D. XLVIII), ed. Oskar Reichmann (Assen, 1972), p. 117.

197. Flandrin, *Families in Former Times*, pp. 24–26.

198. "Ein theils biss in das sibet gelide / eins theils / biss in das zehent und noch weiter / so verne man sie nur wissen und ausrechnen könne." Andreas Osiander, *Von den verpoten heiratten und blutschanden / underricht* (Nuremberg, 1537) [Ox-Bod, Vet. D 1 e. 120(6)], p. B 1 b. Johannes Brenz felt that the traditional prohibitions reached only to the fourth degree but shared Osiander's criticism of many additional arbitrary and irrational cases: "Verboten der gevatterschafft / der weyhe / und der gelübde halben / aus keinem grund des Göttlichen worts." *Wie in Ehesachen*, p. E 1 a.

199. "Hat er [the pope] villeicht ein auffsehens gehabt auff das gelt und nutzung der kisten / Daher hat er etlich grad verboten / aber wenn man gelt hat geben / so sind sie widerümb auffgelösst worden." Ibid.

200. J. J. Scarisbrick, *Henry VIII* (Berkeley, 1968), chs. 7 and 8.

201. Wendel, *Le mariage à Strasbourg*; pp. 125–143; Luther, *On the Babylonian Captivity of the Church*, in *Three Treatises: Martin Luther* (Philadelphia, 1960), pp. 226–232 (= *Luthers Werke in Auswahl*, I, ed. Otto Clemen [Berlin, 1959], 490–494); *On the Estate of Marriage*, *LW*, 45, pp. 22–30.

202. *On the Babylonian Captivity of the Church*. p. 226.

203. *On the Estate of Marriage*, *LW*, 45, pp. 22–23.

204. *On the Babylonian Captivity of the Church*, p. 228. In 1530 Zurich forbade a man to marry his mother, stepmother, halfsister or stepsister, granddaughter, sister, aunt, aunt-in-law, daughter-in-law, sister-in-law, stepdaughter, daughters of stepchildren, and daughters of his sister-in-law; a woman was forbidden to marry her father, stepfather, stepbrother, grandson, brother, uncle, uncle-in-law, son-in-law, brother-in-law, stepson, sons of stepchildren, and sons of her brother-in-law. Köhler, *Zürcher ehegericht*, p. 80.

205. *On the Estate of Marriage*, p. 24.

206. Ibid., p. 25.

207. *On the Babylonian Captivity of the Church*, p. 229; *On the Estate of Marriage*, p. 26. Kettenbach also decried the foolishness of a penance that required an adulterous spouse to abstain from sexual relations with his or her mate, apparently a common punishment of adulterers by confessors. *Ein Sermon bruoder . . . Kettenbach zu der loblichen statt Ulm zu eynem valete* (Bamberg, 1523), in Clemen, *Flugschriften aus den ersten Jahren der Reformation*, II, 113.

208. *On the Estate of Marriage*, p. 26; *How Confession Should Be Made* (1520), *LW*, 39, p. 45 (= *WA*, 2, pp. 59–65).

209. "Faren also (die gmelten falschen hailigen) zu / stellen sich als könten sie nun sonst nicht weiber finden dann unter der blutfreundtschafft / greiffen nicht allein zu denen / die der Bapst allein verpotten hat (das sie doch etlicher mass wol fug und recht hetten) sonder auch zu denen die Got selbs verpoten hat . . . Sonderlich aber volget schon diser un-

christlicher grewl daraus / dieweil hurerey und ehepruch vorhin so gar gemein / und leider an allen orten all zu vil ungestrafft sein / das Weiber und töchter under den blutfreunden / da jr zucht / ehr und keuschheit billich am besten verwart sein solt / schier am aller wenigisten sicher sein." *Von den verpoten heiratten und blutschanden / underricht* (Nuremberg, 1537) [Ox-Bod, Vet. D e. 120(6)], p. A 3 a.

210. Cited by Harvey, "Influence of the Reformation on Nuremberg Marriage Laws," p. 241; Seebass, *Das reformatorische Werk des Andreas Osiander*, p. 191.

211. *Von der verpotten heiratten*, pp. D 3 b–D 4 b.

212. Ibid.

213. Wendel, *Le mariage à Strasbourg*, pp. 137–142.

214. Thomas Max Safley, "Marital Litigation in the Diocese of Constance 1551–1620," *Sixteenth Century Journal* 12 (1981): 61–78.

215. See chapter 2.

2. Husbands and Wives

1. Menius, *An die hochgeborne Fürstin / fraw Sibilla Herzogin zu Sachsen*, pp. C 3 b, C 6 b; *Erinnerung wass denen so sich inn Ehestand begeben / zu bedencken sey* (Wittenberg, 1528) [Ox-Bod, T.L. 51.13], p. B 3 a–b.

2. Hoffmann, *Die "Hausväterliteratur,"* p. 103. On Lutherans and classical educators, see Gerald Strauss, *Luther's House of Learning: Indoctrination of the Young in the German Reformation* (Baltimore, 1978), ch. 3.

3. "Ein Hausswirth muss ein Gottsförchtiger / weiser / verständiger / erfahrner und wolgeübter Mann sein / der Gott vor Augen habe / fleissig bete und arbeite / und niemands unrecht thue / weder seinen Nachbarn / oder seinem Gesinde / dann also erhält man Lieb und Freundschafft / und einen guten Willen bei allen Menschen." Coler, *Oeconomia ruralis et domestica*, I, 1, v, 3. See also Hoffmann, *Die "Hausväterliteratur,"* pp. 87–89.

4. Coler, *Oeconomia ruralis et domestica*, I, 1, iv, 3–4; Hoffmann, *Die 'Hausväterliteratur'*, pp. 93–94.

5. "Umb alle sach fecht sy jn an / Gleich als ob sy wol sein der man." *Clag etlicher stand / ganz kurtzweylig zulesen* (n.d., n.p.) [Ox-Bod, T.L. 83.9].

6. Especially Stone, *Family, Sex and Marriage*, pp. 126, 138, 141.

7. "Thu dem Reichen wie dem armen / Verteidinge die frommen / straffe die bösen / frevel hasse / mutwillen straffe / handhabe die tugent / untugent meide / den ernst deyner straffe / mische mit sanfftmut / und deine sanfftmut mische mit ernst / mache es also / das dich deine untersassen / nicht allein fürchten / Sonder auch lieb haben / Tyranney fürchtet man / und liebet nicht / Wie widderumb ein frome Oberkeyt / beyde geliebt / und gefürchtet wird." Antonius Corvinus, *Bericht / wie sich ein Edelman / Gegen Gott / gegen seine Oberkeyt / sünderlich in den itzigen krieges leufften / gegen seine*

elteren / weib / kinder / hausgesinde und seine untersassen halten sol / An den Merkischen / Lünenburgischen / Braunschweigischen / und allen Sechsischen Adel geschrieben (Erfurt, 1539) [B.M. 698.e.22(5)], p. L 4 a.

8. Coler, *Oeconomia ruralis et domestica*, I, 1, v, 4.

9. "Der heilig geist wil / solche unsinnigkeit / gar nichts geleret haben / das ainer sein manheit an einem armen / onmechtigen schwachen weibe / mit stettigem schlahen reüssen / schelten und boldern / on alle frientligkait beweysen sol / Sondern wil man sol sie lieben / neren und eren / wie unser aigen flaisch / ya also lieben / wie Christus seine gemaine." Menius, *Erinnerung*, pp. B 4 b–C 1 a.

10. "Es sind aber vil unfleter also geschickt / das sie selbs weder gatzen noch eyer legen können / und wöllen doch von ihren armen weybern nichts weniger haben / das es alles nach der schnur richtig zugehen solle / und mainen / wenn sie nur können mit den armen weybern schewtzlich plodern / fluchen und schelten / rauffen / schlahen / und alles was sie im hause ergreyffen / uber einen hauffen schmeyssen / so haben sie es dann recht auss gerichtet / und jhre manheyt herrlich beweyset / welche für war wol werd weren / das man jhnen zu zeyten auch meyster Hansen zum zuchtmeyster uber die haut schickete / Dann die Schrifft verbeut solche ungeschickligkeyt." Menius, *An die hochgeborne Fürstin*, p. C 5 B.

11. "Denn mancher Mopsus, und mancher Wunderlein und Sawerzapf sich lest bedüncken / Er wer kein Mann / wenn er seinem Weibe nur einmal in viel Wochen solte was freundlich zusprechen / Er gehet umbher / und sitzt zu Tisch / wie ein stumm / und redet nicht ehe / als wenn er ihr etwa womit die Ohren zu rasseln / und das Herz zu trencken / und alles zu beruffeln und zu tadeln weis / was sie redt und thut / wenn es gleich auch offt gut gemeint / und nicht tadelnswert ist. Solche Unholden solten lieber Münch und Claussner und Einsiedler / als Ehemanner worden sein. Solten billig im Wald bey wilden Thieren / als im Hauss bei vernünfftigen Eheweibern wohnen." Cited by Hoffmann, *Die "Hausväterliteratur,"* pp. 127–128.

12. "Wiewol sie ihm unterworffen / und ihn für ihren herrn erkennen müsse / dermassen gegen sie gebere / das sie dennoch für eyne hausmutter / und nicht für eine magd gehalten werde." Corvinus, *Bericht*, p. H 3 a. Recent studies describe women in the Renaissance as "just wives," totally subordinate and subservient to their husbands, lacking any clear identity or vocation of their own, their lot in life being simply to please their husbands by conforming to every command and bearing their children. Ruth Kelso complains that no author argued that women "should have equal opportunity and equal reward for her effort." *Doctrine for the Lady of the Renaissance*, 2nd ed. (Urbana, Ill., 1978), pp. 16–17, 31; Davis holds similar views. "City Women and Religious Change," p. 31. In the sixteenth century being "fraw im Hawse" was looked on by neither women nor men as demeaning in any way to womankind; it was a respected identity and vocation that lifted women above the rank of "just wives."

13. *A godly form of householde government* (London, 1598), in *Womanhood in Radical Protestantism*, ed. Joyce L. Irwin (New York, 1979), p. 80.

14. Ibid. Compare the German proverb: "To strike a woman brings little honor to a man." Sebastian Franck, *Sprichwörter* (1548), in Irwin, *Womanhood in Radical Protestantism*, p. 68.

15. *Of Domesticall Duties* (London, 1622), in *Womanhood in Radical Protestantism*, pp. 98–104. See also Robert Schnucker, "Views of Selected Puritans, 1560–1630, on Marriage and Human Sexuality" (Ph.D. diss., University of Iowa, 1969), pp. 103–104, 116.

16. *Das Buch Weinsberg*, I, 138–139.

17. *Luthers Werke in Auswahl*, 8, no. 4910 (1540), p. 244; no. 5189 (1540), p. 275; no. 255 (1532), p. 36; no. 3692 (1538), pp. 140–141.

18. "Ob dein fraw unkeusch ist und bricht den gelawben an dir gedenck ob du an ir auch nit gebrochen habst. Es sein gar unrecht richter die menner die unkeusch sein und begeren keuschheit von iren weyben der sie selbs nit haben und die sich mit hubschen worten entschuldigen und ire weyber schwerlichen verdammen und straffen die im selbs alle ding erlawben und den weybern verpieten." *Ehebüchlein*, p. 9. Von Eyb appeals to Plato as an authority.

19. Corvinus, *Bericht*, p. H 3 b.

20. *Vom Ehbruch und Hürerey / wie ernstlich und strenge Gott dieselbige verpotten und alweg gestrafft . . . Item V. Christliche predige S. Aurelij Augustini / Verteutscht durch M. Melchoir Ambach / prediger zu Franckfurt* (Frankfurt, 1543) [B.M. 3907.bb.10(1)], p. A 3 b.

21. Ibid., p. H 4 b.

22. Ibid., pp. A 3 a–b, H 2 b.

23. "Hat ein obrigkheit macht ein frawenhauss zu erlauben on sünde / darein nit allein ledige gesellen (die doch schwerlich sünden) sondern auch Ehmanner gehn / und wollen solches dazu khein schand haben / sonder gerhumet sein / warumb erlaubt sie nit auch ein bubenhauss / darein etwo die weyber / so alte / schwache / oder kheine männer haben / gehn möchten? Ist jhenes recht und erlaubt / so were auch dieses recht / Hat man eins zuerlauben warumb nit auch das ander? do mit doch auch bei dem armen blöden weiblichen geschlecht bösers verhüret würde?" Ibid., p. H 2 a.

24. Köhler, *Zürcher ehegericht*, p. 109. The consistorial records of Geneva indicate no favoritism to men in matters of adultery. Robert D. Linder, "Response to E. William Monter, The Consistory of Geneva, 1559–1569," in De Klerk, *Renaissance, Reformation, Resurgence*, p. 90.

25. Safley, "Marital Litigation in the Diocese of Constance," pp. 61–78.

26. Coler portrays husbands and wives in the role of "bloodhounds" (*Spürhunde*), constantly alert to thefts, crimes, and household subversion by servants. *Oeconomia ruralis et domestica*, I, 1, vi, 5.

27. "Es sol auch ein Hausswirt sein Weib schützen und handhaben / und sich mit ihr nicht übel begehen / dasselbe übel halten / lästern / schmähen / schlagen / dann wann solches das Gesinde sihet und höret / so verachtets die Wirtin auch / und hat darnach das Weib keinen Gehorsam bei ihnen / dadurch endlich ein gross Unheil und merck-

licher Schade einem Hauswirt in seiner Nahrung entstehen kan." Ibid., I, 1, v, 4.

28. "Dann gleich wie sie am leybe einer mannes person gleich arbeyt zuthun nicht vermügen / also können sie es auch im syn und hertzen nicht haben / das sie gedulden und verbeissen sollen / was ihnen zuwider gehandelt wirdt. Man sagt / und ist auch / achte ich / fast also / Weyber haben langer Kleyder und kurtze syn / Darumb / so sol ein man der vernunfft seyn / das er seines weybes wisse wysslich zu verschonen / und was anders ichtes leyden wil / ihr zu gut zuhalten." *An die hochgeborne Fürstin*, p. C 5 b. See also von Eyb, who also doubts a woman's ability to be truly rational. *Ehebüchlein*, pp. 34–36.

29. In Irwin, *Womanhood in Radical Protestantism*, p. 80.

30. "Women's rebellion against patriarchy did not occur on any noticeable scale before 1830 because women themselves did not really define their situation as illegitimate until then." "The consciousness of inequality with men that contemporary women feel was virtually impossible before the early modern era because women did not share a broad enough base of experience with men to be able to compare their situations in universal terms." Janet Z. Giele, "Centuries of Womanhood: An Evolutionary Perspective on the Feminine," *Woman's Studies* 1 (1972): 97–110.

31. *Luthers Werke in Auswahl*, 8, no. 3530 (1536), pp. 100–101; no. 5524 (Winter, 1542–43), pp. 318–319.

32. "Man soll die weybsbild beschawen wie die ross / da beschawe man nit satel und zaum / gerayd und fürbieg / sonder man besehe was tugent odder nach thails das ross hab / also sol man ahn den weybern nicht den schmuck und klaidung / sonder gut tugenten / frumkait und eer beschawen." Wolfgang Russ, *Der Weiber geschefft. Ausslegung des ain und dreissigten Capitels / der Spruchen Salomonis / was ein redlich dapffer weib sey / was thon und lassen soll durch W. R. zu Riethen prediger* (1533) [B.M., 3165.ccc.41], p. C 3 b. Among the signs of the newly emergent "closed domesticated nuclear family" of the seventeenth and eighteenth centuries, Stone cites care in selecting a mate: "[The new] sense of control over the environment, and particularly over animal breeding, . . . led men to choose their wives as one might choose a brood mare." *Family, Sex and Marriage*, p. 160. Russ's analogy is far more sophisticated and charitable, although two centuries earlier.

33. See Lutz K. Berkner, "Recent Research on the History of the Family in Western Europe," *Journal of Marriage and the Family* 35 (1973): 398. See also chapter 1, notes 155, 160. Hermann von Weinsberg could describe a man between thirty and forty as still "ein jonk gesel." *Das Buch Weinsberg*, V, 254.

34. Monter, "Consistory of Geneva," p. 69.

35. *Das Buch Weinsberg*, II, 283.

36. Von Eyb, *Ehebüchlein*, 37. See also Hoffmann, *Die "Hausväterliteratur,"* pp. 121–122.

37. *Mich wundert das kein gelt ihm land ist. Ein schimpflich doch unschedlich gesprech dreier Landtfarer* (1524), in *Johann Eberlin von Günz-*

burg, Sämtliche Schriften, III, ed. Ludwig Enders (Halle, 1902), 165.

38. Alan MacFarlane's comment on seventeenth-century Puritan marriages may also be applied to marriages in Reformation Germany and Switzerland: "Despite the importance of financial arrangements, the choice of a marriage partner, the selection of one among a number of possible suitors, still depended on noneconomic considerations, and still lay in the hands of the children rather than the parents." *The Family Life of Ralph Josselin: A 17th Century Clergyman* (Cambridge, 1970), p. 95. Although his parents took the initiative in his first marriage, Hermann von Weinsberg never for a moment thought that the decision was not his own. In the Weinsberg family an "arranged" marriage was one in which the whole family participated and to which it lent its support, not one manipulated by parents for economic gain. Despite his keen eye for a widow's fortune, Hermann von Weinsberg explicitly listed personal traits of his first wife that made the match desirable apart from economic considerations.

39. See Hoffmann, *Die "Hausväterliteratur,"* pp. 112–115, 123, 129.

40. Yost, "Value of Married Life for the Social Order," pp. 32–33.

41. Robert Friedmann, "Hutterite Marriage Practices," in *Hutterite Studies: Essays by Robert Friedmann,* ed. H. S. Bender (Goshen, Ind., 1961), pp. 123–125.

42. *De regno Christi,* in Pauck, *Melanchthon and Bucer,* p. 325.

43. Ibid.

44. "Ein zusammenfügung, nach beyder verwilligung, die freüntlich unnd erbarlich bey einander wohnen sollen, biss inn todt, Sünde zuvermeyden und früchte zu bringen." Cited by Wendel, *Le mariage à Strasbourg,* p. 56, n. 3.

45. *Sententiarum libri quatuor,* bk. II, *dist.* 18 ("De formatione mulieris"), in *Patrologia Latina,* 192, ed. J. P. Migne (Paris, 1855), pp. 687–688.

46. "Es ist auch wyderumb dz weyb Heva nit von den fussen Adams geschaffen / das der mann das weib wolt für einen fucsshader / und dienstmagt achten / Sondern aus der myttel des leybs / als ein mitgesellyn wie sie Adam nennet die in tzur mithelfferyn vonn got vorordnet / sol er sie als seyn / eygen fleisch und blut an und auffnehmen." Caspar Gütell, *Uber das Evangelion Johannis / da Christus seine Mutter auch sein Junger / wären auff die Hochtzeyt geladen / Wass mit worten und wercken daselbst gehandelt. Eyn Sermon dem Ehlichen standt fast freudsam und nutzlich* (1534) [Ox-Bod, T.L. 39.178], p. B 1 a. Gütell admonishes mutual deference, the wife remembering that she is created to be "mitgehulffyn / nit von dem haubt," the husband that she is not given him as a "fuesschemell." Ibid., p. B 3 b. See also Corvinus, *Bericht,* p. J 1 b; and Hoffmann, *Die "Hausväterliteratur," p. 118.*

47. "Da (in dem ampt eines weibs) wirt freylich ein kurtze freud / und ein langer unlust sein / wie man pfligt zu sagenn / das das weib nit sitz / die hend in die schoss leg / den gutten Adam allein zablen / zaysen und zanen lass / sonder das sie es auch angreyffen soll." Russ, *Der Weiber geschefft,* p. A 4 a.

48. Robert Cleaver in Irwin, *Womanhood in Radical Protestantism*, p. 80.

49. Coler, *Oeconomia ruralis et domestica*, I, 1, vi, 5.

50. "Das seind auch die rechte ehelichen werck / so die ehe zieren / die andern werck künden auch huren und buben / dise werck aber kan niemants dann ehrliche Christliche gemüter." Russ, *Der Weiber geschefft*, p. A 4 b.

51. *Letters of John Calvin*, I, ed. and trans. Jules Bonnet (Philadelphia, 1858), 141.

52. Von Eyb, *Ehebüchlein*, pp. 7, 14–16.

53. "Die weyl seines abwesens / alles ihres geschmuckes enthalten / und biss zu seiner widerkunfft / ein gar einsam und trawrig leben gefurt." Menius, *An die hochgeborne Fürstin*, p. E 5 a. Russ writes of the charity and hospitality of Elizabeth and St. Ferena: "Sie trösteten die armen mit worten / mit speiss / mit tranck / sie leissens nicht als an die verordneten mägt und knecht / wir wir thond." *Der Weiber geschefft*, p. B 3 a. On Elizabeth, see Wilhelm Mauer, *Kirche und Geschichte, Gesammelte Aufsätze*, II, (Göttingen, 1970), 231–283, 284–319.

54. Caspar Cruciger, *Herrn Doctor Caspar Crutzigers Auslegung / uber St. Paulus spruch zum Timotheo / Wie die Eheweiber selig werden / nicht allein allen Eheweibern / sondern auch allen Christen seer nützlich und troestlich durch Georgium Spalatinum verdeütscht* (Erfurt, 1538) [Ox-Bod, T.L. 112.7], p. A 7 a.

55. Clemen, *Luthers Werke in Auswahl*, 8, no. 12 (1531), p. 1.

56. "Weiber / sind noch heüt alle Eva / verfüren den man / und haben den apffel noch in der hand." *Davids Eebruch: Mordt Straff und Buss. Ein kurtze verzeychnusz und Ausslegung des xj und xii Capitels / des Andern Buchs Samuelis / von dem Fall / Mordt / und Eebruch Davidis / Widerumb / von seiner Buss / urständ / von sünden / annemung / und gnädige verzeyhung vor Gott / allen gefalnen sündern ain tröstlich handthäbe* (Ulm, 1534) [B.M. 3835.aaa.59], p. E 1 a. This was a marginal comment on David's inability to resist Bathsheba, perhaps written by the contemporary editors of these three sermons, which were Sam's last, preached in 1533 and published posthumously.

57. Maschke, *Die Familie in der deutschen Stadt*, p. 46. Maschke stresses the "gefühlsbetont" character of the late medieval family. For Culman, every marriage was made in heaven: "Gleich wie dem Adam der Herr sein Eheweib schlaffend zufürt ohn sein wissen und zuthun / also gehet es noch auff disen tag zu / das er zwey in ein Ehelichen willen zusamen fürt / on alles jr beyder wissen und zuthun." *Jungen gesellen*, p. B 5 a.

58. *Chronik und Selbstbiographie* (Bern, 1830), p. 202, Wenzel, *Die Autobiographie des späten Mittelalters*, I, p. 139.

59. Platter, *Lebensbeschreibung*, p. 96

60. *Das Buch Weinsberg*, II, 36.

61. MacFarlane, *Family Life of Ralph Josselin*, pp. 106–107, 116.

62. Russ, *Der Weiber geschefft*, p. B 3 a.

63. Russ, *Der Weiber geschefft*, pp. B 3 a–b.

64. "Ein frawe die ir lieb im anfangk dem manne nit versprechen will

und schwere macht als bald sie die lieb hat zugesagt und in ir hertz genomen so ist inbrunstiger und steter die lieb der frawen und uberwinndet den man in der lieb Aber der man als etzlich menner sein als pald er der frawen willen hat erlangt so gedencket er im also. die fraw ist nach meinem willen gewest und allzeit sein wirdet du wilt aussgien vogeln und besehen ob du ein andre auff den kolben bringen mugst und gefahen. und will es fur ein lob haben ye mer er an die zedeln und kerben mag bringen so die fraw fur schenntliche achtet ir lieb mit mer mennern zuteylen." Von Eyb, *Ehebüchlein*, p. 12.

65. "Es ist uber die massen ein schendlich und heslich ding / umb ein trunckens unnd folles weib." *Auslegung*, p. B 1 b. "Eines sanfften und stillen geystes sein" — that is "der aller schönste geschmuck den ein weyb ymmer haben mag." Menius, *An die hochgeborne Fürstin*, p. C 8 b. Russ railed especially at indiscreet clothing, whose purpose is to excite passions and idly amuse. *Der Weiber geschefft*, pp. B 4 b–C 2 a.

66. "Irem Mann soll sie in allen billichen Dingen gehorchen / ihn lieben und ehren / seine Schwachheit und Gebrechen ihm zu gut halten / und ihm nicht gehassig und feindselig auffrucken / wann er etwas gesundiget / oder ein Ding nicht recht gemacht hätte." Coler, *Oeconomia ruralis et domestica*, I, 1, vi, 6.

67. "Das sie den Ehestandt mit jhren wünderlichen / seltzamen / unbetreglichen worten / geberden / und wesen nicht betrübe. Das sie ihren eigen hauswirt / jhr selbs nicht gram mache. Des gleichen mit gedult jhrem hauswirt helff unglück aushalten / unnd das sie jhren hauswirt von wegen seines unglücks nicht verlasse." Cruciger, *Auslegung*, pp. A 6 a–b.

68. "Sie sol nicht unbefohlne sachen ausserhalben jhres hauses ausrichten / sondern ihres hauses warten." Menius, *An die hochgeborne Fürstin*, p. E 4 b.

69. "Damit zubedeuten / und anzuzeigen / das ein hausfraw und Eheweib / stetigs jm haus sein sol / wie ein schneck jhr heuslein allzeit mit ihr tregt." Cruciger, *Auslegung*, p. B 3 b. See also Coler, *Oeconomia ruralis et domestica*, I, 1, vi, 6. Is this also the significance of Botticelli's Venus, standing on a scallop shell?

70. "Gehört zur zucht / das ein weib fleissig sey inn jhrem beruff / und jhre kinder mit vleis erziehe und regiere / und der haushaltung / die ihr befohlen ist / trewlich warte." Cruciger, *Auslegung*, p. B 3 b.

71. *Das Buch Weinsberg*, II, 300.

72. Ann S. Haskell, "The Paston Family Women on Marriage in 15th Century England," *Viator* 4 (1973): 459–471; see also Robert Frank, "Marriage in 12th and 13th Century Iceland," Ibid., 473–484.

73. Russ, *Der Weiber geschefft*, p. B 1 a. Russ apologizes to "pious women readers" of his work for this outburst, explaining that he is here addressing "shameless pigs who seek neither God nor his honor in the estate of marriage, only their own self-indulgence." Ibid.

74. Coler, *Oeconomia ruralis et domestica*, I, 1, vi, 5.

75. Russ, *Der Weiber geschefft*, p. B 1 a–b.

76. Koch, *Studium Pietatis*, pp. 130–131. Koch argues that Bucer

subordinated women to men and wives to husbands and dealt with them on a double standard that denied their moral and legal equality, to the detriment of womankind.

77. Hoffmann, Die "Hausväterliteratur," p. 120. The model of a good wife for these authors was Sara, the wife of Abraham.

78. From Franz Philipp Florinus, Oeconomus prudens et legalis (1702), cited by Hoffmann, Die "Hausväterliteratur," p. 119.

79. A wife who struck her husband in public might be paraded around town bound to a donkey and ridiculed with her (henpecked) husband. Ingeborg Weber-Kellermann, Die Familie. Geschichte, Geschichten und Bilder (Frankfurt am Main, 1976), p. 70. Wife-beaters in Protestant towns and territories were haled before the marriage court or consistory, and nowhere more speedily than in Geneva, which by century's end had gained the reputation of "the woman's Paradise." Davis, "City Women and Religious Change," in McGuigan, A Sampler of Women's Studies, p. 36. See below, note 207.

80. Das Buch Weinsberg, V, 143.

81. The woman in question gave a most emphatic and independent response: "I have designs on no man; nor any plans to remarry, even if I could have the emperor." Ibid., I, 209.

82. Ibid., I, 283.

83. Ibid., I, 282.

84. Ibid.

85. Ibid., I, 283.

86. Her house was located only six houses above Hermann's on the same side of the river. Hermann said he had been there once as a child but had no recollection of it. Ibid.

87. "Dieweil ich auch 30 jar alt war, wolte ich gein jongfrau nemen van 20 jarn, dan micht duchte, das sulte sich besser schicken, das der man jonger were dan die frau, uis ursachn mich darzu bewegende und auch nach des weisen mans leir, das man die kundigen in der nachparschaft sol freien." Ibid., I, 285.

88. "Es had mich auch scheu gemacht jonge frauwen zu nemen, quia metuebam, ne forte partim generationi obesset." Ibid., I, 51. In 1548 Hermann fell from a ladder and tore the right side of his scrotum, an injury Weisgin suspected would hinder his ability to have children ("forte generationi obfuit, ut opinabatur uxor"); Hermann was quick to point out that his left testicle remained intact. Ibid., V, 3.

89. "Das sei aber kinder hatte, dess moist ich mich getrosten, so hatt sei dargegen narung, inkomst und einen gesatzten stoil; dan wer kan alle hecken scheuwen." Ibid., I, 285.

90. Ibid., I, 328.

91. Ibid., II, 84.

92. Ibid., II, 53–54.

93. Ibid., II, 60–61.

94. Ibid., II, 93.

95. Ibid., V, 23, 92–93.

96. Ibid., II, 298–299.

97. Ibid., II, 94–96.

98, Ibid., V, xi.

99. Ibid., V, 21–22, 25.

100. Ibid., II, 107, 109; V, 24, 26–28.

101. Ibid., V, 31.

102. Ibid., II, 104.

103. Ibid., II, 107.

104. Ibid., II, 103, 142.

105. Ibid., V, 60.

106. Ibid., V, 75.

107. Ibid., V, 71.

108. Ibid., II, 257.

109. Ibid.

110. Ibid., II, 261.

111. Ibid., II, 276–277, 379; V, 256.

112. Ibid., II, 262.

113. When Hermann's stepgranddaughter died in September 1573, her mother, bitter over the inheritance arrangements, refused to receive gifts from Hermann. Ibid., II, 262–263.

114. Ibid., II, 277–279.

115. Ibid., V, 224.

116. For example, Schnucker, "Views of Selected Puritans," p. 256.

117. Again, the famous suit of Henry VIII against Catherine of Aragon demonstrates both the possibilities and the difficulties of this approach to ending an unhappy marriage.

118. *Das Buch Weinsberg*, V, 45, 49.

119. Ibid., V, 56.

120. Ibid., V, 65–66.

121. Ibid., V, 68.

122. Ibid., V, 79–80, 87.

123. Ibid., II, 259–260.

124. Ibid., II, 284.

125. Ibid., V, 104.

126. Ibid., II, 326–327.

127. Ibid., II, 384–389.

128. "Dweil sich in warheit erfint, das Conradt und Sibilla vurg. die neigste acht jar ungeferlich nit samen hausgehalten, dan verscheiden gewont und gelebt, so ist verglicht und vertragen das Conradt vor sich und Sibilla auch vor sich mit der wonung zu bedde und zu disch und der gutter sein sullen und sich dermaissn erlich und wol halten, wie sie das vor got irem herrn zu vertadingen wisten, ohne das ein den andern oder dessen frunde auf der gassen, in der kirchen, haus oder einichem orde binnen oder baussen Coln durch sich oder emantz anders mit worten oder wirken anfertigen oder besweren sol, dan gedultig erwarten, was weiter von got versehen sie oder geschein wurde." Ibid., V, 168.

129. Ibid., V, 170.

130. Ibid., V, 191.

131. Ibid., V, 216.

132. Ibid., V, 217.

133. Ibid., V, 219.

134. Ibid., V, 225.

135. Ibid., V, 236.

136. Ibid., V, 283.

137. Ibid., V, 306–307.

138. *On the Babylonian Captivity of the Church*, p. 236 (= *Luthers Werke in Auswahl*, I, 496).

139. "Dann allein zu bett und tisch scheiden und aber das elich ban lassen blyben, hat kein gute gstalt, sittemal bywonung zu bett und tisch die grösten ursachen der ee sind" (1532). Köhler, *Zürcher ehegericht*, p. 138.

140. Koch, *Studium Pietatis*, p. 140; Wendel, *Le mariage à Strasbourg*, p. 156. Wendel writes of an "abyss" separating Bucer from most other contemporary writers on the subject of divorce. Fellow Protestants, among them Theodore Beza, thought Bucer was too flexible and exceeded the teaching of Holy Scripture.

141. *The Judgment of Martin Bucer Touching Divorce Taken Out of the Second Book Entitl'd Of the Kingdom of Christ*, trans. John Milton, in *The Complete Prose Works of John Milton*, II (1643–1648; reprint ed., New Haven, 1959), 473. "It is certainly the invention of AntiChrist that the promise of marriage *de praesenti*, as they call it, should be indissoluble." Ibid., pp. 446–447.

142. Ibid., p. 465. See also Wendel, *Le mariage à Strasbourg*, pp. 154–156.

143. *Ware erklarung und underrichtung ains Artickels / die Eeschaidung betreffend auss heyliger schrifft bewaret / durch Casparn Schätzger / barfusser ordens wider falsche erdictung Lütherischer leer / in solcher matery* (Munich, 1524) [Tü fiche 98–259], pp. B 5 a–b.

144. *Vom Ehebruch und Weglauffen*, in *Von Ehesachen. D. Mart. Luth. Item Vom Ehebruch und Weglauffen. D. Johan Bugenhagen Pomer / an Königliche Maiestat zu Denemarcken. De arbore consanquinitatis et affinitatis, sive gradibus. Philippi Melanchthonis* (Wittenberg, 1540), p. M 3 b.

145. Ibid., pp. M 4 a–b; O 1 b–O 2 a.

146. Köhler, *Zürcher ehegericht*, pp. 111–112.

147. Ibid., p. 120.

148. Wendel, *Le mariage à Strasbourg*, p. 154; Koch, *Studium Pietatis*, pp. 130–131. Koch berates Bucer for not also requiring a husband to follow a criminal wife, but were there not far fewer examples of this?

149. Vom *Ehebruch und Weglauffen*, p. M 4 b.

150. Bugenhagen, *Vom Ehebruch*, p. N 4 b.

151. See especially Martin Bucer, *Das ym selbs niemant, sonder andern leben soll* in *M. Bucers Deutsche Schriften* I: *Frühschriften 1520-24*, ed. Robert Stupperich (Gütersloh, 1960), p. 57; Wendel, *Le mariage à Strasbourg*, p. 141. Luther argued for using the threat of capital punishment

against a wife who adamantly refused the marital duty because of the sin and social disruption she caused. *On the Estate of Marriage* (1522), *LW*, 45, p. 35; Dieterich, *Das protestantische Eherecht*, p. 71.

152. *Luthers Werke in Auswahl*, 8, no. 6934 (1546), p. 241.

153. Irwin, *Womanhood in Radical Protestantism*, p. 64.

154. *Vom Ehebruch*, pp. M 4 b–N 2 a.

155. "Wenn die Oberkeit und die / welchen es befohlen ist / das unschuldige Teil frey sprechen von Ampts wegen / mit Rechte und Gottes wort / so thuts kein Mensch / sondern Gott selbs." Ibid., p. N 2 b.

156. *Wie in Ehesachen / und inn den fellen / so sich derhalben / zu tragen / nach Götlichen billichen Rechten / Christenlich zu handeln sey* (Wittenberg, 1531), pp. G 2 a–G 3 b.

157. Cited by Koch, *Studium Pietatis*, p. 140.

158. "Wir in diesem . . . falle nichts newes für nemen / Die verstendigesten und gelertesten Papistischen Eherichter / auch Bischoffe vor uns und bey unsern zeiten / haben solchs mit Brieff und Sigel nach gegeben / und habens genennet / Ein Permittimus / und haben in solcher not aus naturlichem Rechte / jre Bapsts krümme Recht hinder sich müssen lassen stehen / das sie den leuten hülffen / wie noch nehest zu Augspurg im Reichstage meinem lieben herrn Philippo / ein solch Permittimus in die hand kam / und war gestellet / das jm von hertzen wol gefiel / Denn es war etwas aus unser Lere besser gemacht / denn für hin." *Vom Ehebruch*, p. O 4 a. Philip married this woman in March 1540 with the grudging approval of Luther, Melanchthon, and Bucer after threatening to return to the Catholic fold if he did not get his way in the matter. The reformers considered a *secret* bigamous marriage the lesser of two evils—lesser than his notorious philandering (which the second marriage did not end) and lesser than his abandoning his wife of seventeen years (the mother of their ten children, three of whom were born *after* his bigamous marriage), which his conscience would not permit him to do. Koch, *Studium Pietatis*, pp. 148–149; William W. Rockwell, *Die Doppelehe des Landgrafen Philipp von Hessen* (Marburg, 1904), especially pp. 19–36; *Argumenta Buceri Pro et Contra. Original–Manuscript Bucers, die Gründe für und gegen die Doppelehe des Landgrafen Philipp des Grossmüthigen* (Cassel, 1878). Bugenhagen's reference to the Reichstag in Augsburg must be to the Diet of 1530 and is somewhat confusing. Philip had sought a way out of his first marriage as early as 1530; in the summer of 1540 he had actively pursued a dispensation from Rome as a condition of peace with the emperor in the matter, since according to the imperial law code of 1532, bigamy was a more heinous offense than adultery and deserved full prosecution. Rockwell, *Die Doppelehe*, pp. 6–7, 99–100; *Die peinliche Gerichtsordnung Kaiser Karls V. von 1532 (Carolina)*, ed. G. Radbruch (Stuttgart, 1967) no. 121, p. 80. If Philip actually received a dispensation from a Catholic official at the Diet of Augsburg in 1530, as Bugenhagen seemed to allege, he certainly did not act on it publicly; and since he was the guilty party in the marriage, it is doubtful that a dispensation would have been forthcoming even from an official whose first allegiance was to natural law. I interpret the reference to Philip's dispen-

sation to be the one received from the Protestant reformers in 1539, although Philip certainly sought one from Catholic authorities also after the Augsburg diet. Rockwell discusses the passage but completely ignores Bugenhagen's reference to Philip's bigamy. *Die Doppelehe*, p. 281 n. 2.

159. *On the Babylonian Captivity of the Church*, pp. 233–234 (= *Luthers Werke im Auswahl*, I, 495).

160. *Catholischer Spangenbergischer Catechismus, für die jungen Christen. Auss der Heiliger Schrifft / und ältesten Kirchen Lehrern / so vor Tausent Jaren gelebt / in Fragestück verfasset* (Cologne, 1561) [Ox-Bod, 1.C.252], pp. AA 8 a–b.

161. Flandrin finds that a high percentage of people remarried within six months of a spouse's death in seventeenth- and eighteenth-century France, evidence, he believes, of "affective unfeelingness and the brutality of marital relationships." *Families in Former Times*, pp. 115–116. This was not true of Hermann von Weinsberg's remarriage within seven months of Weisgin's death. He continued to remember his first wife with affection, as did Thomas Platter, who remarried in his late sixties, three months after Anna's death and a marriage of forty-four years. Platter, *Lebensbeschreibung*, pp. 144–145.

162. Urbanus Rhegius described a crowd assembled to witness a clerical marriage in 1525 as "gaping as if at a new and strange thing." *Ain Sermon vom eelichen stand* (1525) [Tü fiche 65–167], p. A 2 a.

163. "Wir lassen sitzen offentlich Gerichte / die Oberkeit / odder denen es im Lande bevohlen ist / Denn wir haben auch an vielen orten sonderliche Eherichter / Da lassen wir die sache offentlich beweisen und rechtlich bezeugen. Dis geschihet nach einem jare oder lenger dar nach / Ists aber zuvor beweiset so lassen wirs für Gerichte wider publiciren / Darnach erleuben die Richter dem unschuldigen und verwaltigetem Teil wider zufreien / doch also das sie beide / die hie zusamen wollen / zu gelegener Zeit komen für die selbigen Richter / Da verlobet man jnen Ehelich zusamen zu sein / doch also / das sie auff einen gelegenen tag / einen tisch vol Freundschafft neben dem Priester / alleine zu Abendmal / zu sich nemen / und da sich lassen im hause vertrawen. Kirchengang und ander offentlich Hochzeit geprenge gestatten wir jnen nicht." Bugenhagen, *Vom Ehebruch*, pp. O 2 a–b.

164. *Das Buch Weinsberg*, II, 95–96.

165. *Wie in Ehesachen*, p. F 2 b.

166. *Ibid.*, p. F 3 a. Bugenhagen rejected the Israelite "Scheidebrief" as too lax an approach to divorce. *Vom Ehebruch*, p. N 4 b.

167. Brenz, *Wie in Ehesachen*, p. D 1 b.

168. "Wo ein halsstarriger unterthan wer / der sich mit seinem Eheweib jnn keinen weg betragen wolt / und doch kein Ehebruch / sondern allein sonst neid und Hass / so sich offt on Ehebruch hefftiglich zwischen Eheleuten begibt / erfunden wird / das zubesorgen wer / wo man sie wolt zusammen zwingen / sie möchten einander mit gifft vergeben / erwürgen / odder ander unglück zurichten / So wer ein weltliche Oberkeit vor Gott entschuldiget / wenn sie nach dem Exempel Mosi / dem halsstarrigen / so sich

jnn keinen weg keuschlich halten wolt / ein ordenlichen Concubinischen beysitz vergünnet / damit heimlich Ehebruch mit andern Eheweibern / und unordenliche hurerey / jtzt mit dieser jtzt mit jhener / verhutet würde. Ibid., pp. H 2 a–J 1 a.

169. Bugenhagen, *Vom Ehebruch*, pp. N 2 b–N 3 a.

170. Brenz, *Wie in Ehesachen*, pp. J 1 b–J 2 a.

171. See Luther, *On the Estate of Marriage*, LW, 45, p. 35.

172. Brenz, *Wie in Ehesachen*, pp. J 2 b–J 3 b.

173. "Allein solche sorge des Mordes ausgenommen / ists billich / das das Gerichte dem Manne sein Weib wider zuspreche / und gebiete / das sie Ehelich haushalten / wie sie für Gott und der Welt schuldig sind / im friede und ehren." Bugenhagen, *Vom Ehebruch*, p. P 1 a.

174. Dieterich, *Das protestantische Eherecht*, pp. 69–71.

175. Bugenhagen, *Vom Ehebruch*, p. P 4 a. Also in Zurich religious differences were not accepted as grounds for divorce. Köhler, *Zürcher ehegericht*, p. 138.

176. "Concerning Divorce: A Swiss Brethren Tract on the Primacy of Loyalty to Christ and the Right to Divorce and Remarriage," ed. and trans. J. C. Wenger, *Mennonite Quarterly Review* 21 (1947): 114–119.

177. In a pamphlet probably from the 1530s, Melanchthon cited among the unchristian teaching of Anabaptists: "So im Ehestand die ein person rechtgleubig ist / und die ander Eheliche person / nicht rechtgleubig / so sey solcher Ehestand hurerey / und müge die recht gleubige person / die ander verlassen / allein des glaubens halben / und ein andere freien." *Verlegung etlicher unchristlicher Artikel / Welche die Widerteuffer furgeben* (Wittenberg, n.d.) [Ox-Bod, T.L. 51.10], pp. B 3 a–b.

178. "Concerning Divorce," pp. 115–116.

179. Mary Ault Harada, "Family Values and Child Care during the Reformation Era: A Comparative Study of Hutterites and Some Other German Protestants" (Ph. D. diss., Boston University, 1968), pp. 137–138.

180. "Wenn ein Bube stille Schweigens sein fromes Eheweib verlesset / oder mit lügen worten davon lauffet / also das man wol weis / er thue es darumb / das er bey seinem Weibe nicht sein wil / und man weis nicht / wo er bleibet / weis mans / so wil er doch auch wider gefordert nicht wider komen / und stehen zu Rechte / warumb er sie so schendlich verlassen hat." *Vom Ehebruch*, p. R 2 b.

181. Ibid., p. R 3 a; Brenz, *Wie in Ehesachen*, p. J 4 b.

182. "Non debent" does not mean "non possunt", Bugenhagen points out; what the law forbids, people still do, and when willful abandonment occurs, the nature of a marriage bond *is* changed, despite the foolishness of the pope and the common man ("nerrish genug"). *Vom Ehebruch*, pp. P 4 b–Q 2 b.

183. Ibid., p. R 1 a.

184. Ibid., p. R 3 b.

185. "Der Weglauffer setzet sein ehrliches Weib in far der ehren / das offt solches Weib darüber zu schanden wird / zu hohn und spot irem gantzen Geschlecht / und zu unchristlichem Ergernis der Gemeine. . . Des kompt

also ein ehrlich Weib zu falle und mus eine hure heissen / und ire armen kinder hurenkinder gescholten werden / die nie darauff gedacht hette." Ibid., p. S 1 b.

186. Dieterich, *Das protestantische Eherecht*, pp. 76–77, 82–83.

187. Harvey, "The Influence of the Reformation on Nuremberg Marriage Laws", pp. 172–184.

188. Staehelin, *Die Einführung der Ehescheidung in Basel*, p. 51.

189. *The Judgment of Martin Bucer Concerning Divorce*, in *The Works of John Milton*, II, 471–474; Wendel, *Le mariage à Strasbourg*, pp. 154–155; Dieterich, *Das protestantische Eherecht*, pp. 107–108.

190. *Judgment of Martin Bucer Concerning Divorce*, p. 469.

191. Köhler, *Zürcher ehegericht*, pp. 148–150, 154–155; see below.

192. Ibid., p. 109. Although the conclusions remain my own, my dependence on Köhler and Staehelin for data on the Zurich and Basel courts is virtually total, although Köhler's volume on Zurich is so rich in documentation that I have also used it as a primary source.

193. Ibid., pp. 111–112.

194. Staehelin, *Die Einführung der Ehescheidung in Basel*, p. 110.

195. Köhler, *Zürcher ehegericht*, p. 111.

196. Ibid., pp. 113–114.

197. Staehelin, *Die Einführung der Ehescheidung in Basel*, pp. 101–102.

198. Ibid., pp. 104–107.

199. Dieterich, *Das protestantische Eherecht*, p. 104.

200. Köhler, *Zürcher ehegericht*, pp. 111, 116–117; Staehelin, *Die Einführung der Ehescheidung in Basel*, p. 133.

201. Köhler, *Zürcher ehegericht*, p. 117.

202. Staehelin, *Die Einführung der Ehescheidung in Basel*, p. 127.

203. In ibid., p. 129.

204. Ibid., pp. 129–131.

205. "Dann vil unfal in der ee mit einander gelytten muss werden." Köhler, *Zürcher ehegericht*, p. 119.

206. Ibid.

207. Staehelin, *Die Einführung der Ehescheidung in Basel*, pp. 144–147. Drawing on a small sample of cases before the Genevan Consistory between 1559 and 1569, William Monter found that there was great reluctance to grant divorce or even separation; the few divorces that were granted were for willful desertion and confirmed impotence. Wife-beaters appear to have been firmly punished; between 1564 and 1569 the Consistory excommunicated sixty-three spouse beaters, sixty-one of them male. "The Consistory of Geneva," in De Klerk, *Renaissance, Reformation, Resurgence*, pp. 68, 72.

208. Staehelin, *Die Einführung der Ehescheidung in Basel*, p. 117.

209. Köhler, *Zürcher ehegericht*, pp. 121–122.

210. Ibid., p. 128; Staehelin, *Die Einführung der Ehescheidung in Basel*, pp. 118–22.

211. Köhler, *Zürcher ehegericht*, p. 125.

212. Staehelin, *Die Einführung der Ehescheidung in Basel*, pp. 138–39.

213. Ibid., p. 136, 141–143.

214. Köhler, *Zürcher ehegericht*, pp. 125–127.

215. Ibid., p. 128.

216. Staehelin, *Die Einführung der Ehescheidung in Basel*, pp. 127–128.

217. Ibid., pp. 68, 128.

218. Köhler, *Zürcher ehegericht*, pp. 129–131.

219. Dieterich, *Das protestantische Eherecht*, p. 158.

220. Notable exceptions are Roland H. Bainton, *Women of the Reformation in Germany and Italy* (Minneapolis, 1971); and Douglass, "Women and the Continental Reformation."

221. Luther's statement, made at least partially in jest, was: "Men have wide shoulders and small hips, therefore they have wisdom. Women have narrow shoulders and wide hips. A woman should be *Oikoupos* [*häuslich*, domestic]; their very physique—the fact that they have a wide rear and hips—is a sign [from their Creator] that they should sit still." *Luthers Werke in Auswahl*, 8, no. 55 (1531), p. 4.

222. Maclean, *Renaissance Notion of Woman*, pp. 9–10, 18, 27.

223. Davis, "City Women and Religious Change," in McGuigan, *Sampler of Women's Studies*, pp. 35–37.

224. Thomas, "Women and the Civil War Sects," *Past and Present* 13 (1958): 43–47, 53–57.

3. The Bearing of Children

1. "Weyl der man ehe dann das weyb geschaffen / und nicht der man / sonder das weyb verfüret ist worden / und die ubertrettung eingefüret hat / Damit arme / schwache weybliche natur nicht villeicht in verzweyfelung fallen und gedencken möchte / als were sie unter allen creaturen die unseligste / die es allenthalben verderbet / und yederman unselig machete / so setzet Sanct Paulus den trost also bald darauff." Menius, *An die hochgeborne Fürstin*, p. D 5 a. "Denn die weibsbilde sind one das (i.e. rearing children in faith and love, holiness and discipline) von natur blöde und kleinmütig / und geben leichtlich affter und misglauben statt und raum. Derhalben hat auch St. Paul / gleich vor diesen worten gesagt / das er nicht gestatte das ein weib lere und predige. Auch nicht das sie des mannes herr sey / sondern stille sey. Nun aber weiter zeiget St. Paul die rechte Gottes dienst an / so die Weiber recht / und wol lernen verstehen / uben / und halten sollen / Damit sie nicht durch misglauben und unrechten falschen heuchlischen Gottesdienst zu und auff andere nerrische / und unnütze werck verfurt werden." Cruciger, *Auslegung*, p. A 4 a.

2. *On the Estate of Marriage*, *LW*, 45, p. 46; *Luthers Werke in Auswahl*, 8, no. 5458 (1542), p. 304.

3. See the viewpoints of Martin Le Maistre (1432–1481) and John Major (1470–1550) in Noonan, *Contraception*, pp. 370–371, 374.

4. A variety of contraceptive devices did exist in the sixteenth century,

especially sponges and acidic potions, and they appear to have been widely used by prostitutes. Such contraceptive methods as *amplexus reservatus*, the willed suppression of semination on the part of *both* sexes (dry orgasm), and *coitus interruptus*, the diversion of male semen from the womb, were among the sexual practices condemned by confessors. The only form of birth control the Catholic church permitted a lay couple debilitated by childbearing was mutual continence, and that only in theory, as a *possible* pastoral counsel. Church law and catechism condemned contraceptive potions and poisons as instruments of homicide. (Noonan, *Contraception*, pp. 403, 437.) The first generation of Protestants was equally inflexible on this subject; although Luther expressed personal pleasure in his own marital bed and urged others to have no shame about sexual intercourse, as a theologian he excused sex largely as a means to the higher ends of procreation and avoidance of fornication. John Calvin brought up the subject of contraception in his *Commentary on Genesis* only to condemn *coitus interruptus* as homicide and threatened genocide. (Noonan, *Contraception*, p. 423.)

5. Ingeborg Weber-Kellermann, *Die deutsche Familie. Versuch einer Sozialgeschichte* (Frankfurt am Main, 1974), p. 47.

6. The Protestant conception of marriage as a special companionship, the best of friendships, helped make it possible to appreciate marriage for reasons other than the production of progeny, and this created a moral climate favorable to contraception. (Stone, *Family, Sex and Marriage*, p. 262.) By their constant criticism of husbands who beat or neglected their wives and children and of mothers who risked the lives of their infants by putting them out to wet nurses, Catholic and Protestant moralists contributed to a general belief that limitation of family size was a moral course of action, despite official church opposition to contraceptives. (Flandrin, *Families in Former Times*, pp. 216–217, 226–227, 235–237.) Christian evangelizing and education has also been credited with the development of humane ideals of child care during the high Middle Ages. McLaughlin, "Survivors and Surrogates," in De Mause, *History of Childhood*, p. 111.

7. Infant mortality rates during the Middle Ages have been placed at "one or two in three." McLaughlin, "Survivors and Surrogates," in De Mause, *History of Childhood*, p. 111. In early modern Europe as a whole, 30–50 percent of all children under five died, it has been estimated. Lutz K. Berkner, "Recent Research on the History of the Family in Western Europe," *Journal of the Family* 35 (1973): 398. Among German peasants, only one or two of a possible twenty infants are said to have survived. Weber-Kellermann, *Die deutsche Familie*, p. 46; see also Strauss, *Luther's House of Learning*, p. 87. One-third of all children, of both peers and peasants, apparently died before age fifteen in mid-seventeenth-century England. Stone, *Family, Sex and Marriage*, p. 55. Infant mortality in early modern France has been placed at 200–300 per 1,000, with fewer than half surviving to age twenty. Flandrin, *Families in Former Times*, p. 53. It has been estimated that half of all French children died before age four in the seventeenth century. Hunt, *Parents and Children in History*, pp. 116–117; see also E. W. Marvick, "Nature vs. Nurture: Patterns and Trends in 17th Century French

Child Rearing," in De Mause, *History of Childhood*, p. 265. By way of comparison, the death rate for children under five in modern India (1960 statistics) was 257 per 1,000. Donald Bogue, *Principles of Demography* (New York, 1969), p. 586. The premium placed on infant life in the sixteenth century is suggested by the severity of the penalities against premeditated infanticide or child murder. In Bamberg a person convicted of this crime was buried alive and speared (a penalty perhaps designed to approximate the helplessness experienced by the slain infant) or drowned. *Bambergische Halssgerichts und rechtliche Ordenung* (1507), in Klaus Arnold, *Kind und Gesellschaft in Mittelalter und Renaissance*, (Paderborn, 1980). pp. 169–170. Hermann von Weinsberg reports a woman drowned for murdering her daughter's illegitimate child. *Das Buch Weinsberg*, II, 316.

8. Over one hundred editions are today extant, including thirteen English editions, the first of which appeared in 1540.

9. His editor claimed, quite falsely, the Rösslin "had no particular experience" at childbirth. *Eucharius Rösslins "Rosengarten" (1513)*, in *Alte Meister der Medizin und Naturkunde in Facsimile-Ausgaben und Neudrucken nach Werken des 15.–18. Jahrhunderts*, II, *Begleit-Text* by Gustav Klein (Munich, 1910), appendix.

10. "Wiewol solcher schmertz mit keiner vernunfft / weissheit oder kunst gentzlich hingeleit und gehindert mag werden / ye doch wann sich die schwangern frawen vor und in der geburt ordenlich dar zu schicken und halten / auch mit vernünfftigen gelerten frawen und hebammen versehen mag solicher schmertz gmiltert und gemindert werden." *Rosengarten* A 4 a/p. 6 (the first page reference is to the original, the second to the modern edition).

11. Katherine bore three daughters (1515, 1516, 1518) and three sons (1521, 1522, 1526); all but the second son survived into adulthood. Karl von Weber, "Zur Lebensgeschichte Herzogin Katherine von Saxon," *Archiv für die Sächsische Geschichte* 6 (1868): 1–35; S. Issleib, "Die Jugend Moritzens von Sachsen, 1521–1541," *Neues Archiv für Sächsische Geschichte* 26 (1905): 274–331.

12. *Rosengarten*, A 4 a–b/pp. 6–7; B 2 b/p. 11.

13. "Und nit so vil mort würd geschehen / Als offt und dick ichs hab gesehen / Solich farlessigkeit bleip furt." *Rosengarten*, B 1 b/p. 9.

14. Hunt, *Parents and Children in History*, pp. 84–85; Merry W. Wood, "The Early Modern Midwife: A Multi-Faceted Role" (unpublished manuscript, kindly made available to me by the author).

15. These were the manuals of Jacob Rueff, *The Expert Midwife* (London, 1637), and James Guillimeau, *Childbirth or The Happy Deliverie of Woman* (London, 1612). Discussed by Schnucker, "Views of Selected Puritans," pp. 412–416. Both contain illustrations of fetal positions within the womb.

16. M. J. Tucker, "The Child as Beginning and End: Fifteenth and Sixteenth Century English Childhood," in De Mause, *History of Childhood*, p. 238.

17. On Rösslin's performance of actual deliveries, see Harvey Graham,

Eternal Eve (London, 1950), pp. 142–143, 170; discussed by Tucker, "Child as Beginning and End," p. 238.

18. *Rosengarten*, B 3 b/p. 13.

19. See editor's discussion in *Rosengarten*, appendix.

20. *Rosengarten*, C 2 a–C 4 a/pp. 18–22.

21. Ibid., H 1 b/p. 57.

22. Ibid., H 2 a–H 4 a/pp. 58–62.

23. Ibid., H 4 a–b/p. 62–63.

24. Ibid., J 1 a–b/pp. 64–65.

25. Ibid., D 1 b–D 2 a/pp. 25–26.

26. Ibid., D 2 b/p. 27.

27. Ibid., D 3 a/p. 28.

28. Ibid., D 4 b/p. 31.

29. Ibid., F 2 a/p. 42.

30. *On the Estate of Marriage, LW*, 45, p. 40. Platter, *Lebensbeschreibung*, p. 94

31. *Rosengarten*, F 3 a–F 4 a/pp. 44–46.

32. Ibid., F 4 b–H 1 a/pp. 47–56.

33. Ibid., J 2 a–b/pp. 66–67.

34. Ibid., J 3 a–J 3 b/pp. 68–69.

35. Ibid., J 4 a–K 1 a/pp. 70–72.

36. Ibid., K 1 b/p. 73.

37. "Hardly a year went by in this period [between 1660 and 1730] when at least one Haushaltungsbuch or a new edition of an old one did not appear." Hoffmann, *Die "Hausväterliteratur,"* p. 75.

38. *Allgemeine deutsche Biographie*, 4 (Berlin, 1968), pp. 402–403; *Neue deutsche Biographie*, 3 (Berlin, 1956), p. 319.

39. Coler, *Oeconomia ruralis et domestica*, pt. II, bk. IV, ch. iv, p. 342.

40. Ibid.

41. "Die Natur ist ein wunderliche Nachfolgerin aller dinge." Ibid.

42. Ibid., II, IV, v, 344.

43. Hoffmann, *Die "Hausväterliteratur,"* pp. 138–141.

44. Coler, *Oeconomia ruralis et domestica*, II, IV, v, 343.

45. Ibid., II, IV, v, 344.

46. Ibid., II, IV, v, 343.

47. Ibid., II, IV, vi, 344–45.

48. Ibid., II, IV, vi, 345–346.

49. "Wenn ein Weib in der Geburt in ein Ohnmacht geräth / und nicht daraus wieder kommen kan. . . . Soll ihr Ehemann zugehen / ihr freundlich zu sprechen / sie bei der Hand nemen und auffmuntern / das hilfft einem Weib gar sehr / und ist die beste Erquickung / sie höret ihren Mann balde / thut die Augen auff / und sicht wieder umb sich darzu sie denn auch der Mann ermahnen soll." Ibid., II, IV, vi, 346.

50. Platter, *Lebensbeschreibung*, p. 94.

51. Alan MacFarlane, *The Family Life of Ralph Josselin, A Seven-*

teenth Century Clergyman: An Essay in Historical Anthropology (Cambridge, 1970), p. 85.

52. Stone, Family, Sex and Marriage, pp. 57, 116. See below, my discussion of parents grieving over the death of infants and children.

53. Rosengarten, K 2 a–b/pp. 74–75. "Denn es ist gut all Wehetagen / Schmertzen und Reissen des Bauchs." Oeconomia ruralis et domestica, II, IV, vii, 347.

54. Rosengarten, K 2 b/p. 75.

55. Oeconomia ruralis et domestica, II, IV, xiv, 352.

56. Marvick found that swaddling ended after four months in seventeenth-century France because it created too many laundry problems. "Nature versus Nurture," in De Mause, History of Childhood, pp. 270–271.

57. Hunt, Parents and Children in History, pp. 128–132.

58. The Florentine middle classes strongly favored wetnursing as a "symbol of gentility." James B. Ross, "The Middle Class Child in Urban Italy," in De Mause, History of Childhood, p. 186.

59. Flandrin, Families in Former Times, pp. 203–204; Hunt, Parents and Children in History, pp. 116–117.

60. There was strong aversion to feeding a child any form of animal milk, save in an emergency. See Ross, "The Middle Class Child in Urban Italy," p. 187. On the superiority of human milk over bovine milk, both for antibodies (breastfed babies suffer significantly fewer gastrointestinal and other infections) and hormones that promote healthy cell growth in infants, see Graham Carpenter, "The Importance of Mother's Milk," Natural History 90/8 (1981): 6–14.

61. Schnucker, "Views of Selected Puritans," p. 446. "As much as anything else [wetnursing was] a sexual triumph for the father." Hunt, Parents and Children in History, p. 108. Hunt is quick to add, however, that French wives looked on nursing as debilitating and degrading work and desired to be free of it for reasons both vain and conjugal. In Florence a concern to perpetuate the family (by keeping wives regularly pregnant, hopefully with sons) seems to have been the dominant professed motive for wetnursing. Ross, "Middle Class Child in Urban Italy," p. 186.

62. Brundage, "Carnal Delight," p. 382.

63. Marvick, "Nature versus Nurture," pp. 264–265.

64. MacFarlane, Family Life of Ralph Josselin, p. 83.

65. Stone, Family, Sex and Marriage, p. 270; Hunt, Parents and Children in History, pp. 106–108.

66. Flandrin, Families in Former Times, p. 206.

67. William Lazareth, Luther on the Christian Home, (1960), p. 266.

68. Flandrin, Families in Former Times, p. 207.

69. Rosengarten, K 3 a/p. 76.

70. Hoffmann, Die "Hausväterliteratur," pp. 141–142. The Puritan Robert Cleaver accused the mother who refused to nurse her own child of being a "half-mother"; "she breaks the holy bond of nature, in locking up her breast from her child, and delivering it forth like the cuckoo to be hatched in

the sparrow's next." In Irwin, *Womanhood in Radical Protestantism*, p. 84. See also Erasmus's colloquy *Puerpera*, a censure of a new mother for not wanting to nurse her own child. *D.E.R. Opera Omnia*, I (Leiden, 1703, reprint ed., Hildesheim, 1961), 766–774.

71. "Darumb hat auch Gott einer jedem Mutter zwo Brüste gegeben / dass sie ihrem Kinde Milche und Nahrung geben kan: Und die hat er ihr nahe zum Hertzen gesetzt / dass das Kind rechte Kindliche Liebe / Gottesforcht / Weissheit und Verstand / Zucht und Erbarkeit aus ihrem Hertzen säuge und bekommen soll." *Oeconomia ruralis et domestica*, II, IV, viii, 348.

72. *Rosengarten*, K 3 b/p. 77.

73. Ibid., K 4 b/p. 79.

74. "Es soll ein jedere Mutter / so viel immer menschlich und möglich / ihr Kind selber träncken / und demselbigen bei Leibe und Leben keine Amme halten. Nicht allein umb der Amme selbst willen / die bissweilen lose Leute / und mit keiner Speise oder Tranck zu ersättigen sein / balde wollen sie diss / bald jenes gut Bisslein oder Truncklein haben / da sie doch in ihren Häusern offt kaum das liebe Brod und schlecht Wasser zu trincken haben / davon den Kindern grosser Schade / und auch wol der Tod selber entstehen kan. Zudem hat die Milch *genium Matris* und bekommen die Kinder gemeiniglich ihrer Saugammen Naturen und Eigenschafften . . . Kan es aber anders gar nit sein / sonder man muss seinem Kinde eine Amme halten / so nehme man hierzu ein verständig / ehrlich / fromm und Gottsfürchtig Weib / die das Kind lieb hat / und nicht verschlaffen ist / und sie das Kind des Nachts / wenn sie sich voll gesossen hat / gebrächlich schreien läst." *Oeconomia ruralis et domestica*, II, IV, viii, 348.

75. *Rosengarten*, K 3 a/p. 76.

76. Ibid., K 4 b/p. 78.

77. *Oeconomia ruralis et domestica*, II, IV, ix–x, 348–349.

78. *Rosengarten*, L a l/p. 80.

79. Avicenna's *Canon medicinae* (Basel, 1536) is excerpted in Arnold, *Kind und Gesellschaft im Mittelalter und Renaissance*, pp. 100–101. Soranos of Ephesus, an important authority for both Rösslin and Coler, recommended weaning at one and a half or two years, when the child had powerful teeth and a firm bite. Ibid., p. 93.

80. *Rosengarten*, L 1 a/p. 80.

81. *Oeconomia ruralis et domestica*, II, IV, xiv, 351.

82. MacFarlane, *Family Life of Ralph Josselin*, pp. 83, 90.

83. When Edward Shorter discovered a contemporary report that in 1777 one-sixth of the children of Paris (16.7 percent) were with wetnurses, he took this as evidence of parental callousness in premodern Europe. Shorter, *Making of the Modern Family* (New York, 1975), p. 176. Even if this statistic were unquestionably accurate, it would hardly justify so dire a conclusion. In the modern world a good 5 percent of all mothers, one in twenty, are incapable of nursing their own children for physiological reasons. Surely at least this many Parisian mothers also fell into such a category, which leaves

us with roughly 10 percent of parents who placed their children with nurses for reasons of apparent vanity, convenience, and/or patrimonial ambition.

84. *Rosengarten*, L 2 a–b/pp. 82–83.

85. Ibid., L 2 b–L 3 b/pp. 83–85.

86. Ibid., L 3 b/p. 85.

87. Ibid., L 3 b–L 4 a/pp. 85–86.

88. Ibid., L 4 b–M 1 a/pp. 87–88.

89. Ibid., M 1 a/p. 88.

90. Ibid., M 1 b/p. 89.

91. Ibid.

92. *Oeconomia ruralis et domestica*, II, IV, xi, 350.

93. *Rosengarten*, M 2 a/p. 90.

94. Ibid., M 2 b/p. 91.

95. Ibid.

96. *Oeconomia ruralis et domestica*, II, IV, xiv, 351.

97. *Rosengarten*, M 3 a/p. 92.

98. Ibid., M 3 b/p. 93.

99. *Oeconomia ruralis et domestica*, II, IV, xiv, 352.

100. *Rosengarten*, M 3 b/94.

101. Ibid., M 4 b/p. 95.

102. Ibid., M 4 b–N 1 a/pp. 95–96.

103. Ibid., N 1 a/p. 96.

104. Ibid., N 2 a/p. 98.

105. Ibid.

106. *Oeconomia ruralis et domestica*, II, IV, xiii, 354.

107. *Rosengarten*, N 2 b/p. 99.

108. Ibid., N 2 b–N 3 a/pp. 99–100.

109. Ibid.

110. Ibid., N 3 b/p. 101.

111. Ibid.

112. *Das Buch Weinsberg*, I, 22.

113. Ibid., II, 104.

114. Ibid., I, 25.

115. "Das min fatter nachtz duch hat moissen uffstain, mir uff einem becken gespilt und gepiffen, das ich swigen sulte." Ibid., I, 27.

116. Ibid., I, 27.

117. Ibid., I, 32.

118. Ibid., I, 95; V, 25, 29.

119. "Die worme waren mir auch oben und unden abgegangen." Ibid., I, 34.

120. "Hie hat mich nit leif, hie ist ein boif." Ibid., I, 33.

121. Ibid., I, 156–57.

122. Ibid., I, 36–38, 46, 50.

123. Ibid., I, 59.

124. According to Josef Stein, an editor of *Das Buch Weinsberg*, Hermann's father considered "barbaric beatings" at school a possible source of the hernia. (Ibid., V, xiii.) The statement in the chronicle reads: "Min fatter

leis sich bedunken, ich hett ader in der scholen mit hohem und vil kreischen ader mit springen und gratzen es bekomen." (Ibid., I, 50) "Kreischen" here cannot be directly connected with barbaric beatings at the hands of either peers or teachers; literally, it says "much loud screaming." Were the situation as Stein suspects, then Hermann, who is so forthcoming elsewhere about thrashings at school, would surely have commented directly on it. Stein attempts to infer too much. See also above, Chapter 2, notes 87, 88.

125. *Das Buch Weinsberg*, I, 95, 140, 175–176.

126. Ibid., I, 61, 69, 79–80, 151–152.

127. Ibid., I, 64–65.

128. Ibid., I, 77.

129. Ibid., I, 96.

130. Ibid., I, 109.

131. Ibid., I, 96.

132. Ibid., I, 136.

133. Ibid., I, 113–114.

134. Brueghel's famous painting, "Children's Games," depicts at least seventy-five different games, most quite simple, the product of youthful imagination. See Jeanette Hills, *Das Kinderspielsbild von Pieter Breugel der Aeltere* (Vienna, 1957). On children at play, see Max Hermann, "Bilder aus dem Kinderleben des 16. Jahrhunderts," *Mitteilungen der Gesellschaft für deutsche Erziehungs- und Schulgeschichte* 20 (1910): 125–145.

135. "Mehe aus lust dan noit allein, das sie ursach haben, frolich zu sin und mit wein dricken neu bloit zu setzen." *Das Buch Weinsberg*, V, 355.

136. *Oeconomia ruralis et domestica*, I, I, v, 4.

137. *Luthers Werke in Auswahl*, 8, no. 3964 (1538), p. 208.

4. The Rearing of Children

1. Dietrich, *Von der Kinderzucht*, p. 121.

2. Cited by Gütell, *Ueber das Evangelion Johannis*, p. B 4 a–b.

3. Menius, *Erinnerung*, p. C 2 b.

4. "Dann daran ist yhe kain zweyffel / gleich wie man auss jungen kelblin grosse Küe und Ochsen / auss jungen fullen / weydliche streytbare hengste / und jungen zarten pflantzen / grosse fruchtbare baume auffzeucht / Also muss man auch auss der kindheyt / verstendige und tapffere leute auffziehen / die landen und leuten mügen nütz und fürderlich seyn." Menius, *An die hochgeborne Fürstin*, p. E 6 a.

5. The humanist Canon von Eyb expressed a widespread sentiment when he wrote of the love of a father for his son: "A father holds his son more dear than his own life and suffers more in his son than in himself. He sees himself and his son as one person and one flesh. For a son is part of his father's body, and after his death the father lives on in the person of his son." *Ehebüchlein*, p. 20.

6. Hoffmann, *Die "Hausväterliteratur,"* p. 136.

7. Menius, *An die hochgeborne Fürstin*, p. E 6 b.

8. Stone declares that "more children were beaten in the sixteenth and seventeenth centuries over a longer age span than ever before," both at home

and in school, and largely as the result of the application of Protestant principles of discipline. (*Family, Sex and Marriage*, p. 117.) Hunt generalizes from the punishments Louis XIII received as a child to charge the entire seventeenth century with frequent and widespread whipping, food deprivation, and scare tactics, all designed to break the child's will and his "efforts at self-determination." (*Parents and Children in History*, pp. 133–139.) Gerald Strauss has corrected such wild accusations for Germany. (*Luther's House of Learning*, p. 90.)

9. Sam, *Davids Eebruch*, p. F 3 b.

10. Boyd M. Berry, "The First Pediatricians and Tudor Attitudes toward Children," *Journal of the History of Ideas* 35 (1974): 570–571.

11. Sam, *Davids Eebruch*, p. F 3 b.

12. Culman, *Jungen gesellen*, p. E 4 a.

13. Dietrich, *Von der Kinderzucht*, p. 117.

14. "Nicht zu gar weich seyn / noch den zaum zuweyt lassen / das sie mutwillig werden / und die eltern verachten lernen . . . im alter auch die öberkeyt verachten / und wilde / rauchlose / auffrhürische / schedliche leute werden." Menius, *An die hochgeborne Fürstin*, p. E 8 a.

15. Corvinus, *Bericht*, p. J 3 a.

16. Ibid., p. J 4 a.

17. "Nützt solche zucht den untersassen und gantzem vaterland / Die untersassen / dieweil sie tyrannischer weise nicht beschweret / sonder on alle unbilliche beschwerung regirt werden / frewen sich solcher fromen öberkeit halben." Ibid., p. K 1 b.

18. See the discussion by Klaus Petzold, *Die Grundlagen der Erziehungslehre im Spätmittelalter und bei Luther* (Heidelberg, 1969), p. 65.

19. A Carthusian monk since 1510, Brunfels, under humanist influence, converted to the Reformation in 1521 and even served briefly as an evangelical preacher in Steinau and Neuenberg before becoming Strasbourg's schoolmaster in 1524. When he died in Bern in 1534, he was famous as a botanist and herbalist. His *Weiber und Kinder Apothek* (*Pharmacy for Mothers and Children*, Strasbourg, 1535) was an influential Galenic medical guide throughout the sixteenth century. It has recently been alleged that he was the leader of an underground network of advanced intellectuals who simulated orthodox beliefs for safety's sake, while secretly holding more tolerant and "modern" views. See Carlo Ginzburg, *Il nicodemismo: Similazione e dissimulazione religiosa nell' Europe del' 500* (Turin, 1970), whose views are challenged by Carlos M. N. Eire, "Calvin and Nicodemism: A Reappraisal," *Sixteenth Century Journal* 10 (1979): 45–69.

20. Brunfels, *Von der Zucht und Underweisung der kinder / Ein Leer und Vermanung. Item ein underweisung der döchterlin auss der Epistel oder sentbrieff des heyligen Hieronymi die er zum Letam geschriben hat.* (Strasbourg, 1525) [Ox–Bod, T.L. 98.16], p. A 4 b.

21. Erasmus, *Züchtiger Sitten Zierlichen wandels / und höfflicher Geberden der Jugent / In alle weg und nach Ordennung des gantzen leibs / Den Jungen sich darinn zuüben / Den alten / jre Kind nach solichem ebenbild / inn zucht zu erziehen. Ein nützlich Büchlein H. Erasmi Rote.*

Nach der kürtze / so vil der gmeynen Jugent dienlich / new verteutscht
(Strasbourg, 1531) [Harvard-Houghton NC5.Er153.En531z] pp. A 1 a–A 2
b. This is an abridged version of Erasmus's *De civilitate morum puerilium*
(Basel, 1530). I rely on the German abridgment rather than Erasmus's
original Latin because the former conveys Erasmus's views in the mode most
people received them. Throughout this book I favor vernacular writings.

22. "Niemand kan jm eltern oder vatterland erwölen / aber sitten und
verstandt mag er jm wol machen." Ibid., p. C 7 a.

23. Ibid., pp. A 3 a–b, A 5 a–b, A 7 a.

24. Ibid., pp. A 6 a, C 4 a.

25. Ibid., p. A 7 a.

26. Ibid., pp. B 1 a, C 5 a.

27. Comments Hunt: "Adults began to feel at home with the six- or
seven-year-old child who was physically more robust and self-sufficient, and
intellectually more approachable. In other words, he was 'cured' of the
malady of infancy which had made him so incomprehensible and frightening
to his elders." *Parents and Children in History*, p. 186. Parents did see one
side of infancy as a malady, but they understood it all too well.

28. According to Brunfels, such "greetings" were "punishable in a
Christian child," a statement that reveals contemporary Protestant influence
on his thinking. On the other hand, Brunfels appended as an instruction for
girls an excerpt from St. Jerome's letter to Laeta, a classic ascetic guide to the
nun's life. The letter dwelled on the importance of placing a daughter with
learned and exemplary teachers who will teach her Latin and the Bible and
keep her safe from worldly influence. Among the prohibitions: no painted
lips or cheeks, gold or pearl necklaces, jewels on the head, or dyed hair; no
banquets or wine; no organs, lyres, or harps; no friendships with "bad girls";
no games with servants or attendance at their weddings. Indeed, Jerome
even doubted the wisdom of bathing, lest her own nakedness arouse in her
the desires she is struggling in the convent to suppress. *Von der Zucht*,
p. D 2 a.

29. Ibid., pp. A 7 b–A 8 b.

30. "Dann nichts kostlichers ist in disem leben / dann die
zeit . . . Bedenckt das sye unwiderbringlich ist / sye verleürt sich / und
schlychthyn." Ibid., p. B 1 a.

31. Erasmus commented on the patience required of children at table:
"A child should always be made to wait a while, for this teaches him to resist
his [naturally impatient] disposition." *Züchtiger Sitten*, p. B 4 a.

32. Erasmus permitted children to speak at table "when an emergency
arises," ostensibly when a sudden pain or illness struck, and also to laugh
modestly at pleasant stories. He also expected women to be generally silent at
table, although not to the same degree as children (*aber noch meer die
jugent*). Ibid., B 7 b.

33. Brunfels, *Von der Zucht*, p. B 4 b.

34. According to Erasmus, children should peel the egg with a knife,
not with their fingers, nor dig it out of the shell with their thumb, or, worse,
with their tongue. *Züchtiger Sitten*, p. B 7 a. Judging from the amount of at-

tention devoted to it, the proper eating of a soft-boiled egg appears to have been the supreme culinary challenge for the sixteenth-century child.

35. Brunfels, *Von der Zucht*, pp. B 5 a–B 6 b. Erasmus urged parents to excuse children who were full, bored, or tired: "Those parents hate their children, when they force them while still young to sit patiently at table into the night." *Züchtiger Sitten*, p. B 8 b.

36. Brunfels, *Von der Zucht*, p. C 5 a.

37. See my *Reformation in the Cities* (New Haven, 1980), p. 23.

38. Corvinus, *Bericht*, p. J 4 a.

39. Coler, *Oeconomia ruralis et domestica*, II, IV, xviii, 355.

40. Etienne Delaruelle et al., *L'Eglise au temps du Grand Schisme et de la crise conciliaire (1378–1449)* (Paris, 1964), p. 656; Strauss, *Luther's House of Learning*, pp. 35, 55, 100.

41. Quoted at length in Brunfels, *Von der Zucht*, on selecting a teacher, pp. B 8 a, C 2 b.

42. Menius, *Erinnerung*, p. C 3 a.

43. Von Eyb, *Ehebüchlein*, p. 24.

44. They also referred to selfish behavior in a child as "the Devil in him." Hoffmann, *Die "Hausväterliteratur,"* p. 152.

45. Menius, *An die hochgeborne Fürstin*, p. F 1 b.

46. As Hoffmann summarizes this recurring theme in the housefather books, "Immerhin wird das Zu-Viel in der Hauslehre noch lieber gesehen als das Zu-Wenig. Besser eine strenge und harte Regierung des Mannes [even at the risk of limiting the marriage by inhibiting the development of mutual love] als gar keine männliche Regierung." *Die "Hausväterliteratur,"* p. 129. Both wife and children must perceive the husband and father as one who rules.

47. Coler offered the following advice to housewives in dealing with servants—a point of view that may be extended to the rearing of children, should a parent be tempted to praise them unduly. "Ein Hausswirt sol sein Gesinde nicht loben in ihrer Gegenwart / dass es höret / sonst verderbet mans balde / es wird stoltz / und thut hernach kein gut mehr: und so bald es mercket / dass man etwas von ihm hält / so hebts im Hause an zu herrschen und zu regieren / und wil endlich dem Herrn und Frauen / und Kindern nicht mehr gehorsam sein." *Oeconomia ruralis et domestica*, II, I, vi, 5.

48. *The Complete Works of Menno Simons*, trans. L. Verduin, ed. J. C. Wenger (Scottsdale, Pa., 1956), p. 951.

49. See Hoffmann, *Die "Hausväterliteratur,"* pp. 145–148, 152–153. Fifteenth-century Italian attitudes toward corporal punishment ranged from condemnation (Guarino da Varona) to the recommendation of frequent whippings between the ages of three and twenty-five (the Dominican friar Dominici). James B. Ross, "The Middle Class Child in Urban Italy," in De Mause, *History of Childhood*, p. 214. The Florentine merchant-moralist Paolo of Certaldo expressed the universal sentiment of the age: "The man who does not correct his children does not love them." Ibid.

50. Petzold, *Die Grundlagen der Erziehungslehre*, pp. 84–89.

51. Examples are provided by M. J. Tucker, "The Child as Beginning

and End: 15th and 16th Century English Childhood," in De Mause, *History of Childhood*, p. 111.

52. Examples in Hoffmann, *Die "Hausväterliteratur,"* p. 154.

53. Butzbach, *Chronika eines fahrenden Schülers oder Wanderbüchlein* (Regensburg, 1569), in Arnold, *Kind und Gesellschaft im Mittelalter und Renaissance*, pp. 167–169.

54. See Lewis W. Spitz, "Psychohistory and History: The Case of Young Man Luther," in Roger A. Johnson, ed., *Psychohistory and Religion: The Case of Young Man Luther* (Philadelphia, 1977), pp. 70–85; and Roland H. Bainton, "Psychiatry and History: An Examination of Erikson's Young Man Luther," in Ibid., pp. 19–56.

55. *Luthers Werke in Auswahl*, 8, no. 3566a (1537), p. 111.

56. *Das Buch Weinsberg*, I, 37–38.

57. Ibid., I, 75, 104.

58. Ibid., V, 13.

59. Culman, *Jungen gesellen*, p. B 4 b.

60. Ibid., pp. C 1 a–b; Flandrin, *Families in Former Times*, p. 210. See Strauss, *Luther's House of Learning*, pp. 103–104.

61. Stör, *Der Ehelich standt*, p. B 1 a; also Menius, *An die hochgeborne Fürstin*, p. F 2 a.

62. Dietrich, *Von der Kinder zucht*, pp. 116–117.

63. An illustrated bestseller, *Von der Artzney bayder Glück, des guten und widerwärtigen* (Augsburg, 1523), depicts "The Many and Hard Burdens of Children" in a scene that shows a father leaving his family of seven children, resigned to their suffering, because their numbers have become too great for him to support. Paternal hardship obviously increased when a wife died and left a father alone to care for the children. In Ingeborg Weber-Kellerman, *Die Familie. Geschichte Geschichten und Bilder* (Frankfurt am Main, 1976), p. 48.

64. Moeckard, *Ain Christliche ainfältige / und zu diser zeit seer notwendige ermanung / an die iugent darinnen angezaigt wirdt was Kinder iren Eltern zuthun schuldig seind* (Augsburg, 1550) [Ox-Bod, T.L. 81.5], pp. A 4 a, B 1 a.

65. In addition to Moeckard, on this duty see also Menius, *An die hochgeborne Fürstin*, p. F 2 b; Corvinus, *Bericht*, p. G 4 a.

66. *Ains Erbern Rats / der Stat Augspurg / Zucht und Pollicey Ordnung* (1537), p. C 3 a. See also Menius, *An die hochgeborne Fürstin*, p. F 5 b.

67. Coler, *Oeconomia ruralis et domestica*, I, 1, vii, 6. Pastor Ralph Josselin summarized the duties of a child to his parents: "Let them [children] first learne to shew piety at home, and to requite their parents . . . Now to requite, is when that we do, carries a proportion to what we have received. Now what have we received from our parents? We received from them our life under god, and our bringing up, and education, with a great deal of care and labor, and with all love and tenderness, Now to returne that love and tenderness to your parents with all willingness, this is to . . . requite your parents for the cost they have laid out about you; follow their counsells, and

cheer their sperits in their gray haires." In MacFarlane, *Family Life of Ralph Josselin*, pp. 124–125.

68. Moeckard, *Ain Christliche ainfältige*, p. B 4 b.

69. "Diss [David's example] solten dise kind wol betracten / welche / ob sy gelich von Gott unnd jren Eltern alles haben / Eer unnd Gut / unnd was sy besitzend / und gutes vermögens seind / auch jre Eltern mit ringerer müe erneeren unnd hinbringen möchten / weder (= welcher) sy von jren Eltern ertzogen worden seind / und aber unangesehen Gottes gebott / und aller erzaigter Vätterlicher unnd Mütterlicher trew / stossen sy ire Eltern in die Spitäler und Blaterheüser / oder laden sy dem gemainen Seckel unnd Almusen auff auff das erfült unnd war werde das gemainen sprüchwort: 'Ain vatter erzieh bass und mit willigerem hertzen zehen Kind / dann zehen Kind ainen Vatter'." Ibid., p. C 2 a.

70. Hoffmann, *Die 'Hausväterliteratur'*, p. 137.

71. Corvinus, *Bericht*, p. H 2 b.

72. Laslett suspects that this was a widespread practice in England from the sixteenth century on; it was prohibited in early modern France. See the discussion in Flandrin, *Families in Former Times*, pp. 70–71.

73. *Das Buch Weinsberg*, V, 82–83.

74. See Joan Thirsk, "The European Debate on Customs of Inheritance," in Jack Goody et al., *Family and Inheritance: Rural Society in Western Europe 1200–1800* (Cambridge, 1976), p. 29. Pre-mortem transmission of property from parents to children is discussed by Goody, "Inheritance, Property, and Women: Some Considerations," in Ibid., p. 29.

75. "Ist dabei auch unser wil, dat keiner van unsern kinderen den lest levendigen dar untboven besweren sall noch auch zu einicher deilung dringen sall, sonder sall ein jeder zufreden sin mit demselben, dat im der lest lebentiger gift." *Das Buch Weinsberg*, I, 121.

76. Ibid., II, 10–11.

77. *Luthers Werke in Auswahl*, 8, no. 5041 (1540), p. 260; *LW*, 34, pp. 291–297. See also H. G. Haile, *Luther* (New York, 1980), p. 271.

78. Luther, *Ein Predigt, dass man Kinder zur Schulen halten solle* (1530), *WA* 30/II, p. 532. See Werner Reininghaus, *Elternstand, Obrigkeit und Schule bei Luther* (Heidelberg, 1969), pp. 41–43.

79. See Erwin Mülhaupt, "Elternlehre und Elternpflicht in Reformatorische Sicht," *Luther* 35 (1964): 49–60.

80. Petzold, *Die Grundlagen der Erziehungslehre*, p. 91.

81. Flandrin, *Families in Former Times*, pp. 159–160.

82. *Das Buch Weinsberg*, I, 35, 37, 48; II, 57.

83. Ibid., I, 57–58.

84. Ibid., I, 77–78.

85. Ibid., I, 80–81.

86. Ibid., I, 82, 87–88.

87. "Ich ein sonderliche freude in dir haff." Ibid., 90–91.

88. Ibid., I, 104, 108, 116–117.

89. Ibid., I, 131.

90. Ibid., I, 143, 176.
91. Ibid., I, 320.
92. Ibid., I, 321.
93. Ibid., I, 323.
94. Ibid., I, 342–43.
95. Ibid., I, 257–58, 294–295.
96. Ibid., II, 49, 54–55, 83.
97. Ibid., V, 19.
98. Ibid., II, 105.
99. Ibid., V, 48.
100. Ibid., II, 147–148.
101. Ibid., II, 166–167. Some idea of what this amount represents may be gleaned from Hermann's annual household expenditures. Between October 1577 and October 1578, the household expenses for the Weinsberg family as a whole, including siblings and servants, were placed at 667 gulden, excluding outlays for wine and clothing. Ibid., V, 132.
102. Ibid., II, 175, 180–182.
103. Ibid., II, 191; V, pp. 72, 329.
104. Ibid., V, 178, 389–390.
105. Ibid., V, 162, 181, 198–199, 320–331.
106. See above, chapter 3, note 6.
107. Stone, *Family, Sex and Marriage*, pp. 116–117, 125. Stone declares (p. 126): "In the newly sanctified conjugal marriage [of Puritan Protestants] the duty of the wife and mother was to assist her husband in the task of the repression of their children." Philippe Ariès characterizes childhood generally before the eighteenth century as a period of "deliberate humiliation." *Centuries of Childhood: A Social History of Family Life*, trans. R. Baldick (New York, 1962), p. 262. According to Hunt, "in their most pious moments parents [in early modern France] went so far as to equate the child's natural search for autonomy with the principle of original sin." *Parents and Children in History*, p. 139. Hunt would have the reader believe that parents punished children for "autonomous" behavior rather than misbehavior. Luther wrote of infants: "The life of the infant is the most blessed and best, for they have no temporal cares, neither do they suffer nor even perceive the terror of death and hell; they have only pure thoughts and happy speculations." Cited in Georg Buchwald, *D. Martin Luther. Ein Lebensbild für das deutsche Haus* (Leipzig, 1902), p. 354. "The faith and life of infants is the highest because they have only the Word. We old fools have hell and hellfire; we argue over the Word, which they believe in pure faith without argument." *Luthers Werke in Auswahl*, 8, no. 18 (1531), p. 2.
108. Flandrin, *Families in Former Times*, pp. 130–131, 136.
109. See Strauss's refutation of Ariès's views, *Luther's House of Learning*, pp. 180–181; and my comments on Erikson's speculations on Luther's allegedly brutalized childhood, *Age of Reform*, pp. 226–227.
110. Mary Ault Harada, "Family Values and Child Care During the Reformation Era: A Comparative Study of Hutterites and Some Other Ger-

man Protestants" (Ph.D.diss., Boston University, 1968), pp. 143–146, 148–153.

111. In Irwin, *Womanhood in Radical Protestantism*, pp. 131–132. The Hutterites' denial of infant baptism was also decried by Lutherans as a form of child abuse.

112. See Gertrude Enders Huntington, "Children of the Hutterites," *Natural History* 2 (1981): 34–46.

113. See the discussion by Hoffmann, *Die "Hausväterliteratur,"* pp. 152–154.

114. Here I take strong exception to Strauss's conclusions, *Luther's House of Learning*, p. 136.

115. Again, I take exception to Strauss, who draws very negative conclusions about the intent and results of religious instruction in large formal catechisms.

116. "Ym natürlichen wercke nicht versamlen / sie wissen dann dass das Kindt (so davorn kommen wirt) verordent sey zur ewigenn seligkeit." Eberhardus Weidenssee, *Von dem stand der kindlein so on die tauff vorscheyden* (1525) [Ox-Bod], p. B 2 a.

117. Ibid., p. B 1 b.

118. Andreas Althamer, *Von der Erbsund des sye der Christen kynder gleich als wol verdamb als der heyden* (Nuremberg, 1527) [Ox-Bod, T.L. 15.14], p. B 3 b.

119. Weidenssee, *Von dem stand der kindlein*, p. B 1 b.

120. Rösslin, *Rosengarten*, B 1 a–b/pp. 8–9. When twins were born to the wife of Hermann von Weinsberg's nephew in 1586, they were "hurriedly baptized" on the advice of the midwives, who observed that they appeared not to be very strong. *Das Buch Weinsberg*, V, 271.

121. Althamer, *Von der Erbsund*, pp. C 1 a, D 1 b.

122. Weidenssee, *Von dem stand der kindlein*, pp. A 3 b–B 1 a.

123. "Niemand bequemer und geschicklicher zum glauben und tauff ist / dann die jungen kynd / die on list / vernunfft / und fleyschliche geschwyndigkeit sind." Althamer, *Von der Erbsund*, pp. F 3 b–F 4 a. Luther insisted that even unborn fetuses had faith, basing his argument (against the Anabaptists) on the passage in Luke 1, in which the fetus of John the Baptist is said to have leapt in the womb of his mother at the approach of Mary, who was then carrying Jesus—fetus responding to fetus! *WA*, 26, p. 156.

124. Althamer pointed the reader to God's promise to save all who believe and are baptized, while Weidenssee was less gentle in reminding parents of God's sovereignty; he declared that even if a couple knew they would have a hundred children who were to be damned eternally, they still should obey God's commandment to procreate and rejoice in his will. Althamer, *Von der Erbsund*, p. F 3 a; Weidenssee, *Von dem stand der kindlein*, p. B 2 a.

125. Stone, *Family, Sex and Marriage*, p. 57. I think it is equally questionable to argue from remarriages within six months of a spouse's death to the conclusion that marrriage was characterized by "affective unfeelingness."

Flandrin, *Families in Former Times*, pp. 115–116. It rather suggests that the companionship of marriage was held in high regard. See p. 212, n. 161.

126. Sam, *Davids Eebruch*, p. F 2 b.

127. In MacFarlane, *Family Life of Ralph Josselin*, p. 221. See also my *Reformation in the Cities*, pp. 55–56.

128. MacFarlane, *Family Life of Ralph Josselin*, p. 166.

129. Buchwald, *D. Martin Luther. Ein Lebensbild für das deutsche Haus*, p. 356.

130. In ibid., p. 356.

131. Letter of Sept. 23, 1542, *LW*, 50, p. 238. See his pitiable comments upon returning from Magdelene's funeral, when he attempted to console himself by saying that girls need more care and protection than boys and so he gladly gave Magdelene to God's good keeping, although "*secundum carnem* I would gladly have kept her with me." *Luthers Werke in Auswahl*, 8, no. 5500 (1542), p. 313. In his recent study of madness in seventeenth-century England, Michael MacDonald has found that the death of an infant was a leading cause of mental depression among parents. *Mystical Bedlam: Madness, Anxiety, and Healing in Seventeenth Century England* (Cambridge, 1981). The depth and pervasiveness of parental grieving over deceased infants and children suggests that parents did not "limit the degree of their psychological involvement" with their children (Stone); they seem rather to have loved their fragile children all too much. On the other hand, people were expected to suppress feelings of incapacitating grief and to terminate their public grieving at an early date.

132. Letter of May 1531, *LW*, 50, p. 19.

133. Letter of Dec. 1542, *LW*, 50, p. 248.

134. Letter of June 1545, *WABR*, 11, pp. 113–124.

135. Platter, *Lebensbeschriebung*, p. 91.

136. *Das Buch Weinsberg*, II, 196–197.

137. Ibid., V, 312–313.

138. Ibid., V, 352.

139. Alberus, *Zehen Dialogi. Für Kinder / so angefangen zu reden* (Nuremberg, [1550]) [B.M. 3089.aa.42(1)], p. A 3 a.

140. Ibid., p. A 3 b.

141. Brunfels, *Von der Zucht*, p. D 1 b.

142. Alberus, *Zehen Dialogi*, pp. A 4 b, A 6 a–b.

143. Alberus mentioned plans to publish more dialogues for six- and seven-year-olds, a collection based on "conversations" with younger children.

144. Alberus, *Zehen Dialogi*, pp. B 3 a–b.

145. Von Günzburg, *Ein schöner spiegel eins Christlichen lebens* (Strasbourg, 1524), in Enders, *Sämtliche Schriften*, III, 105–106. Despite his ultimately harsh verdict on Lutheran pedagogy, Strauss characterizes Lutheran catechisms generally as "moderate on the subject of sin and generous with promises of eternal bliss." *Luther's House of Learning*, p. 214. Perhaps Strauss's own personal aversion to catechetical indoctrination of children in the knowledge of sin (he claims "one cannot today read these

passages without wincing" [p. 211]) has inhibited his integration of this more positive judgment into his overall conclusions.

146. I suspect that the same may also have been true to a certain extent of Catholic "counter-catechisms" against Protestantism, like that of Jasper Gennep. But this seems not to have been an extensive catechetical genre among Catholics, whose clergy chose more often to reiterate the old than to dwell mockingly on the new religion.

147. *Ain schöne Frag und Antwurt den jungen kündern. Zu underweysen / got zuerkennen / auch in anruffen als ain vatter. Den jungen vast nützlich zu lernen* (1523) [B.M. 3504.c.6], pp. B 3 a–b.

148. Agricola, *Hundert und lvj. gemeyner Fragstücke / für die jungen kinder in der Teüdtschen Meydeleyn schule zu Eyssleben* (Nuremberg, 1528) [Ox-Bod, T.L. 102.13], pp. C 2 a–b.

149. *Kurtze schrifftliche erklärung für die kinder und angohnden. Der gemeinen artickeln Christ. glaubens. Der Zehen Gebott. Des Vatter unsers. Hierin findestu einfeltigen christliche bericht aller stucken / die einem christen nutz und not zu wissen seind* (Strasbourg, 1534) [B.M. 3505.bbb.9], pp. O 3 b, O 6 b.

150. Andreas Althamer, *Anzeigung warumb Gott die Welt so lange zeit hab verplendet und irrhen lassen* (Nuremberg, 1527), pp. A 2 b–A 3 a. On rebellion against parental religion/authority in the French Reformation, see the recent perceptive study of Donald R. Kelley, *The Origins of Ideology. Consciousness and Society in the French Reformation* (Cambridge, 1981), p. 78.

151. Spengler, *Verantwortung unnd auflösung etlicher vermeintter Argument und ursachen So zu widerstandt unnd verdruckung des wortt Gottes und heiligen Evangelions Vonn denen die nitt Christen sein und sich doch Christen namenns rumenn täglich gepraucht werden* ([Augsburg], 1524), in Clemen, *Flugschriften aus den ersten Jahren der Reformation*, II, 362–363.

152. Agricola, *Hundert und lvj. gemeyner Fragstücke*, pp. C 3 b–C 4 a.

153. Flandrin, *Families in Former Times*, p. 136.

Index